The Federal Theatre Project

A Case Study

Drawing upon archival resources, official correspondence and personal interviews, this book provides a detailed examination of the operations of the US Federal Theatre Project in the decade of the 1930s. From the colorful bus tours through the Civilian Conservation Corps camps to the turbulent productions of the Living Newspapers, the book recreates the often chaotic but frequently exhilarating story of Uncle Sam as producer. Special attention is given to the controversial Seattle Negro unit, the prize-winning production of *See How They Run* and the mass spectacles which attempted to incorporate Hallie Flanagan's vision of a truly national project rooted in local culture. *The Federal Theatre Project: A Case Study* illuminates both the ambitions of the program and the day-to-day details of making art from a new model – a subsidized national theatre.

BARRY B. WITHAM is Professor at the School of Drama, University of Washington. He is the author of thirty articles in scholarly journals and editor of *Theatre in the United States: A Documentary History, Vol 1: Theatre in the Colonies and the United States* (Cambridge, 1996).

The Federal Theatre Project

A Case Study

BARRY B. WITHAM

University of Washington

CAMBRIDGE
UNIVERSITY PRESS

PUBLISHED BY THE PRESS SYNDICATE OF THE UNIVERSITY OF CAMBRIDGE
The Pitt Building, Trumpington Street, Cambridge CB2 1RP, United Kingdom

CAMBRIDGE UNIVERSITY PRESS
The Edinburgh Building, Cambridge, CB2 2RU, UK
40 West 20th Street, New York, NY 10011–4211, USA
477 Williamstown Road, Port Melbourne, VIC 3207, Australia
Ruiz de Alarcón 13, 28014 Madrid, Spain
Dock House, The Waterfront, Cape Town 8001, South Africa

http://www.cambridge.org

First published 2003
Reprinted 2004

Printed in the United Kingdom at the University Press, Cambridge

Typeface Adobe Caslon 10.5/13 pt.   *System* LATEX 2ε   [TB]

A catalogue record for this book is available from the British Library

ISBN 0 521 82259 9 hardback

For Peggy, Michael and Drake
and
Robert Bates Witham
1942–2001

"Quemadmodum omnium rerum, sic litterarum quoque intemperantia laboramus; non vitae sed scholae discimus." ... Seneca, Epistle 106

Contents

Illustrations

Acknowledgments

I owe a debt of gratitude to all the librarians and scholars who aided my research, especially Lorraine Brown at George Mason University, Karyl Winn, Nicolette Bromberg, Carla Rickerson and Gary Lundell at the University of Washington and Walter Zvonchenko and Chamisa Redmond at the Library of Congress.

I'm indebted to dozens of students who have shared my interest in this era and this project, especially Ron West, Terry Smith, Sheila McNerney, Mark Farrelley, Tamara Underiner, Jennifer Jones, Theresa May, Mark Weitzencamp, Derek Davidson, Karin Waidley, Victor Holtcamp, Jim Fitzmorris, Sydney Cheek and John Warrick.

To my colleagues in the study of theatre in the United States I also owe special recognition. Rose Bank and Don Wilmeth have been friends and role models, but there are many others who have helped shape my teaching and research including Felicia Londré, Tom Postlewait, Bruce McConachie, Ron Wainscott, Spencer Golub and David Rinear.

There are many faculty colleagues who have been supportive of my interests and my desire to accomplish this task: Jack Wolcott, Sue-Ellen Case, Sarah Bryant-Bertail, Odai Johnson and the late Michael Quinn.

I am especially grateful to Tina Redd for her insights and encouragement, and to Sue Bruns who was invaluable in bandaging my computer wounds, undoing my technical glitches and always pointing me towards solutions I had not imagined.

Portions of Chapters 5 and 6 were originally published in *Theatre History Studies* and part of Chapter 8 first appeared in the *Journal of American Drama and Theatre*.

Photographs appear with the permission of The Library of Congress, Manuscripts, Special Collections, University Archives, University of

Washington Libraries (Fig. 6: UW 9782; Fig. 7: UW 1707; Fig. 8: UW 9825;) Fig. 10: UW 21075, the School of Drama, and the Museum of History and Industry of Seattle.

The publisher has used its best endeavours to ensure that the URLs for external websites referred to in this book are correct and active at the time of going to press. However, the publisher has no responsibility for the websites and can make no guarantee that a site will remain live or that the content is or will remain appropriate.

Introduction

Imagine a new play on Broadway in 1985 subsidized by the United States Congress urging support for the Contra movement in Nicaragua. Imagine the outcry and the storm of controversy. Imagine a similar production in 1999, funded by the Democratic Administration, exposing the sins of the Microsoft Corporation and demanding that the company be broken up for the benefit of the American economy, especially for those companies competing with Microsoft. Imagine the furor. Now recall *The Cradle Will Rock* (1937) with its pro-union agenda as the Congress of Industrial Organizations (CIO) sought to organize "Little Steel." Or *Power*, the same year, propagandizing for government control of public utilities and direct competition with private enterprise. Recall *Big White Fog* (1938) peopled with African Americans advocating communism as the only alternative to racism and a bankrupt capitalist system.

The Federal Theatre Project, which mounted these three latter works, was a unique and influential experiment in American theatre; not just for its outspoken politics, but because it reimagined the very way that theatre was produced in the United States. For the first time in the history of the country theatre was subsidized by the federal government, a practice with widespread precedents in Europe and Asia, but one that was totally out of step with free enterprise business practice and a culture which had banned plays in its Second Continental Congress. Between 1935 and 1939 the United States provided more than 45 million dollars to pay the salaries of actors, directors, designers, technicians and others so they could produce plays. Classics, new works, marionette shows, dance programs, even circuses were performed under the banner of Federal Theatre. And while it would be remembered most for some of its "leftist" productions, they actually made up only a small sampling of the total repertoire: a repertoire that was performed in tents, on make-shift stages in school cafeterias, in CCC

(Civilian Conservation Corps) dining rooms, in Broadway theatres and on the radio. From high school auditoriums in Florida to outdoor theatres on the banks of the Columbia River in Oregon, millions of Americans saw thousands of productions.

The Federal Theatre Project was established by an Act of Congress in 1935 as part of a comprehensive welfare program administered by the Works Progress Administration (WPA). Along with similar programs in art, music and writing, the theatre unit was designated as Federal One in the WPA hierarchy. The specific goal of Federal Theatre was to reemploy theatre artists who were victims of the economic crisis precipitated by the Great Depression. The philosophy guiding the program – as with all WPA endeavors – was work-relief. That is, participants were paid a specific monthly wage by the Federal government for working in the professions in which they were trained. Wages were targeted specifically for labor, however, and thus other costs of producing theatre such as materials for scenery, costumes and lighting – as well as advertising and publicity – were passed along to the private sector.

The director of the project was Hallie Flanagan Davis, Head of the Theatre program at Vassar College and former Grinnell classmate of Roosevelt's WPA chief, Harry Hopkins. Flanagan had attended George Pierce Baker's famous Workshop 47 at Harvard and had won a Guggenheim grant in 1926 which allowed her to tour Europe seeing contemporary theatre. She had gained considerable prominence in the college-art theatre scene because of her work at Vassar and because of the popularity of her original play, *Can You Hear Their Voices?* (written with Margaret Ellen Clifford) which had been produced at several regional American theatres. While Flanagan was not a product of America's highly visible commercial theatre, she was widely respected, and at the time of her appointment she had been offered a prestigious position in Dartington, England, which she declined in order to work for Harry Hopkins. Flanagan was energetic, dynamic and ambitious. Like many of her contemporaries, she was also idealistic about the power of the arts to compel and humanize. She believed in the *idea* of a Federal Theatre and was excited about its potential to entertain and to instruct. It had the power in her imagination to transform both the kind of the theatre for which Americans yearned and the audience who would benefit from that transformation.

The plan was flawed, of course, because the government money came with significant complications. In order to be eligible for the theatre payroll, people had to qualify for unemployment: that is, the real test of their theatrical talent was often their relief status. There were exceptions.

Individual units could "exempt" up to 10 percent of their employees from this relief qualification in order to address specific requirements of production and to insure a degree of "professionalism." But Federal Theatre would always host a struggle between those who were "right for the part" and those who qualified for relief. In addition, production costs for essential items such as paint and canvas had to be raised at the local level. The hope was that, like other WPA projects, local businesses or communities would "sponsor" individual projects and help to defray production expenses. That too was a stumbling block, especially for units outside large metropolitan areas. Eventually box office receipts – which were supposed to go back to the government – were approved for essential nonlabor expenses.

Flanagan insisted that the theatre be professional. She wanted it to reflect the highest quality of American talent and did not want to settle for amateur theatrics. And she wanted it to be truly national. Actors, for example, were discouraged from crossing state lines to apply for welfare because Flanagan wanted to decentralize the project. Good actors were needed in every state, not just New York or Los Angeles. On the other hand, scripts, lighting instruments and other materials could be widely borrowed back and forth among the units in order to reach as "professional" a look as possible. Many scoffed at the very notion of a government-run theatre, supervised by an "amateur" college professor and peopled with unemployed "actors," who might or might not qualify for welfare.

But in 1936, when Flanagan was able to accomplish her simultaneous openings of Sinclair Lewis's *It Can't Happen Here* in eighteen cities across the country, notice was served that the project might just work in spite of all its inherent problems and demands. Lewis's best-selling novel – adapted for the stage by the author – was a Federal Theatre hit, and its multiple productions constituted the equivalent of a five-year Broadway run. Flanagan was instrumental in organizing, supervising and insisting that the production open on time and as advertised. She was talented, tenacious and absolutely masterful at losing battles so that she could win the war. Harry Hopkins had promised her a hands-off stance by the government in terms of play choice and production values, for example, but she struggled with censorship from the very first moments on the job. The government canceled her initial Living Newspaper, *Ethiopia*, because they did not want current heads of foreign governments (such as Mussolini or Haile Salassie) represented on the stage. Elmer Rice, her regional director in New York, resigned in protest of such blatant interference, but Flanagan bided her time and within two years the Living Newspapers were hailed even by her critics.[1] She fought the Stagehands and the other powerful theatrical unions and accommodated their demands. She battled the radicals and communists who wanted to hijack the project for their own ideological aims and made them back down.

The Federal Theatre did not fail. It was stopped. And that's an important distinction. By many criteria it succeeded beyond expectations, perhaps even beyond Hallie Flanagan's. In a depressed economy the Federal One (the Arts Projects) programs provided jobs for the workers in the arts just as its parent organization, WPA, provided jobs for workers on the roads and in the forests. In dozens of cities across the United States actors, directors, designers and stage hands were paid a weekly wage by the federal government to produce plays. And thousands of those plays were shown *free* to their audiences. Other productions had modest admission fees, fees that were eventually funneled into production costs. For a program that was routinely characterized in the press and public media as "boondoggling," it is instructive to remember that federal theatres earned $2,018,775 at their box offices.[2]

It was a national theatre not only because it was located in many states but because it aspired to reach out to a wider audience and to represent their experiences on the stage. Children, workers, Jews, Hispanics and African Americans were all part of the vision and the demographics of the Federal Theatre. In an audience survey conducted in Seattle during the run of *Help Yourself* in 1937 nearly 70 percent of the respondents characterized themselves as "Office or Trades and Manual laborers" and specified their jobs as laundryman, cigarmaker, maid, barber, gardener, etc.[3] The Negro units, in spite of the controversy surrounding their leadership and control, were ground-breaking institutions in the American theatre whose influence and accomplishments are still being evaluated.

The Federal Theatre was dangerous and an affront to many. Perhaps that is why some of its critics were so hostile and its reviews so vitriolic. Here is George Jean Nathan in 1938:

> at least three-quarters of the younger people who have been living off it are spongers and grafters and no more deserving of charity from this particular source than they are deserving of Civil War pensions or Congressional dispensations of *pate de foie gras*. They have clearly demonstrated that they have nothing to give to the theatre – whether in the way of playwriting, producing, acting or scene painting – beyond a puissant and understandable itch to shine in easy and romantic jobs. With no faintest competence whatsoever, and infinitely better suited to humbler and more prosaic work, they are simply stagestruck and theatre struck loafers, and the Federal Theatre Project recklessly affords them opportunity to pleasure their fatuous whim.[4]

For the Broadway crowd they were amateurs. For the unions they were scabbers and a threat to their closed shops. For many of their WPA colleagues they were lazy bums. And for many politicians – at both the federal and local level – they were a visible threat to America, especially American capitalism.

So, when the inevitable congressional attacks came, and the enemies of the project marshaled their forces, there was an impassioned public performance. From Martin Dies, the head of the House Committee on Un-American Activities, to Representative Rush Holt or Senator Everett Dirkson, no charge was too absurd, no analysis too grotesque. In fact, almost as much has been written about the *auto-da-fè* of the project's final days as the productions themselves. And this has unfortunately obscured appraisals of the very genuine accomplishments of Federal Theatre – especially outside New York City. The "A" list of their alumni and accomplishments has been well rehearsed: Orson Welles, John Houseman, Marc Blitzstein, Abe Feder, etc.; *Murder in the Cathedral, Macbeth, Julius Caesar, One-Third of a Nation*. But what of the *thousands* of other productions from Portland, Maine to San Diego? From Miami to San Francisco? How did Federal Theatre operate in the hundreds of communities that were not New York, Chicago or Los Angeles?[5]

I began this inquiry with those questions, and over the course of a decade and a half my research journey took me to Washington, DC several times, to the Library of Congress and the National Archives, to the FDR Library at Hyde Park and to George Mason University in Virginia, as well as state and local historical societies. I eventually decided to use the Seattle unit as a focal point for this study because I was fortunate enough to turn up a great deal of information in Seattle, as well as to interview people who had worked on the project there. Seattle was important because it survived to the final days and thus illuminated all of the tensions and contradictions that were played out across the country. It was by no means the most "successful" or largest unit, but it did embody nearly all the programs which characterized the whole enterprise and provides a vivid snapshot of the work. In addition to producing FTP plays, it developed a thriving CCC touring group, successfully completed the research programs which Flanagan prized, developed a theatre for children and had one of the most acclaimed Negro companies.

Although remote from the power struggles in Washington DC and New York City, Seattle was an active participant in the day-by-day operation of the project: the ongoing requests to raise the exemption quotas so that actors who were not on welfare could be cast in pivotal roles, the constant struggle with the state and local WPA personnel who were both part of the project and exempt from some of its chain of command, the never-ending search for local sponsorship to help cover the costs for advertising and other expenses. Operating within the framework of the WPA agenda and struggling constantly to accommodate regional and local interest and impulses, Seattle is a unique lens for examining the complex character of Federal Theatre and for illuminating its multiple dreams and disappointments.

Imagine, then, *Stevedore* in 1936 with its sweeping and passionate call for black and white dock workers to unite against corruption and capitalist exploitation. Imagine its production in Seattle in the aftermath of a waterfront strike when the aroused longshoremen came out of the audience to help the actors build the barricades for the play's climactic struggle. There, thousands of miles from Washington, DC and New York City, was the embodiment of Flanagan's dream of a national theatre. As the *idea* of racism was contested and then submerged in the power of the Sklar and Peter's script, the actual representation of black and white unity was enacted on the stage with such fervor that the lines between audience and actor were blurred. "Dangerous theatre," Flanagan was fond of saying. And here it was dangerous and *alive*. Alive with the possibilities of forging a new national audience, in Loren Kruger's phrase, "out of diverse and divided regions, classes and ethnicities," and invigorated by a "promiscuous mixing of art and politics, uplift and agitation."[6]

I

A showboat for the people

Edwin O'Connor was convinced that a showboat could save Federal Theatre in Seattle. Since his appointment as acting director in 1937, O'Connor had become increasingly frustrated with the problems of finding sufficient performing spaces and now, in late November 1938, the small movie house that the WPA had allotted them was due for demolition by the highway department. With it would go their already cramped shop and storage spaces.

They had performed, like so many of the units that had survived the economic purge of June 1937, in rented halls, gymnasiums, parks, CCC camps and legitimate road houses. But even those were becoming problematic. The big downtown Seattle houses such as the Metropolitan and the Moore were happy to have Federal Theatre for two or three weeks but would not make space available on a regular schedule. Moreover, high school principals were refusing auditoriums to O'Connor because they were anxious about the WPA affiliation and "therefore administration propaganda."[1]

O'Connor was energetic and persuasive. He would turn 42 in December, and he spent many hours in rehearsals and completing Federal Theatre paperwork. He had been transferred to Seattle from Los Angeles, and while at first uncomfortable with the unit, he wanted Seattle theatre to be respected and his title to be permanent. He had done his homework and was now preparing a proposal which would call for the WPA to build his theatre a permanent floating home.

Throughout the fall of 1938 O'Connor visited the Seattle docks and marine shops talking to engineers, sailors and salvage operators. At first he posed as an entrepreneur interested in acquiring a ship for his own theatricals, but gradually he befriended a group of workers who seemed sympathetic to his mission, and he was able to use his WPA connections to speak to labor leaders and sympathetic union personnel. He studied maritime regulations and abandoned the idea of a power-driven ship since this would require three daily shifts of crew. A boat that was towed by a tug would be immensely cheaper, especially if he could convince the Coast Guard, as a sponsoring government agency, to pull them around for free.

At the urging of several maritime officers, he began looking for a hull rather than a working boat, because it would be much less expensive to begin from scratch rather than pay for the disemboweling of the engine, tanks and decks. He discovered that wood was cheaper than metal because steel hulls were required to be drydocked for scraping every year, while comparable wooden ones were scraped every five years. He trudged from dock to dock seeking an appropriate vessel. "Who says hulls can't be found," he wrote to Ole Ness. "I found seven of them and one of them ideal for our purpose. These seven are old, but seaworthy, and the gentleman who owns them has stripped them of all iron, which incidentally is going to Japan."[2]

O'Connor had worked as a lighting designer and stage manager during his apprentice years with the Rachel Crothers and Leon De Casta companies in New York, and he was confident of his drawing and design skills. Again, to save money he prepared elaborate designs and drawings of his proposed showboat which he planned to present to Federal Theatre officials. He envisioned a boat that would seat up to approximately 600 people. The lower deck would house the stage and auditorium, and the upper deck would be partitioned into approximately forty small sleeping rooms which could also double as make-up and dressing spaces. In this arrangement O'Connor was convinced that they could troupe fifty people, taking out everything from musical reviews to Living Newspapers such as *Power* and *One-Third of a Nation*.

He envisioned a route which would take advantage of Seattle's lakes and canals as well as the vast expanse of Puget Sound. Moving from town to town in short hops and playing mostly one-night stands, O'Connor was confident that he would be able to fill the seats for a seventy-three-night season. His itinerary was ambitious, moving from the comfortable calms of Lake Washington through the Straits of Juan Difuca and down the Pacific coast to the treacherous inlet of the Columbia river. His enthusiasm is evident in the letters that he wrote to his supervisors. "I would like to see it done in real show boat fashion. That is not to be too dignified to ballyhoo. A real gaudy show boat painted in WPA colors, covered with colorful WPA and Federal Theatre flags and colored lights, and on docking the old calliope as an attraction."[3]

As for funding, O'Connor also thought it could be done at a bargain. He had no reservation about finding local sponsorship, and because of the sleeping accommodations provided by the boat, he estimated that the regular

1 The ferry *City of Bremerton*. This was Edwin O'Connor's choice to convert into a Federal Theatre showboat.

$3 per diem could easily be cut in half and passed on to local sponsors. That, along with towing charges (if he could not enlist the Coast Guard), would make them an extremely attractive and affordable package. Moreover, he believed that they might be able to go out without sponsorship, if necessary, and keep all the receipts for themselves, thus making the project self-supporting.

Of course, the boat and the remodeling were certain to be costly, but O'Connor believed that they would be able to negotiate for the hull and use WPA labor for the refitting. His first choice was a former ferry, *The City of Bremerton*, for which he had been quoted $1,000, but which he thought he could acquire for half that. His estimate for the remodel was approximately $5,000, with lumber and heavy equipment acquired through government discount and using WPA architects and engineers. In addition, he requested that WPA construct on an appropriate Seattle dock a frame building which would be large enough for shops, rehearsal and offices. It need not be anything elaborate, O'Connor reasoned. "A sort of barrack effect . . . a Pacific coast Provincetown Playhouse."4 Even if his figures were high, he wrote, it would still be cheaper than playing in an uptown theatre and acquiring comparable headquarters and facilities for another year.

O'Connor's proposal was greeted enthusiastically in Washington, DC. Hallie Flanagan was committed to saving as many of the regional units of the enterprise as she could. By 1938 the South was gone. In spite of heroic efforts by many now obscure workers in Birmingham, Atlanta and Tallahassee, Federal Theatre had not been able to overcome the bureaucracy of overlapping WPA agencies and the deeply rooted apartheid system. In the North and West almost all the projects outside of New York, Chicago and Los Angeles were struggling to stay afloat because the rigid spending restrictions created barricades to advertisement, nonrelief casting and quality productions. Flanagan's hope was that increased emphasis on plays about regional concerns as well as projects which would endear Federal Theatre to local sponsorships would be a stimulant to saving the national character of the whole venture. A year earlier she had written to George Kondolf in Chicago that the Federal Theatre had to be a national program and not two or three big metropolitan shows. She encouraged imaginative thinking, touring and satellite programs such as puppetry and dance.[5] She hoped that touring would give the project a public relations boost as well as combat the perception that Federal Theatre was not carrying its message to rural America. WPA officials had approved a national touring plan in April 1938, and Flanagan envisioned a production of *Prologue to Glory* – E.P. Conkle's dramatization of the life of young Abe Lincoln – on a grand tour co-sponsored by the Shubert organization. But the theatrical unions protested, and touring plans bogged down in red tape and labor squabbles. By September 1938 regional touring, however, was still seen as a way of building an audience for Federal Theatre, and Flanagan was anxious to implement it. But even these plans grew contentious. John McGee, for example, had developed an ambitious Midwest plan using Chicago as a hub, but he was confounded by the number of permissions he had to obtain and eventually abandoned the idea. Jane Mathews describes his frustration:

> According to procedure worked out in July, companies would be permitted to tour, provided that permission had been obtained from the regional director of the Federal Theatre, the state administrator in whose state the touring company originated, the state administrator in whose state the company wished to play, and the regional administrator of the Women's and Professional Division. Now Ellen Woodward further insisted that each state administrator also be consulted about each specific playing date within his state and that his approval be telephoned or telegraphed to Washington. To McGee it was utter nonsense. Furious over this "idiotic duplication of approvals," he notified Howard Miller that he would not move a single company out of Chicago until someone had enough "common sense" to cut through this crippling mass of red tape.[6]

In her most recent visit to the Seattle project Flanagan had despaired at the run-down movie house and meager resources. A touring showboat might work. She told her assistant, J. Howard Miller, to follow up with O'Connor and Ness and get some hard figures.

O'Connor was elated. By mid-December he had arranged with Mr. Bancroft in the state WPA office to visit the hull of *The City of Bremerton* with architects and engineers and began arranging for a drydock inspection. The cost of the boat was fixed at $500, although O'Connor believed that they might be able to go a little lower. He wrote to Miller after Christmas that once the hull had been inspected and cleared to be seaworthy, he would arrange for the architects to do the drawings for the remodel.[7]

By the end of January 1939 the blueprints had been drawn, and O'Connor reported that the local WPA engineers were very excited about the venture and the state office seemed to be behind it 100 percent. When Hallie Flanagan visited Seattle the next month to see *Spirochete*, O'Connor went over the plans with her and promised to let her know as soon as they had the exact figures from which a final budget could be prepared. She suggested that he also get some letters of support from prominent members of the community to append to the whole package when it went to the WPA state headquarters for the director's signature. There had been conflicts in the past with Don Abel, the WPA director, and Flanagan wanted it to be clear that there was community support for the project. O'Connor agreed, and by mid-February the showboat proposal was completed and awaited only Abel's signature.

A month passed. Abel had not been particularly supportive of Federal Theatre, but following the *Lysistrata* debacle two years earlier – when Federal Theatre had allowed Abel to save face after his own blunders – O'Connor believed that his enmity was blunted and he would not be an outright foe.[8] Also O'Connor had involved many WPA personnel in his plans for the showboat and he had encountered no resistance. In addition, Abel's assistant, Wallace Kelso, had assured Hallie Flanagan on her last visit that Abel was supportive of the showboat notion. But there were omens, and O'Connor could not suppress the uneasy feeling that the whole enterprise might blow up in his face. After all the WPA had already built a showboat theatre in Seattle, and while it was stationary and used for student productions at the University of Washington, it was captained by Glenn Hughes, the director of the School of Drama and the man who had been Hallie Flanagan's initial choice to run Federal Theatre in the Northwest. The honeymoon had been brief, however, and now Hughes was adamant that the Federal Theatre, like the rest of the New Deal, was mostly "boondoggle."

O'Connor called the Port Commission, which he had enlisted as a sponsor on the project, and discovered that the supervisor Horace Chapman had discussed the idea with Glenn Hughes and that Hughes was totally opposed to it.[9] A subsequent call from the head of the Stagehands union alerted O'Connor that Hughes was bringing all possible pressure to bear to prevent the theatre from being built. Then O'Connor spotted an item in the society column of a local paper that Mr. and Mrs. Abel had dined with Mr. and Mrs. Hughes and then attended a production at the university Showboat Theatre. "We have never been able to get him to one production here," lamented O'Connor to Flanagan, "even though he assured you he would pay more attention to Federal Theatre."[10]

In spite of all his work and the goodwill and support of many people, O'Connor could sense that the ground was shifting. Glenn Hughes was a formidable presence in the community, and in his brief association with the Federal Theatre he had become acquainted with key WPA personnel. Although many of them did not understand how a *floating*, professional theatre would be competition for a *stationary*, student one, Hughes was the authority on theatre in the Northwest, and people generally respected and acceded to his opinions. If there was to be a battle it might get very nasty because O'Connor shared Hallie Flanagan's current views of Hughes – that he was a vain, dictatorial opportunist who had used WPA funds to build his own empire and then turned his back on Federal One. In October 1937 she had written him a stinging letter demanding that he explain, "on what statistics and what critical judgements you base the statement made at Stanford University characterizing the Federal Theatre as 'the most wasteful and least satisfying experiment ever indulged in?'"[11] In subsequent trips to Seattle, she ignored him.

On March 24, 1939, O'Connor was summoned to a meeting by Abel's assistant, Wallace Kelso, and other WPA officials who told him that the showboat project was not feasible. Their former enthusiasm had been replaced by three specific concerns. First, the money pledged by Federal Theatre for other than labor expenses was inadequate. Second, the plan would require a number of skilled workers, and the local WPA was already beyond its proscribed limit. And, third, since no one could guarantee that there would even *be* a Federal Theatre by July, this was not the time to undertake a new project. O'Connor countered that he was sure that Flanagan could help him find more money if that was the principal objection. But Kelso was firm.

Money wasn't the "prime concern," he said, but rather that "Mr. Abel does not think it a good time to set up a show boat project."[12]

O'Connor was stymied. The decision had been made, and each objection that he raised was dismissed in light of Abel's decision. "It was comic and it was sad," he wrote to Flanagan, "sad in as much as the moment I entered I knew it was doomed, and comic to watch Mr. Kelso struggle to remember his rehearsed objections."[13] What frustrated him most was that no one had raised any serious opposition in the months when he had been preparing the report, and now the WPA was backing out just because the state administrator did not think it was an appropriate time to pursue a new project. O'Connor was convinced that he had been done in by "the Glenn" but he also renounced, "A couple of fearful souls who don't know which way the wind will be blowing in 1940. I hate cowardice when it injures others more than the cowards themselves."[14] While Congress debated the future of the whole New Deal apparatus in Washington, DC, the WPA succeeded in blocking the Federal Theatre in Washington State, a practice they had rehearsed nationally many times in the stormy history of the project.

Understanding the complex relationship between the WPA and the Arts Projects is critical to any study of the Federal Theatre and particularly crucial in Seattle. By September 1935 every state had a WPA director who was responsible for all activity, projects and personnel. When Harry Hopkins created Federal One, however, he promised Hallie Flanagan and the three other national directors full freedom and authority to run the programs from Washington, DC. It was a promise that he needed to make in order to secure the best people, but it would plague him and Federal Theatre personnel because of the awkward reporting structure which quickly emerged.

At first Hopkins tried to finesse the state WPA directors by instructing them of the need to be cooperative and of their *advisory* role in the new organization. On September 29, 1935, he wrote to them that:

> the Directors of these (Art) projects are authorized to select project units within the states which they wish to include in the national project. You are directed to give them and the members of their staffs continuous advice, suggestions and aid regarding professional personnel and projects that have heretofore been in operation or have been organized for operation. The decision as to those units to be included in the national project rests with its National Director or his designated representatives.[15]

In other words, appointments to local Federal Theatre units could be suggested and recommended by WPA officials, but the final authority rested with the national director and her representatives. Hopkins wanted the Arts Projects to be independent of the existing WPA reporting structure, but he also did not wish to build a completely parallel bureaucracy. Thus, as Federal One began to organize on a regional and state basis, Hopkins went back to his state WPA directors and ordered that they "service" the arts programs through their divisions of Finance and Employment.

The result of this directive to "service" meant that the salaries of all Federal Theatre personnel, as well as all expenses associated with materials and space, were paid through the state WPA offices even though these same offices were effectively removed from administrative authority and the command structure. The potential for ill will was enormous, and it did not take long for a mini-rebellion within the WPA.

Directors in Illinois, Indiana, Oklahoma and elsewhere balked at having their authority questioned and others flooded Washington with letters and phone calls of protest. Some state directors were outraged at suddenly finding people whom they didn't even know – or in some cases, didn't like – on their payrolls. In Iowa the state administrator argued that he had been appointed to administer all relief personnel and theatre people were no different from other laborers.[16] But Hopkins backed Hallie and his other arts directors because he had promised them no interference when he had coaxed them aboard the project.

Still, the reporting process of the arts directors to Hopkins was a constant source of confusion and irritation. As early as May 1936, Flanagan, fearing WPA interference, complained to Hopkins that "in New Jersey our state director is called (in order to satisfy some strange, sadistic desire on the part of the state WPA director) a 'special representative' and is not allowed to communicate with us except in the third person through letters signed by assistant WPA officials." She went on to explain that, "I find everywhere in the field, not only from the arts people, but from district and state WPA administrators and professional and service people, many of whom have consulted me on the project, great confusion."[17]

The confusion was due not only to the reporting structure. The WPA was always suspicious of the Arts Projects because the bulk of WPA work was manual labor and the "dole." Many state administrators believed vehemently that the arts programs were boondoggling and wasteful. Because of this many WPA personnel delayed implementing Hopkins's organizational scheme for Federal One completely and seized every opportunity to frustrate or scuttle the Arts Projects at the state and local level. They also believed that the programs constituted a "federalization" of relief to which they were opposed. And while they were willing to accept federal money, they balked at federal control of policy or operation.[18] This attitude – and the subsequent behavior of many state and regional WPA personnel – was the immediate source for the censorship battles which had plagued the Theatre Project as well as the ongoing skirmishes over proposals such as Edwin O'Connor's Seattle showboat.[19]

By the spring of 1939 Hallie Flanagan was consumed with her battle to save Federal Theatre. She had overcome WPA timidity and testified courageously in defense of her record before HUAC (House Un-American Activities Committee). After weeks of red-baiting, innuendo and scurrilous charges, she confronted her attackers with facts, figures, common sense and dignity. But the circus atmosphere carried over into the endless appropriations battles in Congress, and the anti-New Deal battle plan became clear. They would hold the entire WPA appropriation hostage for Federal Theatre. Tarred as "red" and "wasteful" the project seemed doomed, but Flanagan mounted a powerful counterattack hoping at the very least that the project could survive by consolidating its gains and be reorganized as a truly National Theatre.

In such an atmosphere she had to choose her battles carefully and husband her energies. She was fond of the "indomitable" Edwin O'Connor, and she felt that his showboat idea would address some of her original and fundamental notions about the project. It would take theatre – hopefully meaningful theatre – to the people. She was also proud of what had been accomplished in Seattle in spite of continued opposition: the thrilling Living Newspapers; the Negro Company; the exquisite model theatres; the children's productions. She had even sent her favorite protégée, Esther Porter Lane, to help the project get back on its feet after the 1937 recession and cutbacks. In accordance with some of her recent directives, the Seattle unit was working on a huge pageant to celebrate the centennial of the Catholic Church in the Northwest and preparing a new Living Newspaper, *Timber*, based on the commercialization and destruction of America's old growth forests. Plus the New Deal had some allies in Seattle. So perhaps it was time to call for help.

The state of Washington had had Republican leadership for most of its history but that had collapsed in the New Deal landslides, and the Democrats had inherited a host of social problems along with their new political clout. Unemployment, unionization and labor wars had fueled huge schisms in the Party, and in the summer of 1935 the left-liberal wing had been contested by the appearance of the Washington Commonwealth

Federation. The Federation, which was to play a decisive role in Seattle and Washington State politics throughout the late 1930s, advanced an aggressive agenda which featured public ownership of utilities, old age pensions and production-for-use plans.[20] Like many "left" constituents across the country, the Federation wanted to claim the "New Deal" label in the state and, at the same time, not be branded as "red" when the Communist Party embraced many of their political planks. It was a difficult balancing act especially after the declaration of the Popular Front that encouraged the Communist Party to support the New Deal.

Although the Federation was eventually discredited by its silence and then acquiescence to the Hitler–Stalin pact and by the failure of its leader, Howard Costigan, to separate them from the Communists, it had considerable political clout in the spring of 1939 and was anxious to ingratiate itself with the Roosevelt administration. Flanagan appealed to Costigan to see if he could bring any pressure on the local WPA with regard to O'Connor's showboat.

On April 26, 1939, Howard Costigan responded to Flanagan and expressed his surprise that anyone would want to block such an endeavor, but that he had heard that it was largely due to the efforts of a local director and "bitter opponent of the show boat" who sees it as competition. Costigan goes on in effusive terms to describe how important such a venture could be:

> Personally, I think the show boat idea such a swell one that no New Dealer who isn't a block-head could possibly oppose it. It will bring to well over a hundred small Washington towns their first taste not only of the legitimate theatre but a socially significant theatre as well. It offers an opportunity to reach those communities which have under the lash of consistent tory propaganda become convinced that the Federal Theatre is first a subversive force and second is a waste of money. Had this show boat idea been developed prior to the public utility district elections throughout the state, many of the communities not now enjoying public power facilities would be getting their first taste of cheaper power. As I told you, the only way the Federal Theatre, or for that matter all federal agencies, can meet the attack of the budgeteers is not by retreat but by advancement. The quickest way to dispel opposition to the Federal Theatre is to bring Federal Theatre productions to the country. What Washington small towns may think "red" in the abstract becomes upon association common sense in the concrete. By reaching more people, the Federal Theatre has nothing to lose but the public opposition which has developed chiefly because of its absence.[21]

Costigan was an articulate and passionate spokesman for human rights and a leader in Seattle's attempts to address unemployment and fair wages. And while he may wax enthusiastically about the project in that gloomy spring of 1939, it is refreshing to compare his vision of a theatre with that which was being offered on the floor of the Congress in Washington, DC by the likes of Senator Everett Dirkson of Illinois and others. Costigan assured Hallie that he would "take the matter up with Anna" and then they would meet with O'Connor and see what could be done.

Anna was Anna Roosevelt Boettiger, daughter of President and Mrs. Roosevelt, an editor at the *Seattle Post-Intelligencer* and wife of John Boettiger, the publisher of the *P-I*. Sent to Seattle by William Randolph Hearst in late 1936, Boettiger had been charged with the task of restoring the paper's credibility after the acrimonious labor action which had closed the paper for forty-nine days. Caught between the warring forces of Dave Beck's teamsters and Harry Bridges' expansionist ILA (International Longshoreman's Association), Boettiger had steered the paper on a course to gain union representation based upon a majority vote and to soften the virulent anti-New Deal stance of his predecessors. It was a difficult job. In their first meeting Bridges informed Boettiger that he planned to take over the Newspaper Guild and the *P-I*, and that he had no interest in a friendship with Boettiger. "He advised me not to be friendly with labor," Boettiger wrote to FDR, "that labor leaders would rather deal with an employer who was recognizedly their enemy."[22] Of course, Beck was a thug too, in Boettiger's estimation, but he at least was not a communist like Bridges. "I have no idea what Miss Perkins discovered in her investigation in 1934," he wrote to his father-in-law, "but he's a very smelly egg!"[23]

Anna tried to stay out of the political fray. In her capacity as "associate editor," she wanted to remain as objective as she could and devote time to raising the family. Of course, she was courted by a variety of "women's" constituencies and was targeted for special invitations from all factions of the Democratic Party. Shortly after her arrival in Seattle, Anna received a delightful letter from Mary Dewson, vice-chair of the Democratic National Campaign Committee, synopsizing the important women in the state Democratic Party and advising her whom to pursue and whom to avoid: "a real battle-axe...the wealthiest woman in Seattle... she's like Jim Farley, a fixer...supporter of your father...her husband is a poof!"[24] Anna thanked her for her thumbnail sketches and said that she had already been introduced to many of the women on the list. She was anxious to represent her family and the party in the West and was fascinated by the "New Dealers" such as the Washington Commonwealth Federation.

By mid-May 1939, while the House Appropriations Committee was debating the future of Federal Theatre and Flanagan was once again planning a spirited defense, Edwin O'Connor met with Howard Costigan to plan a showboat counterattack. O'Connor was impressed with Costigan's vigor and enthusiasm for the project, and his spirits were lifted again. They discussed the route of the proposed tour, the kinds of plays to be presented and the WPA objections to the proposal. After an hour reviewing the principal concerns, Costigan agreed to speak to Don Abel while O'Connor huddled with Anna Boettiger to see what additional support they could rally.

With Costigan, Abel seems to have been much less rigid. He reviewed the financial proposal and told him that he did not believe that $5,000 was sufficient to accomplish the work. Moreover, with the present uncertainty in Washington, DC he simply did not think that it was a good time to mount a brand-new venture. Costigan pressed him on the financial issues and inquired whether the local WPA would be more cooperative if additional funds could be secured? Although this point had been rejected in earlier discussions, Abel paused. If the National Office was really behind the project then perhaps "it would be a good idea."[25]

With Anna, however, he was much less hopeful. After O'Connor had briefed her on the showboat history, she too met with Abel to explore areas of cooperation. While she was always cautious of intervening where she had no expertise, she was convinced by both Costigan and O'Connor that this was an extremely worthwhile project. Abel returned to his favorite two themes: that this whole idea did not appeal to him very strongly, and that the Federal Theatre did not have enough money to carry out the job anyway. Then he introduced a new wrinkle which had not been discussed before and which did appeal strongly to him. He complained to Anna that, in the current construction jobs that he was supervising in the state, the army and navy engineers were providing the construction plans and drawings and he "did not wish to change this custom or rule."[26] Anna very likely did not know that WPA engineers had drawn the plans four months earlier.

By mid-June the fight to save Federal Theatre was at flood tide in Washington, DC. At the beginning of the month the *Washington Post* had leaked a story about the Federal Theatre being discontinued before the WPA budget was approved, and Flanagan had mounted a final campaign to save the program. With telegrams and phone calls pouring in from around the country and Talullah Bankhead working her oratorical magic in front of the

Senate Appropriations Committee, Flanagan was determined to halt the attacks against Federal Theatre.[27] On June 13 she took a moment and wrote to Howard Costigan about her hopes that the showboat would survive in Seattle. It had always been her goal to have a truly national project and to have local sponsorship for the regional theatres. "I am glad to hear that you have not given up," she wrote, "neither have I and neither apparently has Mrs. Boettiger." She indicated that more admissions money could be allocated to the project and added that, "I believe a show boat with the season guaranteed by the Commonwealth Federation and the *Post-Intelligencer* might be a wonderful way of swinging it."[28] Two weeks later, however, it was a moot point. By Act of Congress the vision of a nationally subsidized theatre – free, adult and uncensored – was as dead as the NRA (National Recovery Act), the FERA (Federal Emergency Relief Administration) and countless other New Deal programs.

The visionary but ultimately futile attempt to launch a showboat in Seattle encapsulates many of the tensions that were inherent in the Federal Theatre Project, especially in the dozens of projects outside New York City. Imagined and pursued by men and women of talent and commitment, showboat was an idea that embodied the best of Federal One. At inexpensive prices and with limited production costs, live and meaningful theatre could be brought to people who might never have experienced it before. And, ideally, that theatre would address and reflect the regional concerns of its actors and its audience. Ultimately it would be self-supporting, or at least freed from the requirements of a national subsidy. But the venture was constantly plagued by a triumvirate of woes that haunted many projects: scarcity of funds for material costs (other than labor); local jealousies about who was "qualified" to present theatre in the community; and finally, WPA roadblocks from the "umbrella" group which the theatres should have been able to turn to for support and encouragement.

Still, its failed history is emblematic of the vigor and imagination which characterized much of the Seattle project. When the closing notices were finally posted that summer of 1939, rehearsals were already underway for a new Living Newspaper about the timber industry in the United States, the "white" company had received rave notices for staging a huge pageant commemorating the centennial of the Catholic Church in the Northwest, and O'Connor had revived the Negro Company which was already nationally recognized for a world premiere of *Natural Man* and a stunning *Stevedore*. In four years Seattle had compiled an enviable calendar of striking productions such as *An Evening With Dunbar*, *Spirochete* and *One-Third of a Nation*. It had confronted and shocked audiences with their "Ethiopian" *Lysistrata* and had engaged the electorate in the public utilities debate over public ownership in *Power*. It had articulated and accomplished a vigorous historical research project and created a thriving children's theatre. And in spite of the active enmity of their first director, Glenn Hughes, it had succeeded in approaching Hallie Flanagan's dream of creating a theatre that entertained and debated issues relevant to the nation and the local community.

2

Glenn's plan

It was Gordon Craig, the legendary English designer, who mentioned Glenn Hughes to Flanagan. "He's got a great plan for theatre in the Northwest," he wrote her.[1] It was August 1935 and Flanagan was putting together the team which would establish professional "Federal" theatres across the country. Although she had met some initial resistance on Broadway, she had been able to recruit influential people in the "regional" theatre, and she was delighted with Craig's recommendation. In the Midwest she had signed up E.C. Mabie, the head of theatre studies at the University of Iowa, and in the Southeast she had tapped the University of North Carolina for playwright Paul Green and Frederick Koch, an important advocate of folk and regional drama. Her roster included some of the country's most important regional producers and directors: Gilmore Brown from the Pasadena Playhouse, Jasper Deeter from Hedgerow Theatre and Frederick McConnell from the Cleveland Play House. Hughes would complement these imaginative and active people, who were not closely allied with the commercial Broadway establishment and who were a strong force in trying to rally a federation of national theatres.

Flanagan's decision to accept the directorship of the Federal Theatre had not been an easy one partly because of the tensions she foresaw between this venture and America's professional theatre. Certainly the Broadway stage had been impacted by the market crash and the subsequent depression, but there was still a very active theatre in New York, and newly emerging organizations such as The Group Theatre demonstrated that quality work could still be done even in the depths of economic disaster. Surely the answer was not to provide competition for the stage at a time when it was still adjusting to the threats from radio and motion pictures? In addition, many theatre people believed that the project, by focusing on relief artists, was only insuring its mediocrity.

When she convinced the highly respected playwright Elmer Rice, however, to head the New York City unit, the Project gained some credibility, especially with young people and left-wing artists who admired Rice's passionate commitment to social causes and freedom of expression.[2] And in spite of the fact that many Broadway professionals never supported the idea of "government theatre" – and that Flanagan was never able to win important concessions from Equity and the Stagehands union – many agreed with Barrett Clark's characterization that, "very little good can come to the theatre through this scheme, but we may be able to prevent some harm."[3]

The reason that Flanagan was able to move so quickly and effectively in establishing a national network that summer was because a "shadow" organization was more or less in place. Although it is frequently overlooked in studies of the Federal Theatre, the history and activity of the National Theatre Conference provided a skeleton upon which Hallie erected the edifice of her new organization. The NTC had emerged in the late 1920s to fill the void left by the demise of the Drama League and to accommodate a burgeoning number of university and community theatres. Inspired by a series of meetings at Carnegie Tech (November 1925), Yale (February 1927) and Northwestern (June 1931), the leaders of America's "Little," community and college theatres had banded together to address common concerns as well as the state of the art across the country. With grant support from the Carnegie Foundation, they established a federation of working theatres which would address common concerns and problems including sharing new scripts, building local play libraries, circulating and publishing new books and generally combating what many of them sensed as working "alone" in the vast territory outside New York City. In 1932 they elected a board of directors and officers and outlined a constitution to govern the operation of their activities. George Pierce Baker, now director of the Yale Drama School, was the first president of the National Theatre Conference with E.C. Mabie and Gilmore Brown as vice-presidents and Kenneth Macgowan and Frederick McConnell as members of the board. Edith Isaacs served as corresponding secretary and provided a rent-free headquarters in the offices of her *Theatre Arts Monthly* in New York City.

Because of its commitment to the regional theatre, the National Theatre Conference divided the country into nine geographical areas and appointed a director for each section. The goal was not only to "decentralize" the theatre but also to provide a mechanism for encouraging and supporting production and related activity in each area. They saw themselves as producing not only theatre but also books, newsletters and as consulting on matters of theatre architecture, fund raising and equipment. It was an ambitious project and only fitfully successful, but it was to Edith Isaacs, E.C. Mabie and others in the National Theatre Conference that Flanagan turned in the summer of 1935 to plan the federalization of the professional theatre. And it was principally National Theatre Conference personnel whom she relied upon to develop the regions of the emerging Federal Theatre Project.[4]

Flanagan knew of Glenn Hughes's reputation as a theatrical entrepreneur because of his participation in the NTC, and Gordon Craig's endorsement convinced her that he was the most appropriate person to direct the Northwest region of her Project. On August 9, 1935, she wrote him a long letter in which she outlined the parameters for the program and inquired about whether he would consider serving as regional administrator. It is an important document because she makes it clear that *relief* is central to the mission of the program and that its nature is to be thoroughly *professional*. In light of subsequent misunderstandings and quarrels in all regions of the country, however, it is instructive to examine the initial correspondence to see what positions were advanced, what promises made. Or, in Dorothy Parker's metaphor from the bridge table, "to review the bidding with the original emphasis."

The most frequent critique of the entire Federal Theatre Project is that it was flawed from the outset because of its impossible mixture of art and relief. How could you possibly hope to produce first-class *professional* theatre when you were casting almost entirely from welfare rolls? It was a dilemma that each region wrestled with and which Flanagan and her advisors constantly addressed with innovative changes, easements of WPA requirements and special exceptions. But it was always there, lurking in the background of every casting call, frantic rehearsal period and last-minute preparations for opening nights.

A week before she was sworn in as national director, Hallie Flanagan submitted a plan to begin spending WPA money as soon as she was authorized. The central premise of her plan was "that the re-employment of theatre people now on relief rolls is the primary aim."[5] A week earlier she had written to Glenn Hughes:

> the project will work through regional theatres. In each case any theatre enrolled would have to absorb a certain number of unemployed actors, technicians, etc... About 1 percent could be *not* from relief rolls, working on small administrative salaries... You understand that the government would pay wages and allow a small production budget... Admission fees would accrue to your own project.[6]

While there is nothing untrue in any of this, it is important to note that "a certain number" is actually a huge number, and admission fees only accrued to local projects if there was a "sponsoring organization which is a public enterprise or a non-profit-making co-operative."[7]

Glenn Hughes was 41 years old, making $4,000 per year directing dramatics at the University of Washington in Seattle and was in the midst of building an impressive theatrical program. Through his participation in the National Theatre Conference he had met George Pierce Baker, E.C. Mabie and others of his generation who were instrumental in introducing theatrical practice into the traditional curriculums of American colleges and universities. He had succeeded in spectacular fashion, and his practice-based theatre training, in which his students performed constantly, would earn him many plaudits and a share of controversy. He was bright, articulate and capable of sustained periods of hard work. And while he was not especially sympathetic to "New Deal" politics, he did realize – as did his colleagues at Chapel Hill and Northwestern and many other places – that federal dollars to support theatre arts were a very rare commodity and not to be taken lightly. Accordingly, Hughes cleared his desk and spent the next few days drawing up a comprehensive "Plan for a Federal Theatre Project in the Pacific Northwest Region."[8] He completed it on August 17, 1935 and mailed it to Hallie Flanagan. Its conception and detail are meticulous and imaginative; the financial projections are sound; and the local analysis, thorough and provocative. Ironically, much of it seems at odds with what Hallie Flanagan was proposing.

Hughes begins by outlining the "premises" on which his plan is based. A "strictly" professional theatre cannot compete with the motion pictures, he contends, so the hope for the future of legitimate theatre in America rests with "community" (amateur) theatre. Moreover, these community theatres should begin modestly and grow "naturally" around the concerns of the community and not be imposed with "pretentious, subsidized starts." Ideally there would be a series of modestly supported theatres offering work to the community which had been made there. And these theatres must have their own spaces, their own "homes."

Hughes was opposed to large "Civic" theatres and preferred a neighborhood concept. He believed that communities with a minimum of 15,000 people could support a theatre, and for metropolitan areas such as Seattle (population 366,000) he proposed four in "different parts of the city."[9] In a section titled "The Nature of the Proposed Theatres," he stresses that no new structures need to be erected. Instead old buildings – stores, garages, churches and barns – would be leased and "converted by relief labor" into theatres. Equipment would be portable. Seating would vary from 100 to 500.

In terms of personnel and budget, Hughes proposed that a "trained theatrical director" be employed on a nonrelief basis at each theatre. He would report to a regional board of five who would also be paid and who would advise on matters of play selection, design, technical direction, business and production. This board would additionally employ a relief staff of thirty, which would include draftsmen, stenographers, clerks, etc. At each theatre the director would train and supervise a company of thirty-two relief people: sixteen actors and sixteen production (including electricians, stage managers, board operators, carpenters, props and janitors). To deflect the criticism that the companies were "just relief," Hughes proposed two additional strategies. A percentage of nonpaid volunteers "like students" could be used and "some" actors could be paid out of receipts, "although no more than 50 percent of the gross receipts should be used for this purpose."

The repertoire would be a balance between nonroyalty classics and modern low-royalty plays, although each theatre would be encouraged to develop original nonroyalty works. With an efficient staff a new production would be ready every five weeks, which would allow a month's run and a week of final rehearsals. There would be a minimum of two performances per week with a maximum of six. Admission would range from 25 to 50 cents.

Hughes then provides Flanagan an elaborate financial breakdown with an "estimation of earning power and suggestions as to disposition of resources." Based upon an average of 125 seats sold at 35 cents for three performances over forty weeks he projects gross annual earnings of $5,250. After an initial outlay of $4,000 for equipment he projects annual expenses at $3,600 (excluding all labor) for such items as rent, printing, royalty, utilities, telephone, etc. He then cites his own recently opened Penthouse Theatre as an example of just such an operation. Since April they have been grossing $104 per week against expenses of $72. Because it was constructed with WPA labor, its initial debt to the university was only $1,500, which Hughes projects will be entirely paid for in eleven months. Finally, returning to labor costs he estimates that the cost to Federal Theatre (using thirty-two company members at relief wages of $50 per month plus directors and advisors) for twenty-seven theatres throughout Washington, Oregon, Idaho and Montana will be $826,800.

Hughes's bold plan for a federation of amateur theatres in the four states of the Northwest is a complicated and sometimes conflicted document, but it had a breadth of imagination combined with attention to detail that was impressive. Moreover, as Hughes was careful to point out, it was rooted in the reality of successful producing and buttressed by his experience in running two profitable houses to public acclaim at the University of Washington. Hughes knew that smart, persuasive people could extract money from the government for local projects, and his own success in gaining WPA support for his Penthouse Theatre was a valuable model. In the days ahead he would repeat this venture with federal support for his "stationary" showboat. For now, however, in the waning summer of 1935, he had a vision of his producing skills magnified many times in a theatre "writ large" across the Northwest. And although the asking price was ten times what would eventually come to Seattle in their first federal allocation, and although the entire enterprise was grounded in an "amateur theatre," Hallie Flanagan loved it.

"Your plan is magnificent!" she gushed. "I want to appoint you regional director for the Northwest."[10]

In Washington, DC there was incredible turmoil. Flanagan's office was literally being built around her. "Bombarded by the sounds of electric fans, riveting machines and hammering workmen, she alternated between hope and despair as she read the letters of men and women pleading for work and struggled with red tape, confusion and delays in working out financial and labor policies."[11] As summer turned into fall, she fashioned her national team, tried to find shortcuts through the maze of WPA forms and sought to placate theatrical labor unions. Hughes's plan must have seemed a marvel of clarity and precision, and she hoped that he would accept her job offer. Many of her NTC colleagues who had full-time positions were willing to donate their time or work for a small honorarium. But she was willing to pay to get accomplished administrators. She wrote Hughes that his "splendid project" was awaiting the development of proper government forms, and that she was authorized to pay him $3,000 per year if he'd join the team full time or $2,000 if he wanted only part-time status. If he wished to "volunteer," she would pay him $1 plus traveling expenses and $5 per diem. "We want you, whatever arrangements you are willing and able to make."[12]

In the meantime she had asked Hughes – along with all of her other directors – to begin investigating how many theatre people were certified for relief in their cities and regions. Determining how many unemployed there were was central to the implementation of the whole project, and she was already getting conflicting numbers. New York City was no problem. They were already lining up there. But the numbers varied widely from state to state. In addition, getting an accurate count was further complicated by the fact that many theatre people had recorded other occupations when they had originally signed up for relief. Furthermore, Flanagan was unsure how to deal with people who now suddenly announced that they were qualified in "theatre." What would be an appropriate audition process that they could implement nationwide?

In consultation with Harry Hopkins, Jacob Baker and other WPA administrators, Flanagan planned a meeting of all her national and regional personnel in Washington, DC on October 8, 1935. Slowly the structure was emerging: Charles Coburn, the professional actor and director, would supervise in New England, joining Gilmore Brown from Los Angeles, John McGee from the Birmingham, Alabama Little Theatre, Jasper Deeter from Pennsylvania, E.C. Mabie from Iowa and Fred Koch from Chapel Hill. All the appointments had to be approved by the administration, and they went through quicker if accompanied by a political endorsement. Flanagan believed that Senator Lewis Schwellenbach, a New Dealer from Washington State, would be the appropriate party to speak for Glenn Hughes who also had to have the approval of Dr. Lee Paul Sieg, the president of the University of Washington. Schwellenbach told Sieg that it would be helpful if Hughes could demonstrate a connection with the Democratic Party. In some apparent frustration Hughes wrote to Flanagan, "this I cannot do... I have few political contacts, and as a rule few political interests. I have no record with either political party."[13]

But Hughes had been doing his homework in preparation for setting up Federal Theatre in the Northwest. He had made official inquiries to the state directors of Federal Re-Employment for Idaho, Oregon and Montana asking about numbers of theatrical people registered for relief. The Montana office reported that they had *none*, which did not surprise Hughes but which did spur him to write a lengthy letter to Flanagan in which he reviewed his objections to the way the plan was being envisioned. In light of subsequent developments, both in Washington State and in other projects all over the country, it is instructive to examine this letter and Flanagan's response to it in some detail.

After reviewing the dearth of theatre people on relief in the Northwest, Hughes explains:

> What this means is that we have no problem of theatrical people on relief, in the sense that they have theatrical people on relief in New York and California. It is perfectly natural. Professional actors, directors, etc., would hardly stay in a territory such as this where there are practically no professional theatre activities.
>
> This does not mean, however, that there are not many persons on relief who would be interested in working in the theatre and in learning the

various arts and crafts of the theatre. My original plan, as you may recall, was not based on the establishment of a professional theatre, but on the foundation of a number of small amateur community theatres. In other words, in a region such as this a theatre project must be thought of as a social-artistic institution and not at all a professional institution. And personally I think it is a mistake to stimulate professional stock and road companies with government money, and to raise the hopes of hundreds of actors, when there is such a slim chance of their being able to live from the practice of this profession after the government subsidy has been withdrawn...

I may be wrong, but from what I have read of the theatre relief work in New York, I am inclined to think that hundreds of persons are being encouraged to follow the theatrical profession when they should be discouraged...

As you see, I am all for the amateur theatre. And this may not be in line with your thought entirely, or with the aims of the administration.[14]

Hughes goes on to say that he is continuing to gather data and also to compile lists of capable directors and supervisors to be employed on a nonrelief basis.

Two days later he telegraphed his official answer to her offer to become regional director in the Northwest. "Will accept Regional Director... without pay...Best wishes."[15]

Flanagan wanted a national theatre. From the outset it was important that the theatre not only be professional but also that it be nationwide. In her ideal model these theatres would be embraced by their local communities, develop plays and pageants out of their local concerns and eventually survive and prosper without federal support. The tension between a national theatre and a "professional" one, however, was formidable and – as Hughes's letter demonstrates – one that was raised clearly *before* Federal Theatre ever had a formal meeting or a premiere performance.

Flanagan was elated to have Hughes on board. "There was general rejoicing in this office when your telegram arrived," she wrote him. She also reminded him that "re-employment is the goal working through existing theatres," however, in the event there are none, "*independent theatre companies may be formed with a production program capable of becoming integrated into community life.*"[16] It's an intriguing idea, fraught with contradiction and confusion. A professional company could be created, if necessary, from relief rolls virtually void of theatre people. It was a notion that would haunt them. But time was pressing; Flanagan needed to assemble her team and demonstrate to Hopkins and the WPA bureaucrats that she could spend their money.

In October they assembled in Washington, DC for two days of orientation and exhortation. WPA officials reviewed for them procedures for identifying, hiring and paying qualified personnel. They were given sample forms, manuals and lists of instructions. Reporting channels, especially those in which Federal One overlapped with the WPA offices already in existence, were carefully explained. And Hallie Flanagan outlined for them her vision of a great national theatre sensitive to the issues of the day and reflective of the struggles that were going on all across America. She spoke of a three-fold artistic policy which would concentrate on putting theatre people back to work at reduced prices – or free – and which would be, "national in scope, regional in emphasis, and democratic in allowing each local unit freedom" in setting their goals and making their choices.[17] Her words were exhilarating and, in spite of what many perceived as an inordinate amount of red tape and paperwork, her team left with a vision of theatre which would reach out to all – blacks, children, poor and all the political and class shades that made up the United States of America. Her rhetoric still crackles on the page: "man is whispering through space, soaring to the stars in ships, flinging miles of steel and glass into the air. Shall the theatre continue to huddle in the confines of a painted box set?"[18]

Glenn Hughes rode the train back to Seattle. Like others he was energized by Flanagan's oratory, but he was having doubts and several concerns were nagging at him. Could one really create and then run a theatre with this much bureaucracy? Requisitions with five carbon copies? Requests to continue projects – even after they had been approved – every two weeks? Payrolls processed through state and local WPA offices that had played no part in the interviewing or hiring of the people being paid? Production costs that were limited to 10 percent of your budget with little apparent concern for advertising, promotions and the various devices that Hughes had learned about putting people in seats? Freedom from censorship but proscribed by a codicil that forbade anything "cheap, vulgar or that the government could not stand behind."[19] And all this to be carried out by a handful of paid supervisory personnel and relief rolls that would yield, Hughes suspected, principally vaudeville actors, amateur poseurs and motion picture camera operators. Before Yellowstone Limited reached Seattle, he had decided one thing emphatically. He would need an assistant to help launch this venture; perhaps more than one.

Flanagan's official notification empowered Hughes to "approve or disapprove, on the basis of artistic integrity and social desirability, projects calling for the employment of actors, directors and all types of theatre workmen."[20] Since the summer announcement that the government was going into the theatre business, WPA offices had been flooded with inquiries, and now that the structure of Federal One was in place the mail and referrals came to Hughes. Toinette Swan proposed to Hallie Flanagan directly that the government should undertake a Gilbert & Sullivan festival at her Tacoma Civic Theatre and cites local rumors that if Glenn Hughes gets control of the money he would only "use his own people."[21] Flanagan replied that, of course, he wouldn't and turned the correspondence over to Hughes. Florence and Burton James, founders of the Seattle Repertory Playhouse and former colleagues of Hughes in his drama department, also wrote directly to Flanagan calling her attention to the work they had done in developing a theatre program for the schools in Washington State, and that any plans for government support in the Northwest should certainly consider them and their avowed mission of creating new audiences.[22] Again Flanagan asks them to contact Glenn Hughes. As the list of suitors multiplied, Hughes realized that he was in danger of being overwhelmed by the sheer amount of the requests and responses. "I am swamped with work," he told Flanagan and, "must therefore have an assistant approved immediately if I am to make any progress with theatre projects in this territory... there are about a thousand things that need doing immediately."[23] His was not a unique situation. As her directors fanned out following the October meeting in Washington, DC, they all encountered the incredible task of putting theatre programs into place where talent was limited and bureaucracy was paramount. One of their greatest obstacles was local WPA officials who, in spite of Hopkins's directives and pleas, thwarted and frustrated the idealistic theatre directors. Plagued by the conflicts between local WPA units and the demands of the new reporting structure and the need to discover talented performers among the confusing relief rolls, many of the original directors were unable to sustain their original enthusiasm. Even the indefatigable E.C. Mabie, plagued by red tape and meager relief rolls, finally threw in the towel after barely three months on the job. Six months after the Washington, DC meeting only eight of Flanagan's original twenty-four directors were still working for Federal Theatre.[24]

But Hughes soldiered on. He had convinced one of his former students, Guy Williams, to take on the "assistant" role and persuaded Flanagan to appoint him officially at a salary of $1,800 per year. Williams, who was 30 years old and had good organizational skills, had been working in publicity and promotion for several Seattle theatres including managing the road tours of the Cornish College Players and doing professional promotion for the local Moore Theatre. He was bright and ambitious and very loyal to Hughes. Together they tried to fight the local WPA resistance and lethargy and push the project forward. "We have some great projects," Hughes wrote to Flanagan, "but we can't get going because the WPA Administrator Gannon is back east and Lahr, the State Director of Professional and Service Projects, must consult him."[25]

In late October Flanagan went into the "field" paying visits to the Boston, Chicago and New York units. There she encountered first hand the frustrations that her regional directors were experiencing nationwide: the frustration over setting up office space and staff; and the increasing perception that there were huge geographical areas where there were few, if any, theatre people on relief. Upon her return to Washington, DC, she met with Jacob Baker and Bruce McClure and tried to ease the "red tape" restrictions. Baker agreed to lean on local WPA offices for help in acquiring competent secretarial staff, and Flanagan authorized the regional directors to add the office expenses to their upcoming project requests so they would no longer be spending funds from their own pockets. As for the second, more central concern of relief actors, she struggled to articulate a response. On November 4, 1935, she wrote to Glenn Hughes, author of the "magnificent" plan which had pleased her so much eight weeks earlier:

If your inquiries prove that there are no people, or few people, who have hitherto made a living in the theatrical profession in a given state, we certainly are not justified in using Federal Funds to start theatre enterprises in such states...We must bend our energies to areas where there is theatrical entertainment.

In that connection, let me say that obviously amateurs are never to be encouraged to get on relief rolls merely in order for us to get them off. This is not and never has been a program for relief of amateurs. We are not justified in advising anyone, amateur or professional, to go on relief; [although] we may, at the discretion of directors, sometimes take people who qualify for relief under the laws of a given state.[26]

To his credit, Hughes did not abandon ship although it must have been clear that accomplishing the plan that he had proposed – and was so heralded for – was out of the question. Flanagan realized the impossibility of what she had proposed before the curtain had risen on a single production, but she was caught in the midst of a government juggernaut. The personnel and reporting structure were in place, the money had been appropriated and she had promised Hopkins that she would spend it. In the big cities there was a chance that it would work, but in the smaller markets adjustments would have to be made. There would not be thirteen theatres in the state of Washington as Hughes had proposed, but there might be one in Seattle. And there might be other, creative ways in which federal dollars could be spent on "theatre projects." Hughes did not resign because he had already realized the futility of trying to establish theatres inside a web of government bureaucracy and the frenzied idealism of Flanagan's dream. But he also knew that there was money that *needed* to be spent, and as regional director he could have considerable influence in where it went. We do not know at what point he gave up on his "magnificent plan," but we do know that by November 1935 he was already moving forward on at least one plan which would benefit his rapidly expanding drama department.

3

Hoofers, mystics and a singing bird

In November they held auditions. Hughes, Guy Williams and four other "professionals" watched in amazement as the relief rolls and word of mouth yielded a parade of applicants. "Hoofers, mystics, Hill Billy balladists, dialect comedians, tappers and a singing bird," marveled Williams as he struggled to keep notes on the passing show.[1] There were "black out"[2] comedians, former Gilbert & Sullivan players, minstrel troupers and assorted refugees from the Pantages and Keith-Orpheum vaudeville circuits. Some were certified for relief. Others were eligible but not enrolled. Some had "retired" but in the pinch of hard times saw this as an opportunity of going back to work or of resurrecting failed careers.

Hughes had hoped that they could form a small company dedicated to new plays since he – along with others in the Seattle and university communities – had written some original scripts. He knew that the creation of new work, especially regional plays, would appeal to Flanagan. But on first viewing he was convinced that such a venture would have to wait. What confronted him and Guy Williams was the enormous task of making sure that the approximately seventy-five "actors" who had successfully auditioned were now properly certified by the WPA and then somehow cast in an appropriate vehicle. In the meantime he had to deal with the ire of the local motion picture owners and operators who were protesting this whole enterprise as unfair labor practice and "just plain stupid."

The idea of Uncle Sam competing with private enterprise was explosive, and when the WPA wasn't being called "boondoggling," it was being skewered for unfairness and "socialism." For those who had been rigidly raised on notions of private enterprise and personal initiative, it was unthinkable that the federal government should be allowed to manufacture a product in direct competition to private industry and then sell it at a price that undercut the going market rate. Thus, for all the material benefits of

the Tennessee Valley Authority (TVA), for example, the Tennessee Power
Company was outraged that a by-product of the Wilson Dam (electricity)
was being offered cheaply to rural residents in Tennessee. No matter how
much New Dealers talked about the plight of the poor and the dispossessed,
many Americans viewed "State Capitalism" with distrust, suspicion and
hatred.

When rumors began to fly in late 1935 that the federal government was
going into the entertainment business, many professional theatre people
were chagrined and then angry. As Hallie Flanagan negotiated with their
unions and sought their help, new rumors spread that the entertainment was
also going to be "free," further upsetting the private enterprise advocates.
And while there was not an abundance of professional theatre companies in
America's smaller cities and towns, there were hundreds of movie theatres.

In Seattle, as in many cities, the people who ran the movie theatres were
organized. As the news unfolded of Glenn Hughes's plan to establish a
network of low-priced theatres, representatives of the MPTONW (Motion
Picture Theatre Owners of the North West) requested a meeting with WPA
officials to protest this misguided enterprise.

They met with George Gannon, Don Abel's predecessor as WPA state
administrator, in January 1936 and outlined their concerns. Vaudeville was
dead they urged and, "to bring out these old people again would only falsely
brighten their hopes and then they would sink back into oblivion and total
discouragement."[3] Moreover, and probably more to the point, the thought
that these performances might be free alarmed the owners. "Only trouble
and plenty of it will ensue if these free shows are given in cities and communities where there are properly licensed theatres now paying considerable
taxes to the government."

Gannon was sympathetic with their concerns and, like many WPA administrators, not particularly supportive of Federal One. He wrote to Glenn
Hughes that, "we would accomplish our purpose of fitting the relief people
for gainful work in private industry by expending our efforts in teaching
these persons who classify themselves as actors, some clerical work such as
typing, filing and general office work."[4] Furthermore, Gannon stated that,
"Since the projects are set up and beginning to function, I am asking that in
the State of Washington you do not permit any entertainment except for the
benefit of other project workers, including their families and CCC camps;
these to be given without an admission charge." These kinds of directives
constantly frustrated Federal Theatre personnel because they needed the
cooperation and goodwill of local WPA offices in order to function, but

they also were required to report to Hallie Flanagan through her national network and were responsible for carrying out her policy.

Hughes and Williams decided that they would divide up the performers who had successfully auditioned and create two "umbrella" companies: one devoted to "Variety" and one to "Revue." Each of these companies would then be partitioned into smaller groups with a specific entertainment focus. This would also facilitate the demands of touring since a principal target were Civilian Conservation Corps camps throughout the state.

The idea of Federal Theatre entertainers touring CCC camps was not unique to the Washington Project; indeed it was popular in many states. In *Arena*, her history of the Project, Flanagan provides some brief but delightful snapshots of the joys and frustrations of touring the CCC camps. In St. Louis she watched a sixteen-act vaudeville show prepare for a tour of camps and hospitals. In Syracuse she was delighted with the *CCC Murder Mystery* which was presented as a "real" event before the startled occupants of a camp dining hall. From Minnesota she read with disgust the newspaper account of a "fan dancer" who had reportedly performed at one of the CCC units. The story spread from an unfounded rumor but had such notoriety that it eventually doomed all Federal Theatre in the state of Minnesota.[5] Flanagan believed that the camps were natural venues for touring units, and the programs could be provided for free without complaint from private enterprise. In addition the camps, frequently located in isolated outposts, were eager for visitors and provided enthusiastic audiences. And those audiences were people whom Flanagan wanted the project to reach. As she later wrote of her St. Louis experience, "Only one who has seen such a troupe in action and watched the audiences at these performances should have the temerity to say whether such work is useful and needed as a part of a theatre in this country. Certainly such performances and such audiences are the antithesis of our usual conception of the theatre – metropolitan productions attended by the privileged and affluent few."[6]

The CCC was one of the great success stories of the whole WPA enterprise. Founded originally in 1933, the camps survived throughout the entire decade in spite of considerable controversy. Designed to provide employment and to address conservation issues, such as creating forests, fire barriers and other tasks, the projects were supervised by civilian personnel, but the camps themselves were administered by the War Department. Like many New Deal projects, they were originally opposed by conservative forces and private enterprise. Organized labor believed them capable of preparing a huge apprentice labor force which would "flood the market" or of establishing the "dollar per day" wage as some kind of benchmark for skilled union workers. Antimilitarists and isolationists objected to the army supervision of the camps although the War Department was a logical choice to deal with the logistics of preparing hundreds of barracks. Some even saw them as an attempt to dilute enthusiasm for a second veterans' march on Washington, DC. But as proponents of the CCC repeatedly pointed out, the service was voluntary, the rewards were for families on relief, and the projects from tree planting to fire fighting were laudatory.[7]

Volunteers were unmarried men between the ages of eighteen and twenty-five from families certified by states for relief. They were provided with clothes, housing, food, medical care and paid one dollar a day. They were required to send approximately $22 per month home to their families, keeping the rest to buy script at the camps or party in a local community or "roadhouse" on Saturday nights. For forty hours per week they were supervised by civilian project personnel from the Agriculture or Forestry Departments. But before and after the work day, they were under the command of the United States Army. Men initially signed up for a six-month tour and could reenlist depending upon their records and state unemployment quotas. There were no stockades, weapons were not allowed and discipline was largely a matter of common sense and the experience of the camp commandant. After-hour idleness was the most common problem, and in spite of a variety of activities, there were complaints about gambling, drinking and, occasionally, theft.[8] But in general they were enthusiastic young audiences, enormously delighted at seeing faces from the outside world or of performing their own dramatic sketches.

The National Recreation Association provided tips for camp administrators by publishing a manual of activities which included traditional games (volley ball, horse-shoe pitching, etc.) as well as guidelines for dramatic activities. One of the most popular of these was minstrel shows, and the precision with which the guidelines were spelled out provides a fascinating look into the CCC camp culture.

> Have the end men and the interlocutor go over their jokes at odd times other than at regular rehearsals. Don't let the circle hear the jokes until the night of performance. It will not do any harm if the circle members do laugh, and on the other hand, if they do hear the jokes before the performance, then the outsiders are apt to hear them also![9]

There are wonderfully detailed instructions about how to rehearse, costume and conduct a minstrel show as well as practical hints about the staging.

"The interlocutor and the end men will find it helpful to keep the cues for their jokes pasted on a palm leaf fan." As for blacking up, campers are cautioned that, "it is better to use plain English rather than to try Negro dialect, unless the end men can do the latter exceptionally well. Many a good joke has been lost on the audience because it was smothered in an unintelligible dialect." In fact, one of the most interesting suggestions from the same source is that campers might want to consider alternatives to the "traditional black-face comedy of the first part of the show." Some other suggestions include: Circus minstrels with clowns, freaks, ringmaster and other characters; Hobo minstrels with tramps, bums, weary Willies and cops; or Newspaper minstrels with comic-strip characters, an editor and reporters.

In April 1936 there were forty-eight CCC camps in the state of Washington with a volunteer population of 1,267. The median age was 18.73.[10] The majority of the camps were carrying out projects for the National Forest Service. Others were contracted with the Department of Agriculture in soil conservation work or with a variety of tasks for the state park system. Among the daily activities were rodent control, estimating timber, checking soil erosion, building trails and telephone lines, and fighting forest fires. In addition to their physical labor, the men were required to dedicate ten hours a week to various "educational" programs, a nationwide provision in response to the alarming rate of illiteracy that the CCC had discovered when they began their enrollment. Entertainment was largely confined to pool playing, fly tying, musical instruments and singing. A minister or priest was available on a rotating basis, depending upon proximity to a town, and the local taverns were required to serve only 3.2 beer. In such circumstances the boys were eager for show business.

By mid-January, 1936, Seattle performers – appropriately certified and classified by the WPA – assembled to begin rehearsals for their debuts as Federal employees. The CCC Revue group, which varied in size from twelve to sixteen, began rehearsing short comic routines and brief one act-plays along with songs and sketches. They developed a "number one routine" which ran for approximately an hour and fifteen minutes and a second routine which could be used if they had to layover longer than required. While they worked, Guy Williams began arranging for transportation and touring dates for their springtime foray into the camps dotting the lower Cascade range and the Olympic peninsula. The logistics were daunting. Since the camps were controlled by military personnel, there were a variety of rules and regulations governing civilian conduct on their premises. Women were not allowed to stay overnight, and thus accommodations had to be found in nearby towns. The roads connecting the camps were often pitted and/or under repair and made exact scheduling extremely difficult. This was particularly troublesome in getting the performers fed each day because they had to eat according to the mess tent schedules and with WPA vouchers which were subsidized against prevailing meal rates. They were often asked, for example, to pay full meal fare for the bus driver because he was not technically certified for relief. There were disputes about their sleeping quarters, about having the sides of the tents rolled up or down and about "rowdy" behavior. But once under way the adventure of the road and of being paid to act was an enormous stimulant, and the records of those tours illuminate in rich detail trouping in the Federal Theatre:[11]

> *Camp Narada* (August 12) Company of 16 composing the CCC Revue arrived at 5:00 P.M. in time for dinner. All members of the troupe well and happy. Captain Brown in charge. Camp received the company with open arms and greatly enjoyed the show. Slept in clean tents, clean linen, plenty of blankets, electric lights, wood stoves, in a word, camping de luxe. Meals very good – wonderful scenery. Show ran one hour and fifteen minutes with 175 people enjoying it. Morale of company good as newness of traveling had not yet worn off.

> *Camp Tahoma* (August 13) Arrived at this camp at 1 P.M. Good, clean camp, meals and accommodation O.K. The only incident of interest was that Mr. Shepard, cello player, was a very sick man and had to be sent back to Seattle that evening. I was afraid that he was going to have D.Ts. His illness was due to alcohol in my estimation. Good trip so far, no bad reports. Show ran one hour and fifteen minutes with 165 in attendance. Some insubordination was shown at this camp when Sgt. Kelly ordered all tent sides rolled up. Our boys said it was too cold and wanted to stay in the tents and sleep and told Sgt. Kelly that they would not roll up the tent sides. This left a bad impression with the Sgt. in charge. I then explained to the boys that we were under military orders in these camps and should obey orders.

> *Camp Ohanapecosh* (August 14) Captain L.A. McMurtie and Lt. E.T. Buckholdt in charge. This is a most beautiful place, fine food, wonderful officers and most cordial reception. The show was put on in the mess hall which was not large enough to hold all the people. At least eighty transients camping in that vicinity were guests at the show and the CCC boys gave them their seats and watched the show from the windows outside the mess hall. These transients were from all parts of the United States. There is a large mineral springs near Ohanapecosh and most of the

people at the hotel came to the show. Many compliments were received from the visitors as to the fine quality of the show. Unusually fine meals served at this camp. Everyone entered into the spirit of the occasion and community singing was a very popular part of each of the programs on the entire tour. Running time was one hour and fifteen minutes.

Camp Lower Cispus (August 15) Very clean camp running the year round. This was our first night in barracks. All camps after this had barracks. Show ran one hour and fifteen minutes with only 60 men in attendance as the rest of the CCC men were out on fire duty. Those that saw the show enjoyed it and want it back again. Nothing of particular interest at Cispus except the eagerness with which the CCC boys received our entertainment.

Camp Rainier (August 16) After a ride of three hours and fifteen minutes we arrived at Camp Rainier at 4:30 P.M. Put on the show at 7:30 P.M. A good show with some outsiders looking on. All enjoyed it and like the other camps wanted to know when we were coming back. All members well and happy. Officers nice and treated us fine.

Camp Elma (August 17) Capt. Byron W. Gray and Lt. K Johnson in charge of a fine, clean camp. Capt. Gray is something of a musician himself and after the show he and Mr. Metcalfe and Mr. Lombardi played trios. It was at Camp Elma that insubordination really showed itself. Capt. Gray and Lt. Johnson were at the office when we arrived. We drove in front of the office and the boys jumped out of the cab and started wrestling causing a little commotion at the trucks while I was talking to the Captain. He looked over my head as much as to say, "What is this nonsense?" I paid no attention to this. Capt. Gray called the sergeant and told him to show us to our quarters and told us what time we were to play. It seems as though Capt. Gray is very strict on dining room discipline. He wants it very quiet and orderly. As he told me later, it was a hobby with him to have respect for meals. At supper time our boys entered the dining room with the rest of the company. Our boys sat down and the sergeant came over and said "Stand up." The boys immediately stood up and one, Thomas McLean, started talking under his breath to the man across the table. When the whistle blew we all sat down. That is part of Captain Gray's discipline.

I noticed this place was very still during meal time. Our boys started talking, not too loud for any of the other camps but apparently too loud for Capt. Gray. The sergeant again came over and said to be quiet, which brought a remark from Tommy. The sergeant took offense and apparently reported it because the Capt. waited until I had finished and then told me that he would not stand for any boisterous conduct in the dining room or any disrespect shown any of his officers and if it was continued he would order the man or the men out of the camp. He said he wanted us to enjoy ourselves, have a good time, that the camp was ours, but he was strict about the dining room.

The boys wanted to leave and not play, as they had been insulted they felt, and their feelings hurt. I said we would play the show – which we did. It proved to be the best thing because later the officers proved to be fine men and one of them made a remark that he was sorry the trouble had been caused regarding the dining room. We put on a wonderful show and after when the Captain played the violin in trios he had Tommy McLean come up and sing several songs.

Camp Millersylvania (August 18) Played a good show. Only sixty men at this camp but they had about sixty-five Camp Fire Girls from Millersylvania State Park as their guests. The audience filled every seat in the mess hall where we played. The Camp Fire Girls ranged in age from six to sixteen. They invited us to their camp where we again put on several individual numbers for their entertainment. The day after the show they came back and took some pictures of our players. They wondered how they could get us to come to their little town of Unalaska to play for them again. It was after this show that a little girl asked her mother if we were real men! It was the first time many of these children had seen a vaudeville show in their lives.

From all available evidence it seems that the CCC unit was a big success in its barnstorming through the Washington camps. Monitored closely by both their leaders and military personnel, Unit 818-(1), as it was officially designated, traveled thousands of miles and entertained thousands of boys with their songs and skits. As Guy Williams reported to Hallie Flanagan, "except for one complaint about their going 'blue' before the CCC lads, they have made a fair record.[12] It is difficult, of course, to assess the quality of the work – as it is for many of the Federal productions – since many of the official reports tend to be self-serving and exhibits for renewed funding. But occasionally a more objective voice can be detected in the discourse. In May 1936, for example, one of Flanagan's most trusted aides, Howard Miller, wrote her the following evaluation of the Seattle activities:

> Seattle on the whole is a very fine project. Unfortunately, when they first began operations, they were under the impression that the idea was to have a program whether or not actors were available; therefore, like practically every other project, they have a number of semi-professional and amateur workers, many of questionable ability. Project morale is splendid

and what they lack in ability they make up in energy and enthusiasm. Vaudeville rehearsals were very ragged indeed. CCC units were also ragged but evidently are greatly enjoyed by the boys in that district. I suggested several changes to Guy Williams and am sure that they will be able to do some reorganizing now that the State Administrator, who as you may have gathered was not altogether friendly, has finally been discharged.[13]

It's quite likely that the "ragged" quality was ironed out as the number one routine was relentlessly performed, running almost always seventy-five minutes, in camp after camp, town after town. Indeed many of the reports barely mention the songs and skits, concentrating primarily on the exigencies of travel, sleep and eating:

At North Bend the company carried cots, mattresses and all bedding a full city block to the barracks assigned to them and the next morning returned same, to the supply department. Officer of the day wanted fifty cents for the ration rate but after seeing the letter regarding rate, accepted forty-two cents.

Left North Bend after dinner. Upon arrival at Camp Kachess Lt. Koch advised me that most of the men would have to sleep in the mess hall. This arrangement would leave us with no facilities whatsoever and also necessitate the men rising very early to allow the tables to be set up, so we left Kachess after the show. The men paid twenty-five cents for a very ordinary supper.

Arrived at Camp Taneum about 10:30 P.M. Capt. Johnson fixed us up for bedding but ten of the company had no pillows. At Camp Ginko the company carried all bedding and cots to barracks and returned them next morning. (NOTE) From Camp Taneum until end of the tour we had to leave immediately after breakfast and get over the road as quickly as possible in order to get the three meal a day ration rate. This arrangement was very hard on the company.

Camp Gold Creek gave us no supplies until after three p.m. I returned several cots that were in bad order, which were replaced. Ration rate in this camp, forty-three cents. Camp Icicle supplied a number of worn out cots. I had to ask for lights and other necessities. Each camp seemed surprised to see us and appeared unprepared. Meals at Ginko meager and not too good. When food put on table was gone it was impossible to get more.[14]

While it is possible that this particular tour was the victim of poor planning and unannounced arrivals, subsequent reports confirm that the interface between the Revue companies and the camps always had the potential

2   The Hill-Billies were a featured act of the Variety shows and one of Seattle's most popular attractions.

for inconvenience and misunderstandings. A few weeks later the company manager was still complaining about carrying bedding, bussing food trays and erratic meal prices in this same circuit of camps. "The only bright spot was the good work of the boys in the company and their fine morale during the entire trip."[15]

While the CCC Revues were negotiating the rural roads of western Washington, the Variety units were playing spot bookings in and around the Seattle metropolitan area. Staffed with a wide variety of former vaudevillians and specialty acts, Unit 819-(1) was divided into two groups: Variety and Hill-Billy. The latter specialized in popular country music and broad comic routines and developed a considerable following in the Skid Road section of the city where they played for free at the shelters and soup kitchens. There were usually fifteen performers and the show lasted fifty minutes from the opening chorus to finale. Singing was the principal attraction but there was also dancing – including a tap routine – as well as comic sketches and blackouts.

Guy Williams watched them perform at a transient shelter in February 1936 and left the following description:[16]

The Transient Shelter, 84 Union Street, is Seattle's "Dead End." Outside in the street there is snow. The hall is warm, but the warmth is laden with the pungent reek of disinfectant. Almost palpable are the dolors of discouraged, homeless road-weary men.

The waves of disinfectant penetrate back to the improvised dressing rooms where director Harry Pfeil is superintending the make-up of his Hill Billies. The odor becomes more pungent as the ranks of wooden benches in the shelter recreation hall begin to fill with shuffling, despair-numbed men. Pfeil is an old showman. He has sung tenor leads in Gilbert and Sullivan, performed in big-time vaud, doubled in brass with tent Tom shows. He has sopped up applause in the elegant, gilt-proscenium theatres of the halcyon days – he has played on rough boards to rough-necks in mining camp honky tonks. He is of the showman's breed which gets the laughs and the effect, (even) if it brings blood from his every pore.

In the Hill Billy troupe are other old timers. Florence Bradbury, singing star of road productions of "Merry Widow," "Price of Pilsen" and "Oh Boy," is emceeing tonight's performance. Bill Anthony, once a character man in Laurette Taylor's Company is strumming his guitar and doing specialties. Musical Director George Metcalf is the accompanist. Mr. Metcalf, then fresh from the American Conservatory Violin class of Joseph Willem, broke into show business as pit violinist at Chicago's Grand Opera House . . .

But those days are past. Tonight George is batting out "Coming Round the Mountain" for the opening chorus of the Hill Billy show, which is going after laughs from as dour and lumpish an audience as a trouper ever faced. Out front the men are banked, each absorbed in his own pain, his own troubles, his own private set of poignancies.

In the audience are young men – "punks" – who have never had a job or a semblance of security, ranged beside the older labor-gnarled "stiffs" who helped build the railroads they now bum their way on...

By now, on the improvised box stage, Metcalf has swung his ridge-runners band into a Hill Billy fantasia of his arrangement which mingles such tunes as "Watermelon Vine," "Home on the Range," Alexander's Rag Time Band" in a pounding rhythm which quickens the feet of the derelicts into jig time.

Elsie Smith and Jimmy Graham, one of George Cohan's song and dance men, tap out a rural routine. LeRoy Wilson and Edward O'Neil do a sure fire black-out which has to do with O'Neil's digging a ditch so that he can get money to buy food so that he can be strong – to dig a ditch. This gets a laugh from the ex-muckers out front, who have been riding freights around the West to do just that...

By now gaiety is competing with disinfectant for possession of the room. With O'Neil mugging it, company and band bring out the guffaws with a mock ballad called "And the Pig Got Up and Slowly Walked Away," which tells the tale of a dipsomaniac who sank so low that the pigs, who shared his gutter, began to broad-A him.[17]

Pfeil and his troupe know that they are not playing the YMCA boys and risk cleaned up versions of a couple of Carroll's old black-outs. Whistles, more feet stamping, wild applause. Company on for finale and six curtain calls.[18]

Williams reports that there were 600 people in the audience that night and that every act was "enthusiastically received." Their popularity almost certainly accounts for the fact that that Spring they were also booked onto the CCC circuit and between April 28 and May 7 performed their number one routine in eleven different camps. Unlike some previous – and subsequent – FTP tours their arrival was well publicized, and they seem to have encountered no hardships. Toby Leitch, their spokesperson and later an important player in several "straight" productions, reported that the troupe was treated very "royally" and that at Camp 25 Mile they "had a good show, a fine reception and were living in the officer's quarters."[19]

The counterpart to the Hill-Billies in Seattle 819 was the Variety unit, by far the largest group in the initial project. Formed to take advantage of the disparate talent that had shown up for the first auditions, Variety employed approximately seventy-six government-sponsored performers who could be sent out on spot bookings with as little as three singers or could be mustered into a full-scale vaudeville show complete with a "spoken drama." They played for free in schools, parks, legion halls, prisons and wherever an organization requested their presence. They entertained for Boy Scout Troops, Goodwill Industries and Veterans' organizations. The following report from May 1936 is typical of the thousands of performances that they gave:

> April 27: John Paul Jones Post, American Legion, at the Civic Auditorium Annex were entertained for 55 minutes by the Musical Comedy Unit consisting of 32 members and two in the stage crew. This production included the opening and finale numbers by the entire company, fourteen musical numbers and three talking scenes. Between 90 and 100 enlisted men vociferously applauded each and every number on the program.

> April 29: 26 members of Musical Comedy Unit went to Sand Point Veteran CCC Camp on Wednesday evening. The program was opened with the comedy drama, "Foiled, By Heck!" for the first part, and continued with seventeen Specialty acts of songs, dances and three scenes. The comedy drama running time was 27 minutes and the time for the Specialty numbers just one hour. Approximately 100 men enjoyed this presentation, after which the Educational Advisor of the Camp arranged for the company to be served refreshments.

> April 30: On Friday six members of Musical Comedy Unit entertained the Boy Scouts of America, Post #1, at the Bailey Gatzaert School. They furnished ten musical numbers intermittently with speaking and other entertainment which had been planned by the Scouts. Their part of the program took one hour. Fifty Japanese Boy Scouts and their parents made up the audience, and they were most pleased with the Federal Theatre Project entertainment.

> May 1: 30 members of Musical Comedy Unit entertained Veterans of Foreign Wars, Post #1416 in the National Guard Armory. One hundred twenty [sic] Veterans applauded and encored all of the numbers presented. Several of the numbers on the routine of eighteen acts took two encores and several bows. The entire program was a hit and all received enthusiastic applause. Coffee and cake was served after the show.

> May 1: On this same day, eight members of Musical Comedy Unit reported to the Rehearsal Hall at 5:30 P.M. and dressed in costume, went to the Georgetown Hospital to entertain the Disabled Veterans there. Eight

Specialty acts comprised this group who walked around the beds and sang
and played for the sick men. This was enjoyed by about 50 invalids over
a period of 40 minutes ...

We have in rehearsal several skits and musical numbers that will be ready
for presentation [.] [I]n the event that we repeat any prior engagements
we can take an entirely new show to that group. Every unit has at least
two routines and the specialty acts are all working on new business.[20]

By the second year of their operation the Variety unit had moved away
from spot bookings and was able to schedule several weeks in advance.
One of their most successful offerings was *The Curtain Goes Up*, a sketch
and musical revue which opened on November 9, 1936 at the Repertory
Playhouse. The ten scenes featured a company of thirty-nine performing
two comic sketches (*For the Good of the Team* and *Mother Goose is on the Loose*)
and eight song-and-dance numbers. Two of those songs ("Transom Blues"
and "Heavens to Betsy") were sung by a Negro quartet who were one of the
most popular acts in the unit. Known as the Baron Knights, the four singers
had originally been assigned to a Negro Minstrel unit which was designated
to tour CCC camps, but the unit did not materialize and the Knights
were incorporated into Variety. They became very popular as a separate act
and were often requested by fraternal and social clubs and organizations.[21]

The popularity of the Variety unit was substantial by 1937, so Guy
Williams began to promote stateside tours to capitalize on their appeal.
As with all the touring operations, there was hilarity and hardship as they
struggled to meet deadlines and deal with local conditions and surprises.
In Sunnyside, Washington, for example, in June 1937 they agreed to take
part in a "Fete Day" celebration where "at 10:30 A.M. nineteen of our members appeared in the parade which was an hour and a half long." This was
followed by specialty acts on a flat bed truck and then another parade at
6:00 P.M. where they led townspeople out to the fairgrounds. Their show
was a big success, playing to "over eleven hundred paid admissions." There
was a carnival in town so the next day they delayed their departure for a few
hours so that the company could enjoy themselves. Unfortunately a problem
developed when, "Sandy Harper proceeded to get about two thirds drunk
and started to raise hell on the bus as we were pulling out by taking any seat
that he desired, telling me to go to hell and that he would do as he damned
please, using filthy, obscene language in front of the girls." The anxiety was
especially acute because Harper's daughter was also on the bus and "his
insubordination was so flagrant" that the company finally cried him down.

3 The Baron Knights (Tom Hanns, Ralph Lamar, Vernon Wade and Frank Freeman) here perform their popular "Transom Blues" with Syvilla Fort.

There is no record of what eventually happened to Mr. Harper although it is recorded that "everybody else in the company conducted themselves as ladies and gentlemen throughout the entire trip."[22]

On another occasion the Variety Company traveled to the Reformatory in nearby Monroe, Washington, where they were vigorously applauded by more than twelve hundred inmates. Buoyed by their sizzling performance and "wild applause," the company was deflated to learn that there had been a riot just prior to the performance – "in the manner of the mess hall riot in *The Big House*" – and they had been the unknowing recipients of this "violent disorder" converting the "nervous excitement" into sustained applause.[23] Fran Power reported that the Reformatory nonetheless was pleased with their production and requested a return booking.

In that same report Power added a note that synopsizes the activities of the Variety unit in the first year and provides a wonderful summary glimpse of the Seattle project. By his estimate Variety had played to a total audience of approximately 62,224 people and had traveled 14,000 miles. In prisons, orphanages, schools, soup kitchens and on dozens of improvised stages they had performed their routines carrying their own sets and costumes. This unit, Power points out, has traveled over a thousand miles every month by "truck, automobile and streetcar" and been most enthusiastically received.

Like similar units all across the country, Variety became the staple item in the first years of the Federal Theatre. Peopled with former vaudevillians and youngsters looking for a "break," they provided free entertainment for thousands of Americans. From children in parks and schools to disabled veterans in homes and hospitals, they performed their theatre magic. Some, such as a youthful Burt Lancaster, would go on to be stars; others such as Seattle's Toby Leitch would become standout straight actors, but most would be returned to retirement and obscurity when the project ended. Along the way, however, they wrote a colorful chapter in the theatre of the 1930s, and the surviving record is replete with their accomplishments, anxieties and failures. Especially noteworthy are the dozens of Specialty Acts which were a constant source of amusement to audiences and frustrating to administrators. How do we pay two guys in a "perch act?" wondered William P. Farnsworth to Lawrence Morris. "They only take ten minutes to perform and a half hour to get ready."[24] In Seattle, Ardella was advertised by her owner as the "world's only singing parrot" and apparently she did manage a surprising mezzo-soprano, but her repertoire was limited and she had a tendency to sulk at critical moments. There was always the possibility that she would simply tell everyone to "go to hell" or erupt into editorial comment – frequently blue – in the midst of her favorite number, "Everybody's Doing It."

4

Typists and models

Glenn Hughes was a shrewd businessman, and by the mid-thirties he had created a theatre program at the University of Washington that was envied and imitated nation wide. His papers are filled with inquiries from colleagues and other interested parties about how to emulate his success. His formula was simple. Using student talent, he would run his productions for six weeks in two or three different spaces simultaneously for thirty weeks per year. Each theatre catered to a different kind of play or genre. The Penthouse was for drawing room comedies, the Showboat for classics and the Studio for more experimental work. The university provided general upkeep, heat and utilities so the overhead was not substantial. Hughes would then sell weeknight performances to various social clubs. They, in turn, would resell the tickets for whatever price they deemed appropriate. He reserved the weekends for general box office, and the combination filled his treasury.

For years he was able to protect his income from the general budget of the University of Washington. He did this primarily by reinvesting profits in a drama library which featured a spectacular collection of nineteenth- and twentieth-century play scripts. "He was very clever about money," said one of his former students whom he later hired to watch over the library, "and he was not very sympathetic to waste or red tape."[1] At the outset he was very enthusiastic about Federal Theatre, but his impatience grew as he realized how difficult it was to accomplish even the slightest tasks. Moreover, his own very full-time job at the university necessitated that he delegate more and more of the work to Guy Williams and others. Still Hughes maintained his position as principal administrator because he knew there was money to be spent, and he knew that his own institution – acting as sponsor – could benefit from the Federal Theatre largesse. Thus, while he labored to get the production end of the enterprise running through the vaudeville and variety units, he also undertook two additional programs which would have long-lasting results for his department and for Federal Theatre.

The first of these was an ambitious research project which was designed to provide the data for a comprehensive history of theatre in the Northwest. Flanagan believed that one of the benefits of Federal Theatre could be a record of past theatrical activity in all regions of the United States. This research would provide the raw data for new plays and for the creation of a "grass-roots" mentality which would enable many individual units eventually to coalesce into a truly National Theatre. Centralized under the National Service Bureau, the various research projects operated in a number of states gathering records, clipping newspapers, studying genealogy and typing reports. In Oklahoma, for example, researchers drawn from the ranks of unemployed theatre artists were put to work compiling information about the history of the Southwest. These Federal Theatre workers uncovered documents and oral tales from the Comanche and Kiowa peoples which became part of a "folk history" of the area. Co-sponsored by the drama department at the University of Oklahoma, this research project was designed to provide materials for future plays and histories of the area. Stories about the native peoples and the pioneer settlers were amassed by the research project and soon, Flanagan reported, "requests for scripts on historical subjects flooded our small Oklahoma office and that office began a service which ultimately furnished plays, radio scripts or dramatic source material to more than two hundred dramatic clubs in educational institutions."[2]

The research activities of the National Service Bureau were particularly important to Flanagan because she felt that the research mission truly encapsulated her goal of stressing regional and local efforts within a national plan. "A locality is apt to ignore local material," she wrote, "only a national plan can emphasize and correlate different parts of the country as parts of a nationwide pattern."[3] Her Service Bureau encouraged research in all the Federal regions with the result that new Living Newspapers were developed which spoke to the hopes, concerns and fears of millions of Americans outside the principal metropolitan areas.

Glenn Hughes established a research project for the Seattle unit as one of his first acts as regional supervisor. While he had not envisioned such a program in his original plan for a federal theatre in the Northwest, he quite quickly realized that it was an efficient way to get money appropriated and expended. And he also realized that it might have excellent benefits for his own drama program. Accordingly on December 17, 1935, Guy Williams (now signing himself as "Assistant Regional Director") informed Flanagan that he was processing the appropriate forms to establish a research project in the state of Washington that would employ twenty relief personnel and one nonrelief supervisor.[4]

The supervisor was Howard F. Grant who had been a student in the drama department and who in 1934 had published a compilation of newspaper clips, magazine articles and other references documenting theatrical activity in Seattle from 1852 ("the beginning") to the present. The book, *The Story of Seattle's Early Theatres*, was published "for the Division of Drama" by the University Book Store and contained a generous Foreword by Glenn Hughes. "I can testify to the author's painstaking research and to his conscientiousness as a chronicler. His work is as unpretentious as it is interesting, and I shall not be surprised if its success leads him to further work in the same field."[5]

A year later it did. Of all the research projects undertaken by the Federal Theatre, the Washington State project was one of the most ambitious and one of the most successful. Under Grant's direction the work began on January 2, 1936, with a staff of twenty. Using Odell's *Annals of the New York Stage* as a model for their taxonomy, they proposed to gather the material for a complete history of the theatre in Washington State from 1852 to 1900 and for the City of Seattle to 1914. They also provided staff to make specific entries for Olympia, Tacoma, Spokane, Walla Walla and Port Townsend. Their goal was to examine newspapers, magazines, journals and other printed material to uncover references to theatrical activity and then pass that material along to a team of typists who would synopsize the information and compile lists for future research. They also proposed to conduct interviews with "old-timers" and made an appeal for photographs, diaries, theatre programs, letters and other ephemera.

In the original request thirteen typists were required to record the work of six researchers who spent their days exploring back issues of local Washington newspapers and magazines. Working five days a week for approximately six hours per day, the typists recorded the material and then filed it chronologically in ten-year blocks by city and theatre. As the files grew they began to make additional subheadings: "Variety and Vaudeville," "Theatre Conditions," "Theatrical Syndicates," "Managers," "Personalities" and "Individuals," "Companies," and "Anecdotes and Observations." The work and the results were prodigious and each bimonthly report of the Seattle Federal Theatre Project attested to the growing bulk of documentation. By September 17, 1936, Howard Grant reported that they had personally examined 42, 800 "sheets" of material from which they had synopsized and typed 1,223 pages.[6]

As the documents mounted, Grant realized that they had at their fingertips materials to provide annals for not only a record of professional production in the state but also for a host of amateur and vaudeville-related performances including "backwoods troubadours, squaw dance halls, box houses and variety theatres with semipermanent houses."[7] Materials could also support studies of local fights with the national theatrical syndicates as well as biographies of outstanding managers, actors, actresses and playwrights. The project intrigued Glenn Hughes because he realized that these histories could become a lode stone for future academic work, particularly masters-level theses which would further legitimatize his division of drama and earn it the full-time departmental status that he desired.

Because of the relative suddenness with which the Federal Theatre was terminated in the summer of 1939, many projects were interrupted and left unfinished. Indeed the Seattle unit was busy on a new Living Newspaper about the depletion of forest lands in the United States called *Timber* which never opened. The research project, however, not only finished its work but did so on time and within budget. By December 1936 Grant reported that his team had examined 52,570 sheets of material and prepared a typed manuscript of some 2,010 pages.[8] In addition he reported that he was preparing a manuscript outlining the work of the project to be published in *The Pacific Northwest Quarterly*.[9]

The research project, as Flanagan and Hughes both suspected, generated tremendous interest in the history of theatre in the Northwest. In the years following its completion it became the basis for several academic studies in the department of drama and a resource for numerous theatrical events. In 1944 Hughes inaugurated a series of monographs published by the University of Washington which drew directly from the research material. The initial offering – *A History of Variety-Vaudeville in Seattle* by Eugene Elliott – is largely based on the work of Howard Grant's research group and bears a "Foreword" by Hughes which places the study in its historical context:

> For several years it has been our hope to publish some of the outstanding results of our graduate research in the School of Drama... This series is made possible by the co-operation of the School of Drama and the Graduate Publications Committee of the University. I feel sure it will prove a worthy contribution to our knowledge of American life and institutions.[10]

A year later *The History of Seattle Stock Companies* by Mary Rohrer appeared with Glenn Hughes now listed as "Editor" of the series. This volume, which was also a masters thesis in the School of Drama, is very explicit about its relationship to the research endeavors of the Federal Theatre Project. "I have used these files constantly," she wrote, and "have given the original source, newspaper name and date, for each item, accepting the authority of the files."[11] In his "Foreword" Hughes notes that the public reaction to the first volume was "most gratifying" and that he is "pleased" to make this research from the School of Drama "available to the general public." He does not mention the Federal Theatre.

The tension between Hallie Flanagan and Glenn Hughes was played out in numerous ways during his tenure on the project and continued after his departure. On a train from Seattle to Portland in November 1937 Flanagan confided to Ellen Woodward that, "I now see clearly that he never really pushed our company because he had no desire to build up a rival. He did develop two remarkable projects for us, both of which enhance his own department."[12] The first of these, the historical research, only mildly illuminates the struggle between federal and regional interests. The WPA did pay for the labor and the School of Drama was the recipient of the "product" as well as the resulting academic and historical prestige. In the second instance, however the beautifully designed and museum quality theatre models – the tensions between the federal government and local interests provoked a paper war over ownership and the integrity of both Glenn Hughes and Federal Theatre.

The theatre models

Today they are abandoned, crammed into the corner of a former Sears store which serves as storage space for the University of Washington. They are tightly wrapped and stacked in their glass cases – at least not destroyed – victims of a lobby redecoration which featured a "new carpet and a Chihuly." The historian always confronts the cruelty of passing times and fading memories. "Nobody cares about them but you, Barry," a Dean said. That's not quite true, but we had no momentum and so they were nearly lost again.

Once they were splendid and splendidly regarded. Here is Hallie Flanagan after first viewing them:

> I have seen the model theatres in the Crystal Palace in London, and also those of the Comedie Francaise, but nothing here or abroad compares with these models of the great periods of theatre...They are absolutely accurate, and marvelous as to workmanship. Each detail is worked out exquisitely...In my opinion they should be in the Smithsonian or the Folger.[13]

4 Model of the Acropolis including the Theatre of Dionysus.

5 Model of a "generic" Roman stage based on the Theatre at Orange.

Their physical presence is imposing. The Theatre of Dionysus at Athens is four feet long and nearly that wide rising to a height of twenty-six inches. The stunning Acropolis is eight feet long and the Elizabethan Fortune Theatre is nearly four feet high. The detail is remarkable. Hand carved and painted by work-relief cabinetmakers, painters and sculptors, the individual statues of the Teatro Olympico gaze out over their auditorium just as their originals do at Vicenza. And each of the columns at the Theatre at Orange bears a striking resemblance to its Roman counterpart. It's no wonder that Flanagan wanted them at the Smithsonian or that Harry Hopkins wanted them for the opening of Treasure Island in San Francisco. Even in the gloom of Sears they are still redolent with theatre history and with WPA strife.

The first mention of them is in October 1935 in a telegram from Hughes to Flanagan. He apparently had conceived of them as a wonderful teaching tool for his fledgling department and as part of the package that he and Guy Williams were preparing for the inaugural FTP proposal in the Northwest. The wording of the telegram is crucial in understanding the confusion that followed. Hughes proposed the "construction of a set of historical theatre models for *permanent* exhibit at the University, eleven persons, five thousand nine hundred and six dollars."[14] In the same telegram he asked permission to continue the project without having to await the "Washington paperwork." Apparently pleased with the action in her Northwest region, Flanagan wired her approval of the plan ten days later. When Guy Williams submitted their first comprehensive plan in December, the Historical Models were listed as requiring ten relief workers and one nonrelief supervisor.

The work began immediately in 1936 under the direction of Hughes's colleague, scene designer John Conway, and their shop foreman, James Hicken. A list of sixteen historical theatres was prepared and work began on the initial project: the Theatre of Dionysus from classical Greek history. While carpenters and cabinetmakers framed in the outline of the Athenian stage, others began studying pictures and plans for the Roman Theatre at Orange and the Stoa of Eumenes. John Conway, who designed the Penthouse Theatre which became the signature performance space for the university, designed each of the theatres and then turned the plans over to a crew of artists and artisans who completed the work. It is not clear what prompted concern in Washington, DC about the status and disposition of these little theatres, but before a month was out Hughes received a letter from Lester Lang, Flanagan's assistant, reminding him that "any work executed with Federal funds becomes Federal property."[15]

The sheer size of many of the models – Dionysus alone weighs 240 pounds – precludes "touring" them easily, but the tug of war about who "owned" them began almost immediately. Hughes obviously expected them to remain in "residence" at the university just like his Penthouse (and later Showboat) theatres, both built with considerable WPA support. But he was also politically astute and did not wish to jeopardize the whole project before it could be completed. Accordingly he consulted with Guy Williams who wrote a conciliatory letter to Lester Lang:

> The word "permanent" was an unfortunate description of the exhibit of theatre models being built by Federal Theatre project unit 813-(1) under the sponsorship of the University of Washington.
>
> Mr. Hughes and the University authorities are perfectly aware that the models constructed by the Federal Theatre project unit become Federal property. They hope, however, that it can be arranged to exhibit the models here on loan from the Federal Government in space provided by the University and under conditions where they may be viewed by the general public. The University, also, under this arrangement should be appointed curator of the models which are already attracting considerable interest from both the student body and the public. Will you please ignore the word "permanent" in the project as now drawn up as it is not at all what we mean?[16]

If there was an official response to this request it has not survived in the record and the building went on. By April 1936 Dionysus was completed and work was well along on the Fortune and Orange. Ten people were paid weekly to mold the forms, carve the statues and paint the auditoriums. Along with twenty people on Howard Grant's research project and nearly 190 in various performing troups, Federal Theatre was employing 220 people in Seattle and, in those early days, was threatening to be one of the most robust units.

The controversy about ownership continued to bubble, however, and some WPA officials began to complain about the University of Washington's contribution to the models project. Since it was being executed in their shops and under their supervision and since they were to be the beneficiaries of the results, perhaps some of the labor costs might be assumed by them and not all packed into the WPA budget? In July Flanagan's new assistant, J. Howard Miller, wrote to Guy Williams that it might be "wise" for him to look into the model project and see if some of the labor costs might be separated from it. Sensitive to Williams's closeness to Hughes, however, Miller cautioned him not to "take any steps until I arrive, but Mr. Abel brought the matter up again at the Salt Lake Conference, and I am inclined to agree with him in his opinion that the Project is costing too much money."[17]

Like everyone else who saw the models taking shape, Miller was impressed. Hughes assured him that the artists working on them were legitimately certified for relief, and in the event of employment opportunities they would be returned to the private sector. He also underlined that the university was functioning as a sponsor on the project, and that the models certainly did belong to the federal government. Miller was appeased and a deal was struck. The building would go forward, but one position would be removed from WPA relief status. The project was redesignated as 7002-D and funds approved to continue construction.[18]

By the end of the year several of the models were finished. The Fortune, Dionysus, Orange and an English pageant wagon were reported as "entirely completed" and others were in various stages of assemblage. A December report from the agent-cashier to Guy Williams records some of the details of the construction. "The Olympic Theatre model is practically complete, except for finishing touches and the decoration. There will be approximately 100 figures in this model when it is finished, and thirty-five of these miniature statues are now done."[19] A Chinese theatre was also under construction, and Power reported that "the decorative railings are done; the roof rafters are cut; the three main walls have been built; the foundation is completed; and the stage is almost finished."[20] Progress was also being made on Drury Lane, a Roman Naumachia, a Commedia stage and others. Sometimes they apparently took shortcuts to the elaborate painting demands. Power also records that a Victorian model was recently finished because "Mr. Conway of the Division of Drama sent to London for a paper model of this stage, and our workmen built a plywood model on which they pasted the paper."[21]

The building continued in the early months of 1937. In April, Power reported that the stage of Drury Lane was completed and partially decorated, that all the seats in the auditorium were done and that "decoration as far up as the ceiling was three-fourths finished."[22] The Commedia was done and progress was being made on the Japanese Noh Theatre. References to them through the summer and fall are cursory, largely because so much focus was on the effects of the "Roosevelt depression" and the massive WPA cutbacks. The Federal Theatre, like all other WPA projects, writhed and withered as productions were postponed and labor unrest captured the attention of the public. By the beginning of a new fiscal year budgets had been trimmed, programs eliminated and exempt positions had been slashed back to 5 percent for a number of the FTP units.

In November 1937, Hallie Flanagan spent three and a half days in Seattle assessing the project and trying to enlist more support from both the community and the WPA bureaucracy. She had lunch with Anna Roosevelt

Boettiger who seemed interested in lobbying for a theatre that was not controversial. She toured Glenn Hughes's theatres at the university and watched a Federal Theatre production of *Androcles and the Lion*. Everywhere she saw the effects of the recent cuts, especially in nonrelief status, and felt that many good people had been lost, including the tireless Guy Williams who had agreed to a promotion in order to supervise touring FTP production in the Western Region.

As for the theatre models, after praising their appearance, she wrote to Ellen Woodward that, "they would make a marvelous addition to our spring exhibit." She asked for figures on how much it would cost to move them to Washington, DC "for I do not consider it right that the University retain them." She believed that Hughes was anxious to keep them and that they would be costly to crate and ship. However, in her opinion, "they represent Government property unique and valuable."[23] Hughes hosted a party for her attended by his colleagues in English and Drama, and she visited the president of the University, "who expressed interest in the Federal Theatre, especially the theatre model project."[24] But when she left she was determined to see if the models could be moved away from their "permanent" location at the university and exhibited and admired by larger audiences.

Shortly thereafter her western regional director, Ole Ness, wrote to George Hood, who was the acting director for the state, requesting that blueprints and working drawings for the model project be submitted to the regional office in Los Angeles. Hood notified Hughes of this inquiry and Hughes promised to look into it. Approximately two weeks later he wrote to Hood that he had looked into the matter of the blueprints. Specifically he had spoken with Jim Hicken who was supervising much of the building and (in one of the great rejoinders of the whole theatre project) informed Hood that we'll "get on it when Jim has the time."[25] Jim was also the technical director for Hughes's ambitious production program, and it is difficult to imagine when he would ever have "time."

He certainly didn't in the next year and references to the models controversy are sparse throughout 1938. This is principally due to the fact that they were completed and no longer a line item on anyone's budget requests. Federal Theatre in Seattle was concerned with finding a permanent home, producing plays and trying to build a children's theatre. The research project and the models were both done and no longer preoccupied the new director Edwin O'Connor, who was pursuing his elusive dream of a showboat theatre. But the enmity between Hughes and his former "boss" Hallie Flanagan was palpable, and neither was reluctant to comment. Following her visit to

Seattle in February 1939, Hughes wrote to Howard Miller, "I noticed in the papers that Mrs. Flanagan was here the other day, but I did not hear from her. Sorry. I dare say she was crowded for time."[26]

Hughes also was not reluctant to criticize Federal Theatre for their real or imagined offenses to him or his program. On the occasion of the university hosting the National Theatre Conference in the winter of 1939, he wrote to Edwin O'Connor expressing his concern over the way some tickets for *Spirochete* had been handled:

> At the 27c price agreed on between you and me for balcony seats they were offered only gallery seats. I know two or three who were irritated to the extent that they refused to see the play and went elsewhere. I am sorry to hear of this, and I think it poor policy on the part of the Federal Theatre to offend out-of-town delegates for the sake of a few cents.[27]

In a masterful reply, O'Connor points out that they have no gallery, and that so many out-of-town delegates wanted to see the show that he provided the $1.15 seats – rather than the agreed upon forty-two center seats – for 27. "Of course, we did not point out that we were favoring them in this way. The Federal Theatre, rather than disappoint, does many such things without publicizing the fact... Of course you KNOW it is not the policy for the Federal Theatre to offend any patrons for the sake of a few cents."[28]

In January 1939 Howard Miller made a final stab at resolving the ownership of the Theatre Models. At the urging of both Flanagan and Ole Ness, Miller met with Hughes to discuss a plan for touring the models to Portland, San Francisco and Los Angeles on their way to the upcoming World's Fair in Flushing Meadows, New York. "At my last conference with Mr. Hughes," Miller wrote, "he was fully aware of the fact that these models were a loan," but cautioned Miller, "he will make every attempt to keep them."[29]

While they haggled over transportation requirements, moving costs and eventual sites for a more "permanent" display, Federal Theatre was engulfed in a political fight to survive. Hurtling toward a showdown in Congress and forced to defend itself against charges of waste, favoritism, communism and general boondoggling, the Federal Theatre was held hostage for the entire WPA budget. And with its demise in the summer of 1939, there was no longer any pressure to move the models to the Smithsonian or the Library of Congress. Glenn Hughes succeeded in his quest for their *permanent* display in Seattle. His models were exhibited for the next fifty years as a centerpiece of his School of Drama. Thousands of students paraded by their enormous glass cases, treated to an imaginative reconstruction of great theatres from the past. And thousands of audience members later viewed them during intermissions at the University's new public performance center. But increasingly they became the victim of the unknowing and the uncaring, their luster lost in familiarity and neglect. Finally, in 1984 Professor Jack Wolcott led a drive to restore and clean them. In 1992 they were exhibited for the annual meeting of the American Society for Theatre Research. But their sheer bulk made them increasingly difficult to exhibit in one place. In spite of their museum quality, they finally succumbed to the new rug and the Chihuly and were sent to storage. Their present disposition is uncertain.

5

A Negro theatre

Their names float across the programs and reviews of the project, slipping away and then reappearing with a frequency that demands attention and explanation: Sara Oliver, Joseph Staton, Theodore Brown, Howard Biggs. Their faces peer out of faded production shots, and newspaper clippings recall their triumphs and transitory moments of celebrity: *Stevedore*, *In Abraham's Bosom*, *Noah*, *Black Empire*, *Natural Man*, *Androcles and the Lion*, *Lysistrata*, *It Can't Happen Here*. For nearly four years they acted, sang, danced and wrote live theatre in a community whose total Negro population probably never exceeded 5,000. By the autumn of 1938 they had created their own piece – *An Evening With Dunbar* – based on the life and work of the black poet. Who were they? Why were they here?

The record is difficult because no matter what they did they could never shake off the baggage of racism that they had to drag through the rehearsal halls and stages they shared with the "white" company. "You could smell em, you know, when they'd been in the room."[1] And even their praise – and it was considerable – was couched in terms which qualified or undercut their achievements. "I saw *Androcles and the Lion*," Flanagan wrote in 1937, "by our Negro company – amazing how it adapts itself to the primitivism of Negro voices; their apparent childlike belief saves the play from fantasy."[2] For Guy Williams they didn't just sing, they "yammered" out the powerful songs in *Stevedore*.

In spite of their achievements, the Negro unit in Seattle, just like other Negro units in Harlem, Newark and Birmingham, never overcame a perception that they weren't quite legitimate. Although the WPA and Federal One embraced and promoted an equal rights agenda, their own documents betray the belief that the Negro units weren't really about *art*. In the great economic upheaval and financial crisis in the summer of 1937, Harry Hopkins outlined a strategy for saving the best of the New York Federal Theatre should the crisis continue. "The Negro Theatre might be retained as an entity, though drastically cut, on the basis of its socialogical [sic] importance rather than theatrical importance."³

In Seattle, where they had premiered the nationwide *It Can't Happen Here*, survived the humiliating censorship and closure of *Lysistrata*, unearthed a talented new writer in Theodore Brown (*Natural Man*) and a brilliant young composer, Howard Biggs, their white director submitted a chilling and derogatory report on his own production of *The Dragon's Wishbone*:

> The negro unit plays the show. Their diction, a constant problem for us, was not aided by the necessity of using masks for the animals; we were forced to abandon the masks in favor of make-up in several instances. Although the negro has a keen sense of rhythm, it must be his own rhythm. The script, which is done in doggeral verse, suffered from their demand for freedom from stated dialogue, ad-libbing and, in their own terms, "Jive." The negro is very amusing when he can write his own script as he goes along – improvisation – but is at a loss when tied to a script. He can grasp a feeling, but not the exact meaning in dialogue.⁴

It was late spring, 1939. Their next to last show. Many of the same names are still there. They were a company.

The origins of the company are cloudy. There certainly was no proposal for a Negro unit in any of the early correspondence between Glenn Hughes and WPA officials. At some point, however, Burton and Florence James, founders of the Seattle Repertory Playhouse and Hughes's sometime colleagues at the University, proposed the idea of a Federal Theatre Negro group, and Hughes, after first dismissing the idea, eventually forwarded it to Flanagan with a positive recommendation. The relationship between Hughes and "the Jameses," as they were known in the community, was confused and often stormy, but it is central to the events of the period and to its explosive aftermath in the Canwell "un-American" hearings a decade later. Those pre-McCarthyite investigations that were played out in Seattle in 1948 ultimately resulted in the destruction of the Jameses and their theatre.⁵

At first, Florence and Burton James just wanted a theatre that mattered. Trained in New York and committed to the "new" repertory of the Guild and other groups, they arrived in Seattle in 1920 to teach and produce plays in Nellie Cornish's Arts School. By 1928 they had established a reputation for good work in a series of modern plays which included the contemporary "art" agenda of Ibsen, Chekhov and Shaw. In 1928, however, they raised the ire of their board of directors by scheduling Pirandello's *Six Characters in Search of an Author.* Concerned about the play's "immorality," the board closed the production over the protests of the Jameses and some of their strongest supporters in the community. One of those supporters, Glenn Hughes, wrote a strong letter to the president of the board objecting to the closing and expressing his support for the Jameses:

> I have never heard an educated person mention "Six Characters" as even savoring of immorality. I saw the play in New York City, and have since discussed it in my classes, and have yet to discover anything objectionable in it. I admit that one of the central situations is a sophisticated one. But sophistication and immorality are quite distinct from each other.[6]

Hughes goes on to say that, "what I fear is that Mr. and Mrs. James will lose faith in Seattle, and will at the first opportunity desert us." The board remained firm, however, and the Jameses resigned. But instead of fleeing, they founded a professional theatre in Seattle and for the next twenty years produced some of the finest theatre in the Northwest.

Glenn Hughes was on their first board of directors at the Seattle Repertory Playhouse and was instrumental in arranging for a bank loan so that they could acquire a theatre in the university district. Their friendship grew and Hughes – through his acquaintance with Barrett Clark and others – helped the Jameses negotiate royalty rights and obtain manuscripts of new plays. On the eve of sailing to England in August 1928, he wrote to Burton from the Roosevelt Hotel in New York that he had succeeded in negotiations with "French's royalty man over two shows" and sent "all good luck with the theatre, and our best love to you. As ever, Glenn."[7]

But by the mid-thirties their relationship had become estranged and difficult. Professional jealousies, personal and national politics and disagreements about the nature of art, theatre and training drove them further apart. The Seattle Repertory Playhouse and Glenn Hughes's expanding campus venues were literally within blocks of each other, but they were increasingly distant and often openly hostile in their relationship. They squabbled over plays, complimentary tickets and season planning. Florence was a popular teacher in the School of Drama for a time, and her firing by Hughes led to a student uproar. Playhouse personnel resented Hughes's appearances on occasion to "count their houses," and Hughes bristled when they seemed to be luring his better students away.

Typical of their skirmishes was an incident in February 1934 when the Playhouse bank note was due for its annual renewal, and Hughes balked at continuing to be a signer. He made it clear that he was no longer actively connected to the management at the Playhouse and had "worries enough of my own." He also stipulated, however, that he wished no embarrassment for the other signers or for the Playhouse, and if the bank would not accept the note then he would relent and sign. His answer was a rather terse note from their counsel to the effect that they'd all gone into this together and therefore they should all continue. Hughes disagreed. "At the time I signed the original note I was a member of the Executive Board of the Playhouse. Now I am not... It is a professional matter with me to wish to avoid assuming financial responsibility for an institution with whose policies I am so seldom in sympathy."[8]

Meanwhile, the Repertory Theatre was producing some highly acclaimed work. Their production of *Peer Gynt* (1929) was one of the most widely acclaimed in the history of the community and was revived four times. In 1933 they had produced Paul Green's prize-winning *In Abraham's Bosom*, drawing some of their cast from the local Negro AME church. It was a profitable connection and one that would be crucial in the days ahead. Sara Oliver, who was a featured player with the Negro Repertory Company, recalled how important the church and performing were to the small black community in Seattle:

> We always went to church. As far as Negro people are concerned, that is the nucleus of the community anywhere you go. Especially the Methodist Church. The Methodist Church has always kept up with Black history... Harriet Tubman, Sojourner Truth, we did all those people. We had pageants and stuff that portrayed *our* people.[9]

Still, making theatre for a living was a risky business, inexorably bound to the profits of the box office and made still more fragile by an economy in peril. Ever mindful about ways that they could keep their operation afloat, the Jameses worked out an official relationship with the State Board of Education to take theatre into the schools, and through the auspices of a Rockefeller grant were able to fund state-wide tours of their repertory.

Thus in the fall of 1935, as plans for a new Federal Theatre began circulating in the press and over the radio, the Jameses – like many other producers nation wide – realized that such an enterprise might be ideal for the kind of new and far-reaching work that they were already doing. Apparently unaware that Flanagan was courting Glenn Hughes as her regional director (or perhaps trying to forestall such an arrangement), Burton James wrote her a long letter in October outlining the accomplishments of the Playhouse and urging that they receive consideration in the development of any plans for the Northwest:

> What final form your plan will take we of course do not know, but we respectfully suggest that in formulating your project in this area you investigate fully the work of the Playhouse, its various social aspects and, particularly, in respect to the work it has been doing with the high schools of this state.[10]

Burton went on to stress their belief in revitalizing the theatre by creating new audiences, an argument that he must have believed would resonate with Flanagan's stated goals for the project. He was obviously disappointed when she replied two weeks later that, with respect to the Northwest, he should write to Glenn Hughes.

Hughes did include Burton on the committee that he put together to hold the initial auditions for the project, probably because he was a bona fide "professional" and would thus validate whatever decisions they made with their WPA supervisors. The Playhouse staff continued, meanwhile, to discuss ways in which they could become a part of the emerging federal largesse. It is not entirely clear why they finally seized upon a Negro Theatre as their point of entry. A number of different reasons have been offered, and it is very likely a combination of them that led to the creation of the first cast. The Playhouse was in a difficult financial position and genuinely needed a "winner" to restore their economic credibility. They had had a huge success with *In Abraham's Bosom* two years earlier and had good relationships with some singers and performers at the AME. Moreover, the Jameses had a strong liberal commitment to civil rights and social justice and whether that was opportunistic, utopian or part of their "communist" agenda, it did lead them to found a Negro Theatre in a remote Northwest city where the census listed only 4,000 black people.[11] It is also quite probable that after the initial auditions had turned up a sea of vaudeville performers, both Hughes and Guy Williams had to reassess their priorities. Hughes had been courted and flattered into a position of authority and now he felt compelled to deliver. What that meant at one critical level was appropriating and spending money for government relief. From that angle a Negro company sponsored by the Playhouse made sense. It would not be the centerpiece of the project, but it would be visible and in keeping with Flanagan's politics. And while no one said this on the record, there was probably a feeling that most of the participants would qualify for welfare.

Burton James's plan was to mount a two-play season at the Repertory Playhouse using his own supervisory personnel and casting an acting company and musical chorus from his previous contacts with *In Abraham's Bosom*. He also planned to draw on the YM/WCA and the Urban League to network for auditionees. The executive secretary of the League, Joseph Jackson, had played Abraham in their 1933 production of the Paul Green play and was instrumental in helping the Jameses establish the company.[12] He assured both Hughes and State Director George Hood that there were sufficient personnel for such a venture. While both the Jameses were wary of the bureaucracy of the WPA paperwork, Burton seems from the outset to have had little patience with forms and deadlines. His behavior suggests that he believed that he should identify the appropriate people, cast and rehearse them, and that the state WPA offices should be responsible for insuring that his choices were eligible or else figure out how they could be. Like so many others who worked for the WPA, he would shortly realize the error of his ways.

Burton announced that they would conduct auditions for *Porgy* and *Stevedore* on December 2, 1935, and that the list of acceptable performers would then be submitted to Hood so that he could have the labor management office of the WPA certify them for appropriate relief status. A week later Hood had not received the list but, apparently trying to be helpful and move the project along, he submitted a requisition for personnel form based upon classification with names to follow. This list, with the standard WPA provision of not more than 10 percent nonrelief, committed the project to approximately sixty workers and $20,000 in federal relief.[13]

Meanwhile Burton, who was also going to cast a Negro chorus to support the productions, continued to audition outside the framework of the Federal Theatre committee. On December 13 he reported to Hood that twenty more people had shown up as a result of his work at the YWCA, and Hood urged him to submit their names for classification. At the same time Hood was accumulating applications directly from welfare people who were anxious to apply for the new Theatre program. It was an awkward process but fundamental to the way that the Federal Theatre Project worked. Since it was both art and relief everybody had to be classified, and the relief positions had to be filled before nonrelief – or exempt – positions could be approved. Every unit wrestled with this process because frequently the actor most suited to a particular role might not be eligible for relief. If an exception was made, however, then that worked against the principal goal of the whole enterprise which was welfare for people out of work. At first, in recognition of this dilemma, units were able to exempt 10 percent of the total number of workers from classification. In the early years of the FTP the number crept up to 15 percent as producers and directors struggled with the demands of staging "professional" productions. On January 13, 1936, Flanagan, under pressure from the state WPA, approved a 20 percent exemption for the new Negro unit in Seattle.[14]

This meant that in a company of sixty, Burton could now employ twelve who were not even eligible for welfare. When his list finally arrived at Hood's office, however, there were twice that many proposed for exemption. Hood was frustrated trying to follow the procedures and getting misinformation from the Playhouse. Husbands and wives, for example, were not allowed to be on welfare at the same time. And "priority one" people were to be favored over lower priorities. Burton ignored both these provisions. Then he had his assistant, Albert Ottenheimer, write to Hood in late January and inquire about the hold-ups and when we can "get moving."

In the middle of this, Hood was confronted with a "committee" who complained about the selection of *Porgy* as the opening show. Rumors had been circulating on the project for several weeks about Negro opposition to *Porgy* and about a "whispering campaign" because people did not want to jeopardize their potential jobs in the new company by speaking out. Concerns about the repeated use of the word "nigger" and the general "degrading" nature of the play created an opposition that was difficult to assess or evaluate. Finally a committee representing the King County Colored Progressive Democratic Club investigated the "whispering" campaign and reported to Hood that the rumors were true. "The play is something that is not really wanted in Seattle or in any other place," they told Hood.[15] At about the same time the producing rights to *Porgy* were withdrawn because the Theatre Guild had decided to tour *Porgy and Bess*, so the showdown over the selection never developed. Evamarii Johnson suggests that given some of the language in *Stevedore*, the whispering campaign probably wouldn't have forced the withdrawal, and it was probably the loss of royalty rights which tipped the balance.[16] But it's equally possible that the Jameses, not wishing a confrontation and the subsequent bad publicity, used the royalty issue as a way to substitute Andre Obey's *Noah* for their premiere production.

On February 12, 1936, State Director George Hood provided the Jameses with a "where we stand" list of Negro personnel. He, with help from Guy Williams, had adjusted and adapted the regulations, stretched the boundaries and tried to provide Burton with the people that he wanted. But it was a difficult task. The chorus totaled seventeen; however, only nine of those were actually certified for relief. The rest were either in process, ineligible or in one case, "to be reassigned from sewing."[17] The acting company numbered twenty-five (thirteen men and twelve women) but, again, only nine of those were certified. Fourteen were in various stages of review, and one was "still listed on his mother's certificate and would have to be certified separately." It is instructive to note, both with regard to this venture and the FTP nation wide, that supervisory personnel were ordinarily not eligible for welfare. That is, directors, designers, lead technicians and others who were required to make the productions happen often used up the quota of nonrelief personnel. For those who have a somewhat cynical view of the James's promotion of a Negro company, it is symptomatic that when the first production finally opened a goodly portion of their own Repertory Playhouse staff was on the government payroll.[18]

Noah opened on April 27, 1936, as the first production of the Seattle Negro Repertory Company. Of the forty-five cast members who participated in the premiere only nineteen had survived from the "where we stand" memo of February 12. Some had simply not qualified for relief, but most were people whom Burton had cajoled or auditioned outside the government system and then sent on to Hood for classification. Hood and Guy Williams bent some of the rules and twisted a number of arms. Chorus sopranos Bessie Ward and Nellie Price were "reassigned from the sewing project," and actor Ben Chandler was brought over from "Washington Park." Others would perform as volunteers because of their earlier association with In Abraham's Bosom or the AME choir. It was a large and fluid group with little theatrical experience and little to hold them to a prolonged commitment beyond their weekly pay. Some grew bored with the "waiting around" and left. Others disappeared unexpectedly for jobs as ship stewards, cabin boys or day laborers. They had a professional tap dancer and some holdovers from In Abraham's Bosom, but there was no question that this was a decidedly amateur venture.

But there was some promise: performers such as Theodore Brown who had moved from New York and who had experience in amateur "theatricals." He became a mainstay of the fledgling company, playing the title role in Noah as well as the leading part – Lonnie – in Stevedore. And he wrote the controversial Lysistrata as well as a powerful original play, Natural Man. Hallie Flanagan once referred to Brown as "our only playwright."[19] And Sara Oliver, a local girl, whose mother cleaned houses and who got on the WPA because she could sing and was determined to do something besides manual labor. "So all of a sudden they decided to have me read for

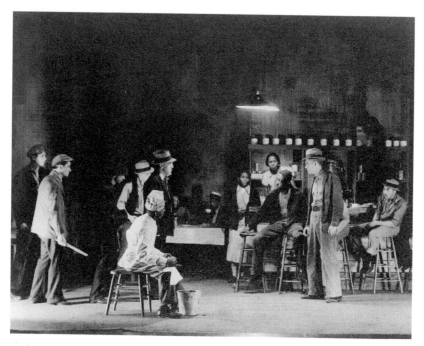

6 *Stevedore* was one of the most successful productions by the Seattle Federal Theatre. Joe Staton as Blacksnake is seated centre.

Momma Noah, and I had three weeks to learn the part, and I did it!"[20] And Joe Staton, young and handsome, a natural leader and gifted performer would become the leading man and eventually "direct" some of their most successful work. Staton had worked at various jobs up and down the West Coast and came to the theatre as a replacement for a buddy who had dropped out of the program. But he would stay to become their inspiration and their dominant personality. His debut as Blacksnake in *Stevedore* was an important moment for the company because Staton, by all accounts, had an instinctively powerful attraction on stage as well as a fertile and vivid theatrical imagination. And there were others: Roberta Walker, whom Florence James found to be instinctively gifted, and the imaginative Robert St. Clair.

Burton and Florence James worked them hard. They cast – and then recast – when problems arose. They started staging the two plays and prepared the chorus for outside appearances and concerts, as well as integrating them into the productions. Committed to a notion that *singing* was somehow fundamental to the performing Negro, they planned for both plays to have choral interludes and underscoring. *Stevedore* featured a dozen traditional anthems and ballads ranging from "St. Louis Woman" to "Water Boy," and during the funeral scene in Act II the entire cast joined in for a rendition of "Shall We Meet." *Noah* was transformed into a kind of dance musical with lots of improvisation and some contemporary references. Although the production report asserts that they remained true to the text, it also admits that after the Ark came to rest on Mt. Ararat, "the younger members, overjoyed at being on land, go through a 'truckin' number, singing improvised words."[21]

And they taught acting. Florence had been a very successful teacher at both Cornish and the University of Washington, and she and her assistant Al Ottenheimer worked with the members of the young company to help them understand the process of performing as well as the social implications of the work they were doing. It was a frustrating task. For some, it was simply "play" for money, and it was at that level that they rehearsed and performed. For others, it was certainly serious business but nothing that couldn't be accomplished by instinct and nimbleness. For a few, however, it was clear that there were secrets which could be learned; a craft that could be mastered; perhaps a career that could be nurtured. Looking back, Sara Oliver remembered:

> What you do in theatre: you, first, try to analyze what the man is putting down. Al Ottenheimer would write out a whole thing about what this play was about, what every little movement meant, what it really meant to you as the person, and everything. Then you'd study it, and they'd ask you what you thought it meant; what did the characters mean... this is the way you become part of the character, and you come to the place where the character is part of you. It's that you analyze what the man is putting down. What did that person do before he ever wrote this play? You have to become involved! This is what they taught us. They also taught us phonics and dancing and body movements. "Pop" James, we called him, would show you how an actor is supposed to walk and what your body movement means, because it isn't only your voice. It's everything – every part of you that you're portraying in front of an audience.[22]

Phonics. Diction. Projection. Less than a year earlier Hallie Flanagan had cautioned Glenn Hughes against "amateurs," and yet here was an awkward, untrained and novice company struggling to establish a theatrical presence on taxpayer largesse. It was one of the great ironies and contradictions in the whole WPA enterprise, and it was played out repeatedly in cities across the country. In almost no circumstance, however, were the results as remarkable as they were with these gifted black performers in Seattle.

Noah was a success, but *Stevedore* was a sensation, a thunderbolt. Curious audiences were charmed by the cartoon folklore of the Obey play and gave it and the new company their approval, but the George Sklar and Paul Peters labor melodrama shook the community. Seattle was a port city and a union town. Its ribald past included the most significant general strike in the history of the United States as well as a vivid record of International Workers of the World (IWW) dissent and agitation. Dave Beck was organizing the Teamsters, and the fiery Harry Bridges was enrolling the dock workers into his powerful International Longshoreman's Association. It was a violent city, not far removed from its gold rush morality or the thugism which attempted to expel the entire Chinese population a few years earlier. *Stevedore*, with its stirring union message and stunning racial critique, found a loud and supportive audience. People came back to experience it two and three times. Its run was extended and extended again. Middle-class Negroes were afraid that its revolutionary message might precipitate a backlash, and conservative whites railed against its apparent anticapitalism, but the audiences kept coming.

Joe Staton remembered how out-of-towners – particularly visiting southern whites – would insure a lively performance. "You know how it started out. Oh, boy! Oh, boy! They used to come backstage and eat Mr. James up. Oh, they used to give him the devil, give him the devil! We'd go out there and see these licenses from various Southern states, you know. And we knew good and well we were going to have a hot time in the old town tonight."[23] *Stevedore* eventually ran for thirty-six performances and was then reprised as part of a summer repertory program along with *Noah* and a musical revue.

The Negro Repertory Company was clearly a success, and, under the guidance of Florence and Burton James, continued to excel. In the twelve months from April 1936 to April 1937 it mounted six major productions, including the national premiere of *It Can't Happen Here* and Theodore Brown's original script about the legend of John Henry, *Natural Man*. Florence James reprised *In Abraham's Bosom* with the company, and in March 1937 revived *Stevedore*. It is an impressive record and emblematic of the camaraderie and technique that they had developed. The same names appear from play to play, a testimony to their growth and commitment. And yet they found it difficult to shake off the stereotypes, to establish themselves as something other than a novelty – even in their own workplace. In reporting to Guy

Williams on the success of the second *Stevedore*, Fran Power, the agent-cashier, observed that the riot scenes had improved to the point that they "no longer resembled an African rodeo."[24]

Their most famous production was also their briefest. The "Negro" *Lysistrata* opened to a sell-out audience of nearly 1,100 on September 17, 1936, and from all reports was a delightful comic romp. Adapted for the company by Theodore Brown, the script was quite faithful to the original with occasional updates such as a rousing rendition of "Ain't Gonna Study War No More" and two Negro spirituals. Brown set the action in Africa, hoping perhaps to suggest parallels with the Ethiopian conflict and to emulate the success of Orson Welles's Haitian *Macbeth* in New York. Tickets sold briskly for the three-night run, the pre-show publicity was substantial and the opening night response was enthusiastic.

Inexplicably, the very next morning, September 18, the state WPA director, Don Abel, ordered the play closed immediately. Abel had not attended the performance, but he had heard that it was "indecent and bawdy." In the ensuing squabble it was unclear who had complained to Abel, although most accounts suggest that it was his wife and secretary who had probably been offended by the sight of black people performing the sexually suggestive comedy. In spite of vigorous protests by the Seattle unit and the fact that Harry Hopkins had visited Seattle the previous week, Flanagan did not put up much of a fight. Her western regional director, J. Howard Miller, supported Abel's decision, although he reported that there was nothing bawdy or offensive about the production. While there is much controversy about this peculiar event, it is clear that Abel had the power to close an FTP production with little explanation. What is curious and indicative of the confusion on this project, as well as others across the country, is why the Federal Theatre administrators let him get away with it.

In the initial outcry following the cancellation, the cast of *Lysistrata* wrote directly to Flanagan condemning Abel's action and charging him with obvious "racial discrimination."[25] At the same time, Guy Williams also wrote to Flanagan praising the quality of the production and requesting what specific action he should take. Williams's letter is enlightening because he cautions Flanagan that, "Mr. Abel also insists that in the future, we should submit all scripts to him for censorship."[26]

This should have raised storm warnings in Federal One, and, although we do not have a complete paper trail in the *Lysistrata* incident, it is possible to piece together a scenario from documents that have survived. Apparently, Flanagan alerted her aid, William Farnsworth, to coordinate events

in Seattle, and then she dispatched J. Howard Miller to do an on-site evaluation in preparation for either reopening the production or moving it to
the Tacoma unit. On September 23 Farnsworth spoke on the telephone
with Guy Williams and was reassured that the show was not indecent and
the press was excellent. Williams believed that if they were to reopen they
would be able to play for four weeks. Farnsworth was completely supportive
as the following transcript indicates:

MR. F: I want you to know that we are behind you 100% in this *Lysistrata*
matter even if it comes to closing the project and removing the money. It
is our contention and we are backed by Woodward that it is not the duty of
the [WPA] State Administrator to guard the morals of the community...
We have had this sort of trouble on a couple of other spots. I want all the
information in every case.

MR. W: I will keep you posted on the whole thing...

MR. F: Keep us posted. Every time an issue comes out shoot it to us right
away.[27]

Harry Hopkins was "burned up" by the *Lysistrata* cancellation and sent one
of his assistants along with Howard Miller to Seattle to confront the local
WPA with a united front of indignation. Unfortunately, Abel had left town
and they had to meet with his assistant, "a choir singer who would cut the
word 'bed' out of any furniture ad."[28] He informed his visitors that the show
was indeed indecent, and had they not closed it the City Council or the
Vice Squad certainly would have. That evening Miller watched a rehearsal
of *Lysistrata* because Hopkins had approved the reopening once the Seattle
negotiations were concluded.

At this point, the controversy veered in an unexpected manner. It isn't
clear what Miller's expectations were, but his reaction to the work was vivid
and negative. He related to Flanagan that it was "badly cast, badly directed,
cheaply costumed and had no focal point."[29] As for the indecent, bawdy
aspects, Miller found that "it was offensive only in a sort of adolescent
writing on the wall way. To anyone who has been seeing vaudeville for a
period of years, the gags couldn't possibly have been offensive, although the
Deputy Administrator dubbed it the rottenest show he had ever seen. My
personal opinion is that he probably has a dirty mind."[30]

The next day he met with Don Abel, and they worked out a compromise.
Abel admitted that he had made a mistake but said that he would have to
resign if the show reopened. Miller did not push for the reopening, but
won assurances that there would be no further WPA interference with the

Theatre Project. In addition, he made it clear that Guy Williams reported directly to Federal One, and that his orders would come from Flanagan or her designates. Miller believed that this decision was in everyone's best interest and would avoid an open rupture between the Theatre Project and the WPA – a rupture that the press was certain to cover in detail. *Lysistrata* disappeared after a single performance.[31]

Miller was apparently nervous about Flanagan's reaction to his handling of the situation and wrote to her that "I am probably in the 'dog house' for not reopening *Lysistrata*."[32] But Flanagan's response was supportive, and on October 5 she wrote that, "Far from being in the dog house . . . we think you handled it very diplomatically."[33] It's very likely that, with the nationwide opening of *It Can't Happen Here* just weeks away, Flanagan did not relish a confrontation with the WPA in a remote corner of her national theatre.

The *Lysistrata* closing is emblematic of the constant battle for autonomy and authority that the Theatre Project fought for in its uneasy alliance with the WPA. In this case the Theatre Project claimed victory because they were able to force the state officials into recognizing their authority and preserve a reporting structure which insured a minimum of censorship. But lost in the congratulatory letters and telegrams and the increasing fervor surrounding the anticipated opening of *It Can't Happen Here* were the cast and crews of the Negro Company's *Lysistrata*. They were censored and silenced directly by the intervention of the state WPA and indirectly by the complicity of their own producing organization.

The decision to entrust *It Can't Happen Here* to the Negro Company – after the *Lysistrata* debacle – was an expedient choice but not necessarily a wise one. It was clearly a "white" play but the "white" company was still an uncertain venture in the summer of 1936. Originally Glenn Hughes had envisioned a company devoted to new works by Northwest authors (including himself). However, that plan was postponed following their initial auditions, and it was not until the spring of 1936 – with the variety units up and running – that Hughes and Guy Williams returned to the notion of a theatre for new plays. In response to repeated requests from the Tacoma (WA) Theatre League, Hughes had authorized a Federal unit in Tacoma, and they had debuted in April 1936 with a production of *Brief Candle* by Robert Hare Powell. It's not clear whether Hughes or Williams actually saw their work, but Howard Miller did and he was appalled. He wrote to Flanagan that, "Tacoma is in very bad shape. Their leading man was a former vaudeville juggler, and their leading woman a speech major who had specialized in phonetics. You can imagine the result when they attempted to produce *Brief Candle*."[34] Miller shared his reservations with Hughes who agreed to "bear down harder" on them. By June he had convinced them to undertake a series of new plays by local authors that failed to generate much enthusiasm or uncover much talent. However, they were active when Flanagan announced her intentions for a nationwide opening of *It Can't Happen Here* and were eager to participate. Williams, Hood and others were anxious to be included in Flanagan's multiple opening night of the Sinclair Lewis adaptation, and since Florence James and the Negro Company were "in place," it looked to be a good match. They were all aware that Miller thought the Tacoma group should be disbanded, but rather than hang the whole reputation of the Northwest on the Tacoma production, Hughes decided to give the Seattle premiere to the Negro Company.

Unfortunately the company, as well as the press and public, viewed it as essentially a "white man's play," and that tension was underscored by some of the choices that the Jameses made. Anxious to localize the events, Florence set the action in the Negro district of Seattle and substituted Seattle names and places for those in the Lewis script. She also changed the Canadian border reference to Blaine to take advantage of the nearby British Columbia port of entry. Senator Windrip, Sarason and the Presidential Aide were played by white men in an attempt to "show the ravages of dictatorship upon a minority,"[35] but it tended to cast the conflicts of the play into racial terms. In spite of good performances by Theodore Brown as Doremus and Joe Staton and Sara Oliver (as Shad and Mary), the production seemed to confuse rather than clarify the issues. "Played by a Negro cast, the local production had a couple of strikes on it at once. They played it with no compromise to color yet it was necessary to keep reminding yourself that the scene was really the United States and not some remote village in Africa," observed the *Seattle Argus*.[36] And the critic for the *Commonwealth News* commented that some "thought the Negro cast unsuited to the play," although "the reviewer from her lofty perch felt no sense of race whatever."[37] *It Can't Happen Here* was received in a generally positive manner by the press and community, but it provoked laughter in places where the intent was clearly serious, and it did not provide the kind of vehicle which could showcase the talents of the emergent Negro Company.

Natural Man, however, was entirely different. And while it did not attract large audiences to the Moore Theatre, it was truly a preamble to some of their finer work and a marker of how far they had come. It exhibited all their strengths: Theodore Brown's lyric writing; Staton's powerful performance as the steel-driving "natural man;" a superb chorus to carry the audience from one scene to the next and to underscore the tragedy of this legendary black folk hero; an excellent supporting cast and original music by the young Howard Biggs, a composer in the raw whom they had discovered in their midst. Inspired partially by the thirties' fascination with "folk plays" and partially by Eugene O'Neill's *The Emperor Jones* and *The Hairy Ape*, *Natural Man* opened on the eve of John Henry's famous contest with a mechanical drill and then flashed back to scenes of his past, including chain gangs and jail time. Unlike some treatments of the legend, however, Brown's was not gentle and folksy.[38] This John Henry was rebellious and outspoken, a giant, powerful figure who would not buckle under to white taunts or racist attacks.

But it too traded in stereotypes of black representation: Memphis hookers and cruel pimps; satanic white jailors and gambling; shiftless Negroes. And these stereotypes, in turn, reinforced a perception about the Company in the eyes of Seattle audiences as well as many of their peers and supervisors in the Theatre Project. So widespread were accepted attitudes about what constituted *Negroes* in the 1930s, that other representations were not perceived as authentic or valid. Most members of this Northwest US company had no notion of the kind of "southern" dialect or folk music knowledge that directors assumed they knew. Sara Oliver remembered that Florence James, "was so surprised that here we had this Negro dialect in plays that we were supposed to do, but Seattle people didn't speak Negro dialect. These people didn't even understand the Negro dialect *she* was speaking! So she says 'Well, just speak like yourself. Don't try any dialect. Speak the lines.'"[39] Members of the company grew to be fond of Burton and Florence, although it was always clear that the Jameses were in charge. Still, Sara Oliver claimed that "Mrs. James tried not to affect us with White culture, but to let us bring out our Black culture. Now she may not have realized that she was doing it that way, but that was where she was coming from."[40] But what was allowed to be brought out was probably quite curious at times. Especially given the fact that *she* in Oliver's line-reading account seems to be Florence James, and that the productions were always framed with choral singing. There is no question that the Jameses were impeccable liberals, but they were also ideological prisoners of a kind of unexamined paternalism that was repeatedly enacted in their Negro productions and which was understood as authentic by most of their audiences. Thus, while the Negro unit was evolving into an excellent *company*, there was no corresponding sense that they could accomplish anything significant without white supervision. The financial crisis of 1937 and their own beautifully lyrical production of *Dunbar* would both undermine and challenge that assumption. But first, their director, Florence James, would plunge the entire Federal Theatre unit and the city of Seattle into the throes of *Power* and the debut of the Living Newspaper in the Northwest.[41]

6

Power *and control*

Living Newspapers, the most successful venture of Federal Theatre, were born out of passion and necessity. Necessity dictated that some productions provide enough roles for large numbers of unemployed performers. The passion was supplied by Hallie Flanagan, who had created one of the prototypes for this intriguing format while teaching at Vassar College in 1931, and who believed deeply in the theatre as a place to debate issues of public concern. *Can You Hear Their Voices?*, written by Flanagan and Margaret Ellen Clifford, details the effects of an Arkansas drought on dirt farmers in the south. Based on a short story by Whittaker Chambers and drawing upon congressional transcripts, newspaper stories and magazine articles, the play effectively dramatized the plight of farmers radicalized by climate and the injustices of the capitalist system.[1] After a successful production at Vassar, *Voices* was produced at a number of American theatres, including Hedgerow and the Cleveland Play House, and was instrumental in establishing Flanagan's reputation as a theatrical connoisseur and innovator in the early years of the depression.

Flanagan was intrigued by what she called "the entertainment value of the fact,"[2] and from the beginning of the project – and the ill-fated *Ethiopia* – she was devoted to the development and production of documentary plays modeled after the pages of the morning news. Like *Can You Hear Their Voices?*, these plays would not rely on scenery or special effects, but rather on actors portraying scenes from actual events, supported by music and light. The episodes in the play would be drawn from newspaper stories, committee reports and eyewitness observations, gathered by a team of "reporters" and then fashioned into a dramatic format by a skilled playwright/editor. Each production would focus on a particular and pressing social issue: poverty, labor unions, housing, etc. In time, Flanagan believed, theatre units all across the country would produce these living newspapers and then develop others that addressed the concerns of their individual regions.

Power – one of the most successful – opened in New York City in March 1937 at the height of the national debate over ownership of electric utilities. Focusing on the controversy surrounding the Tennessee Valley Authority, *Power* argued for public ownership in a panorama of highly theatrical scenes which depicted how electricity had been co-opted by private interests and business trusts. The play dramatized the plight of rural farmers who were ignored by the private companies and of urban dwellers who were victims of price fixing and fraud. In addition, it exposed the abuses of the holding companies who had threatened, bullied and blackmailed their way into a virtual monopoly of what *Power* claimed was a natural right of all citizens.

The production was highly controversial, of course, arriving as it did during the battles between Little Steel and the CIO and in the wake of a Supreme Court decision which had ruled TVA constitutional. In fact, the last scene of *Power* is open-ended as the actors and the audience await a ruling on whether that decision is subject to an injunction from another federal court. The end of the story had yet to be told when the play closed and each evening's performance concluded with a giant question mark projected onto a scrim.

The debate over private versus public ownership of the utilities was one of the major battles of the 1930s and nothing typified it more than the struggle between the Tennessee Valley Authority and a host of private companies, the most prominent of which was TEPCO, the Tennessee Electric Power Company. The contest gained national attention when Wendell Wilkie, head of a large utilities holding company (Commonwealth and Southern Corporation) and later Republican presidential candidate, emerged as the major spokesperson for TEPCO and foe of public ownership of the utilities. Arrayed against him were David E. Lilienthal, a board member of TVA and later chair of the Atomic Energy Commission, Arthur Morgan, the chair of TVA, and a host of New Deal administrators and politicians.

The issues were complex, but essentially President Roosevelt believed that it was in the consumer's interest to have access to relatively cheap hydroelectric power produced as a by-product of the Wilson Dam. TEPCO objected to the cheap power because it put them at an unfair advantage and because they believed that such actions allowed the government to enter the private sector unfairly. It was also a major step, Wilkie argued, toward socialization of the entire utilities field. The battle was bitter. Private companies who had virtual monopolies on much of the industry now saw small communities organizing themselves into municipal Public Utility Districts (PUDs) and buying government power. In the larger cities, such as Chattanooga, TVA threatened to string parallel utility lines, thus forcing TEPCO into submission. The government assailed TEPCO with charges of monopoly; TEPCO responded with cries of communism.

The Living Newspaper supported TVA without reservation. Even a cursory reading of *Power* today is startling in the degree to which the private sector is hounded and vilified. Electric power is repeatedly represented in the play as a right of all citizens, like the air we breathe. The consumer is depicted as frail, ignorant and, often, an easy mark for the machinations of private enterprise. And the private companies are portrayed as willing to stoop to any level of bribery, blackmail and lying to get their way. Although the scenes in the play are based upon actual incidents, the broad brush with which Arthur Arent and his team paint illustrates a technique common to the Living Newspaper. What begins as a fact frequently becomes "dramatized" into New Deal propaganda.

It should not be surprising, however, that this Living Newspaper is dominated by its editorial page. In spite of Flanagan's repeated protestations and disavowals of political preferences, it is obvious in retrospect – as it was to many at the time – that this branch of the Federal Theatre was solidly committed to New Deal philosophy and WPA points of view, especially in Seattle, which in 1937 occupied an almost textbook position in terms of the scenario of the play. The Bonneville Power Authority was viewed by many as the TVA equivalent in the West, and Seattle itself was serviced by two competing utility services: City Light, which was a public company, and Puget Power, which was privately owned.

Florence James was chosen to direct the Seattle premiere even though most of her work had been with the Negro unit. The challenge was huge because it was scheduled for the "White Company" that up until that time had done little to distinguish itself and which was principally known for doing some bad original plays in Tacoma. Although race was not foregrounded in the discussions of *Power*, the whole FTP unit was segregated along clear racial lines, and the Negro Company had received an enormous amount of publicity. James knew that they could never produce the play without all the resources of the project, including the vaudevillians and the Negroes.

Seattle, like many Northern cities, was genteel about its racism, with a smallish population of black people who knew their place and stayed there. In some ways it appeared to be progressive. Interracial marriage was not illegal; there was an active National Association for the Advancement of Colored People (NAACP) and Urban League; and a network of social clubs, churches and popular entertainments. At the same time, however, opportunities for Blacks were limited and the city was rigid in its social codes and geographical boundaries.[3] For Florence James then, the task was not only to "integrate" the project but also to produce this huge, sprawling play which would clearly side with City Light in a community rife with factional debate.

To appreciate the controversy surrounding *Power* in Seattle it is critical to recall the intense rivalry between the two companies in delivering electricity to homes and businesses. In a survey published by the Seattle *Star* in January 1936 it was reported that the duplication of facilities was costing thousands of unnecessary dollars.[4] Several neighborhoods had poles and lines for each company on opposite sides of the street. City Light had 2,100 miles of lines in the city; Puget Power, 1,500. There were more than 17,000 line transformers delivering power in a community where only 9,000 were required. City Light estimated that if they could buy out Puget Power they could bring rates down to 0.02 per kHz. In fact, debate over ownership of the public utilities had become so heated that City Light had undertaken a series of Friday night radio broadcasts that were devoted to educating the public about the costs of duplication. Each of these programs, which ran between 9:30 P.M. and 9:45 P.M., was introduced by an announcer who stressed that there were more than 43,000 customers paying over five million dollars for Puget Power services that essentially were the same as the public utility.[5]

Moreover, with the prospect of the Bonneville hydroelectric project adding to the already enormous resources of Coulee Dam, the Northwest was ripe for the same kind of controversy that was raging over TVA and which had become the dramatic subject matter for *Power.* Mayor John Dore, who had recently won reelection with the aid of Dave Beck's powerful Teamsters organization, recognized the similarity and proclaimed a National Power Week to coincide with the production of *Power.* On opening night in a speech from the stage he said that Seattle was the logical city for the play to premiere on the Pacific Coast.

The Seattle Federal Theatre was so enthusiastic about the production that they mounted a huge campaign in cooperation with City Light to overwhelm the population with the rightness of their cause and the ideology of the play. While there was a good deal of talk in the early years of the Living Newspapers about updating the scripts with news of the day, the rush of production deadlines rarely allowed this to happen. The Seattle promptbook suggests that little was changed after the passage of four months and three thousand miles from the New York production.[6] "Boulder" Dam became "Coulee" on occasion and the scenic design was simplified by a single unit. With one other exception, the text was virtually the same as it had been performed on Broadway.

But that exception is both fascinating and clearly illustrates the determination of the Seattle unit to adapt the play to local conditions. Under the direction of Florence James a film was made which dramatized the virtues of public utilities:

> We felt the comparative Costs scene ended flatly, and to correct this and to point up the show locally an Eisenstein montage was made from the film library of Seattle's City Light Company to top the scene. As this film was run (approximately two minutes of clouds, rain, snow, ice, glaciers, etc. with finally double exposure of energy coursing though turbines and out over transmission lines) Loudspeaker continued with descriptive patter.

> Mountains-snow-ice glaciers
> Nature's reservoir of potential power
> Who put it there?
> Who rightfully owns its resources?
> Who is most entitled to its possible potential benefits?
> You – the public
> Streams-Rivers-Waterfalls,
> Ideal energy
> Energy that is the property of every man
> Who guides its course?
> Who governs its destiny?
> Man can
> Man has
> Water power – the property of every man.[7]

This material, prepared exclusively for the Seattle production, illustrates a theme that was popular between the public utilities and which is still reflected in City Light publications. But the extent to which City Light was involved in the Seattle production of *Power* throws more interesting light on the relationship between the two institutions and the political agenda of Federal Theatre in producing *Power*.

City Light records of this period reveal some fascinating details. The Federal Theatre, for example, approached City Light with the idea of "sponsoring" them in the production. This was a fairly common practice.

Sponsors were local companies, organizations or individuals who were perceived as being sympathetic to an upcoming play and who might be counted on to help with publicity, technical advice or even nonlabor costs. In some cases sponsors simply permitted their name to be used. In other cases they contributed financially since the Federal Theatre was initially limited to 10 percent of the total labor costs in their production budget. Many of the agreements were not formalized, but in the case of *Power*, an assistant superintendent wrote to his boss following the initial meeting and described what had taken place:

> The performance to be given here will be adapted to the local scheme of things and they are working into the script the public ownership theme. They want our cooperation and sent five of their directors down here to see me today, bringing with them the entire manuscript. They would like to borrow some washing machines and some other electrical appliances to use for props, they want us to insert some advertising in with our bills and help them publicize the play. They would also appreciate assistance in the way of technical advice such as Roy Leonard could give... I have already given them copies of "The Romance of City Light" and am going to see Ed Kemoe to have the directors taken up to the Skagit so as to thoroughly imbue them with the ideals of City Light.[8]

City Light formed an advisory committee to work with the Federal Theatre, and on May 25 William McKeen reminded Superintendent Ross that "they are asking for whatever help we can give including technical advice, moral support and a City Light Night on June 22."[9] Apparently no money was involved, which is not surprising since the sponsorship of a public company often allowed the Federal Theatre to apply their box office receipts to such nonlabor expenses as sets and props.

City Light was enthusiastic in their support. They saw it as an opportunity to be bathed in the positive propaganda of the play ("I think this is a wonderful opportunity for us to dramatize and publicize our work")[10] as well as a marketing device to use against their competition:

> We are making every effort to put Power Week over as a big success. In order to create further interest we are putting on a $10.00 range wiring program and have invited the dealers to cooperate. I wish we could get everyone in the City to see the play called "Power" and immediately afterward take a trip to the Skagit. I believe our troubles would be pretty well over.[11]

The troubles, of course, refer to their competition from the private sector and their ongoing attempts to buy out Puget Power.

City Light also supported the upcoming production in a number of other ways. Interoffice memorandums reveal that they provided spotlights outside the theatre for the opening; that they granted a request from the Federal Theatre to place advertising placards on their ornamental light posts throughout the city; and that they allowed special invitations to be sent out which looked like their electric bills.[12] In fact, City Light had sold so many tickets for the production "in house" that when they received word that the opening – and thus Power Week – would be postponed owing to WPA cutbacks, they telegraphed Superintendent Ross, who was in Washington, DC, to see if he would intervene with Harry Hopkins on their behalf.[13]

This attempt to lobby the WPA on behalf of the Seattle production of *Power* provides a wonderful vantage point to view the Federal Theatre from a regional perspective and helps to contextualize one of the most controversial moments in the history of the project. For it was this very same postponement that has been widely reported as the excuse for "censoring" the Orson Welles–John Houseman production of *The Cradle Will Rock* which was about to open in New York City. Since the prohibition also "shut down" dozens of other production all across the country playing on "Federal Theatre stages," one must be judicious about accepting the romanticized accounts that have circulated in the wake of Welles's penchant for publicity and Houseman's recollections in *Run-Through* and other books. This is not to suggest that many people in Washington, DC – including WPA officials – were not relieved at the "postponement" of the highly pro-union *Cradle*, but rather to caution that *Cradle* was not the sole target of an action with nationwide consequences.

In her unpublished memoirs, "Fists Upon a Star," Florence James provides a wonderful inside view of the pressures involved with the production of *Power*. Her biggest difficulty was finding a cast. Since she drew upon the talents of the Negro unit as well as the vaudevillians to fill out the huge number of male roles demanded by the script, she was constantly inventing. The vaudevillians, many of them out-of-work old-timers with little understanding of modern theatre, were often perplexed by the demands of the play:

> One man came to me one day and asked what mug I wanted him to use. I did not know what he was talking about. He then explained that he had 46 mugs and wanted me to see them so I could tell him which one. I explained to him that he should memorize his lines and say them, and the mug he wore every day would be just fine.[14]

Still, casting the play proved to be fraught with all kinds of difficulties and Mrs. James records that she finally had to resort literally to pulling people off the street.

> One morning I came into the building housing the WPA project and saw a man mopping the floor. He was very personable looking. I asked him if he would like to be transferred to the theatre project. He looked startled. "Oh, mam, I can't act." I said, "we'll see." So I arranged his transfer. I did not know what he could do, but at that point I needed men. When I tried him out I discovered that he could not read, actually could not read... His lines had to be read to him, and he memorized them that way. He played the part of Wendell Wilkie, and looked every inch the man when he was costumed in an elegant cutaway.[15]

Rehearsals were chaotic. It took nearly a week to convince the cast members that the script was indeed a play. *Power* has over 200 speaking roles as well as slides, scenic projections and a complex musical score. Mrs. James records that the previous experience of the man who conducted the orchestra was playing "Pal O'Mine" for the rope artist in the vaudeville show. The slides which had been sent from New York cracked in the projector and had to be remade with glass frames. There were 162 light cues. Negro technicians and assistant stage managers were required to "give orders" to white personnel and after some initial tensions, "mixing the races" went well (although the action would come back to haunt her in the McCarthy days).[16] When the opening was postponed two weeks the company had additional time to integrate the production elements and rehearse the show. Even with this added time, however, the orchestra, which had been augmented by eleven musicians from the Federal Music Project, had only one complete runthrough with the cast prior to opening.

On July 6, the curtain finally went up on *Power* and it was a great success. With the mayor in attendance and the house packed with sympathetic fans, the appropriate villains were hissed and heroes cheered. One observer recalled that after about the third scene the audience caught the rhythm and the play never failed to get at least four curtain calls. Word of mouth was so positive that the play could have run a second week were it not for more WPA cutbacks. The reports back to New York were glowing, and Hallie Flanagan reports in *Arena* that it "struck Seattle right where it lived."[17]

The press was caught in a dilemma. Two of the three major dailies were Hearst papers and thus opposed to New Deal politics. But both were also supportive of Seattle's low electric rates and thus City Light policies.

Moreover, both papers were endorsing J.D. Ross of City Light for director of the emerging Bonneville Power Authority. They solved their dilemma by ignoring all of the hoopla surrounding Power Week and simply assigned their drama critics to review the play. The friendly paper, ironically, was hit by a labor strike a week before opening and did not publish during *Power*.

In spite of the ideological stance of the papers, the reviews were relatively favorable. Unlike some of the New York press which had praised the factual nature of the production, however, the Seattle critics commented on the blatant propagandizing of the event.

From the Seattle *Times*:

That Old Debbil, the Power Trust is the villain and the TVA is the hero in as fine a piece of overdone propaganda as ever trod the boards ... The play has the subtlety of a sledgehammer and the restraint of a groundswell.[18]

From the Seattle *Post-Intelligencer*:

Above all it is propaganda for public ownership. The private companies are assailed, satirized, ridiculed, exposed, attacked and condemned... The audience was large and friendly and every time the economic royalists were verbally hit on the head there was a howl of delight out front. Last evening was "City Light Night." No night for the Puget Sound Power and Light has been set as yet.[19]

But the critics were impressed by the technical apparatus of the production: the projected scenery, slides, music and loudspeaker. And they praised a number of the individual actors and Mrs. James's direction, thus reinforcing other perceptions that the play generated excitement for its audiences and excellent word-of-mouth publicity.

Flanagan characterized the newspaper coverage as an "attack" on the project, although she apparently had no difficulty with the support of City Light. She hoped that regional projects would ultimately be taken over and supported by their own communities and thus "sponsors" were constantly sought out to encourage local participation. Frequently the sponsors were volunteer workers, or important local dignitaries or civic organizations. And their contributions varied widely. In the case of *Power*, City Light's participation, however biased, was very likely viewed as similar to the way in which many organizations supported the Project all over the country.

City Light was also a public institution and that gave them a certain kinship in the great New Deal debate over national priorities. The notion of debate is central to understanding *Power* because the play was a response to the alarms raised in the private sector over the whole WPA agenda: that government meddling would lead to inefficiency, undermine the free enterprise system, and ultimately create a nationalized network of public utilities and industry. The Hearst newspapers, which attacked *Power* in Seattle, were very articulate in their opposition to the New Deal and often inflammatory in their reporting. One day after the play opened, for example, the savage murder of a young girl in Los Angeles was reported on the front page of the *Seattle Post-Intelligencer*. The killer was identified in a bold headline as the "WPA Crossing Guard Murderer." And another conservative paper editorialized in racist terms about WPA ranks being swollen with aliens who should either get real jobs or go home.[20] In this context it is not surprising that the Living Newspaper articulated their positions clearly and vehemently.

Meanwhile, the Puget Power Company – that hated private concern – reported annual earnings increases of 34 percent in the month that *Power* opened.[21] Much of that money was distributed to shareholders who held stock in the company, stock that thrived on consumer rates that were significantly higher than City Light. But merger talks persisted, and by December City Light's campaign to buy out Puget Power was receiving support in all the Seattle papers. Although the final agreements and last of the transfers did not take place for another fourteen years, it was clear that public opinion had swung to City Light by the end of 1937.

Whether the Federal Theatre had any influence on City Light's victory is difficult to assess but we can certainly document their participation in the events of July 1937. For Hallie Flanagan, as well as Florence James and others, democracy meant that you had the right to debate issues such as the most efficient way to distribute electricity. Their forum was a public theatre and an examination of *Power* in Seattle suggests that the Living Newspaper, in production, could be as "political" in that debate as the Hearst press and conservative politicians who opposed them.

The production opened some deep fissures on the project and in the community. Anti-New Dealers and Puget Power supporters cried "foul" and complained about government taxes supporting New Deal propaganda. State officials worried that the Florence James "gang" might take over the project and push it in a decidedly "red" direction. And within the theatre there was a renewed rivalry between races and generations; between the men and women who were producing successful variety entertainment and those younger folks who believed that the theatre was on the verge of a modern era. It was a division that appeared in all the units at some point, but it was particularly visible and acute in Seattle because the success of *Power* emboldened both sides.

Guy Williams, who had taken over as director of the Seattle unit after Glenn Hughes tired of the Project, had succeeded in moving the enormous amount of WPA paper and had enabled talented – and disparate – people such as Florence James, Harry Pfeil, Clarence Talbot and Joe Staton to flourish. But he did not have deep support as an artistic director, and the national office was anxious that there be someone in charge who could develop an aggressive social and artistic agenda. Williams was also perceived by many as one of Glenn Hughes's boys, and there were factions who wanted the theatre to establish its own clear presence separate from the university.

Following the success of *Power*, the lines were drawn. The youngsters wanted to capitalize on the impact of the production and the notoriety of the Negro unit and install Florence James as director. They also wanted to democratize the proceedings and have more autonomous control of the artistic agenda – free from Washington meddling. The more conservative elements, including the WPA state officials, wanted to name George Hood, the current state supervisor as director. While much of the correspondence from this period is "coded," it's clear that the battle was both generational and ideological.

Returning from the Federal Theatre Summer Camp – for which he had been selected by Howard Miller – Clarence Talbot assessed the current situation in a letter to Miller:

> Guy Wiliams is planning to leave the project. Already Fran Power (agent-cashier) is inquiring if we don't think Florence James would make a good director in Guy's place...Fran and Florence have recently aired their views on letting the State Director become only a figurehead and let the project be run by a "committee."...They both questioned your "right" to be able to send who you chose to the Summer Session. They felt that a company "voting" should have been entered into to determine who they *wanted* to represent them...Honest to God, Howard, something is wrong with the local picture and I feel for its longevity. The boat seems to be sinking although you can't find the hole to plug up.[22]

Williams was also busy in his last days on the job relocating the entire project to a new home south of the metropolitan area. He and his WPA colleagues had discovered an abandoned movie theatre which would allow them to consolidate all of the project functions under one roof and establish a presence that was distinct from the university or the Jameses' Playhouse. Although the space was cramped and not in a particularly desirable location, it seemed to many a good solution because the project would have, for the first time, a permanent home. In addition it would bring the "black" and "white" units together and allow then to pursue the kind of "integrated" productions such as *Power*.

Flanagan was not an enthusiastic supporter of George Hood because she considered him basically "old school," but she was also leery of alienating the whole WPA structure in Washington State by pushing too hard for more radical leadership. She recognized the talent and ambition of Florence James, Theodore Brown and others, but she also relied upon the input of Howard Miller who cautioned her about embracing too radical a change. "He (Hood) is typical of a great many people with us," she wrote. "He was once manager of the Chicago Opera for Mr. Insull at a salary of $15,000 a year, but those days are past. It is almost incomprehensible to conceive of him in this capacity. He is honest and hardworking, but he does not have a vigorous imagination or modern ideas."[23]

A compromise was struck. Flanagan agreed that Hood would be appointed *acting* director, and that she would continue to seek someone for the permanent post, perhaps from outside the region. She also moved to appoint one of her former students at Vassar, Esther Porter, as a stage director to assist on various projects and to work with the Negro unit. Hood, however, accepted the leadership challenge and, faced with a new home and a new job, he issued a stirring call to arms to his colleagues on the project:

> In the future let us realize our unity; our oneness... Out of the gratitude for the fruits we have already enjoyed, for our present and future opportunity; for the benefit of those to follow and the pride of accomplishment, we should endeavor to maintain Seattle as outstanding among Federal Theatre Projects. I am proud of the personnel on this project and know that I can rely on each and every one of you to do his bit for Federal Theatre. Thank you.[24]

In spite of the fact that *Power* had only played eight performances it had been a bombshell in Seattle. And in spite of the chaotic rehearsal schedule and frantic casting, it had participated in one of the great public debates in the history of the community. To Flanagan's delight and the chagrin of many WPA officials, it embodied the potential of a truly meaningful theatre. In its wake, however, factions from both the left and the right were energized and the subsequent struggle over who would control this theatre was joined. Hood called for unity and a fresh start, but he was trapped. The conservatives at the state WPA office were willing to support a caretaker, but the liberals and radicals on the project were not willing to go quietly. And in the great debate about public utilities the racial issues were wallpapered but not erased.

7

Dunbar *and the children*

The move to the Rainier Valley brought all of the units under one roof. The new Federal Theatre, however, was hardly ideal. Formerly a movie theatre, the backstage space was cramped and the proscenium small and unwieldy. In keeping with the economic cutbacks announced that summer, the project was reorganized so that all of the separate units would now share a rehearsal hall and auditorium. And while everybody tried to put a good face on it, it was clearly an inadequate venue for their accomplishments or ambitions. After visiting in November, Hallie Flanagan wrote to Ellen Woodward:

> Why should W.P.A. be spending $20,000 in labor to build a Show Boat Theatre for the University of Washington when our own company, after struggling valiantly for two years, has no money to lease a theatre? We have had to move into a little old movie house which needs everything done in the way of repainting and remodeling... You know how I believe in Bonneville Dam. But it struck me as pretty pathetic, thinking of a million dollars being spent there for salmon to run up and spawn, that here, in a shabby, bare old room, with a gigantic picture of President Roosevelt smiling down on them, were the actors we are trying to save. After two years of good work and good press, they still have no place to act – to say nothing of spawn.[1]

For the Negro company the future was uncertain. Although Florence James did stay on to direct the "white company" in an amusing production of *Help Yourself* by Paul Vulpius, her eventual resignation left the company without a director. Moreover, George Hood was not particularly sympathetic to the idea or the existence of a Negro theatre. It is intriguing – especially in light of later events – that no thought seemed to have been given to naming a director from their own group.[2] At any rate, Hallie Flanagan was clearly concerned about the future of the Seattle unit, especially the Negro theatre, and in the summer of 1937 she arranged for one of her brightest young protegees to go to Seattle.

Esther Porter arrived in August 1937 as "Hallie's golden-hair haired girl."[3] She had studied with Flanagan at Vassar, graduating in 1932, and then spent a year on a fellowship from Kappa Alpha Theta observing theatre in Europe and Russia. She then joined the New York City Living Newspaper as a stage manager. Later Flanagan transferred her to the National Play Policy Board as an assistant to Director Hiram Motherwell, and when the Seattle project appeared to be floundering, Flanagan assigned her to be Edwin O'Connor's assistant director with special attention to children's drama and the Negro Company.

Esther Porter was 27 and white. Although she had assisted Flanagan at Vassar and been a stage manager in New York, her actual directing experience was quite limited. Following her graduation from college, she had coordinated a summer creative dramatics program at Bryn Mawr and later at the Hudson Shore Labor School. The bulk of her hands-on experience, however, had been in the few weeks before arriving in Seattle when she worked as a stage director in summer stock at the Robin Hood Theatre in Arden, Delaware.

Edwin O'Connor needed an ally in mending some of the political wounds in the organization and in making the theatre viable in its new location. And while he hoped that they might regain some of the political "bite" that had characterized several earlier productions, for the time being he was content to try and build an audience base through comedy and children's theatre. Esther Porter was ideally suited to this agenda, and O'Connor put her to work devising a children's production based upon *Mother Goose* rhymes, utilizing solo acts from the variety troupe and several actors from the Negro Company. At the same time, O'Connor began readying a production of Bernard Shaw's *Androcles and the Lion* with the principal actors in the Negro unit.

The decision to concentrate on children's theatre came from a number of impulses. First, the unit had to take a substantial financial reduction following the WPA downsizing in July 1937, and Hood and O'Connor realized that since a bulk of the certifiable actors were still ex-vaudevillians, the logistics of keeping them on the road would be immense. It seemed to make more sense now that Federal Theatre was consolidated in one venue to reduce the number of specialty acts and feature them in productions for regular runs at the theatre. Children's plays seemed to be a natural for several of the performers. Second, there was an ongoing interest in theatre for children among several prominent people in the community, and Hood was eager to court them in order to gain patronage and support for Federal Theatre. Third, the local and state WPA seemed to be very receptive to notions of children's drama, and Don Abel had suggested to Flanagan that they might be very interested in building an outdoor theatre in one of Seattle's urban parks for such a venture. And finally, Hood, who was anxious to modify the stridency of the "James faction" and some past difficulties, saw in the theatre for children a much more marketable and non-controversial opportunity.

Consequently, following the WPA reductions, Hood set up an official Children's unit and assigned Harry Pfeil of the Variety Company to stage an adaptation of *The Clown Prince* (from *La Mascotte*, an Italian opera by Edmond Audran). Pfeil, who had a great deal of experience tailoring mate-rial for the Variety shows, condensed three acts into two, added characters to simplify the plot and rearranged a number of the songs. The result was a delightful mixture of color, music and comedy which charmed Seattle audiences and generated some excellent press notices and word-of-mouth publicity. In a laudatory piece in the *Seattle Post-Intelligencer* Anna Roosevelt Boettiger wrote:

> I am very enthusiastic about the Seattle Federal Theatre's new Children's Theatre. In many parts of this country children grow to maturity without having a chance to see "the living theatre." Here in Seattle not much is done in this respect for the average child... Almost every child loves to "act." They have a chance to do this in their homes through charades, and in their schools at times. But it seems too bad that so many of them have to grow up without ever developing a knowledge and appreciation of one of man's oldest forms of art – the theatre. It is, therefore, gratifying to know that our Federal Theatre is starting something of real worth for the children of Seattle. This last Saturday morning 220 children sat, jumped up and down, and laughed and clapped their way through "The Clown Prince." Seventy-seven adults attended with them.[4]

The program for *The Clown Prince* announced that this was the first pro-duction of a new Federal Theatre Children's Theatre which will "perform operettas, plays and comedies for children of all ages at nominal prices." The program also listed a number of important Seattle citizens who had agreed to be patrons for the venture, including Boettigger, Charlotte Heussy, pres-ident of the Junior League, Mrs. Eloise McKinnell, Federated Women's Clubs, Mrs. H.J. Parker, president, Seattle PTA and Lady Willie Forbus of the Bar Association. It is an impressive list, and the work of the Children's unit resulted in a number of successful productions and in establishing a tradition of Children's Theatre which still prospers in Seattle. In reality, however, there were two distinct companies – one black and one white – and beginning in 1937 and throughout the remainder of the project life, WPA Form 330, which requested financial appropriation, identified them as two separate units. By May 1939 they had mounted eight productions, two of them by the Negro Company.

Esther Porter was only in Seattle for a year, and her role as director of children's productions and "caretaker" for the Negro Company was difficult. She defended them to Hood whom she was convinced was prejudiced against the unit, and she tried to select material such as *Black Empire* which would give them opportunities to play something other than "white" roles. But she was obviously out of her depth trying to follow an experienced director such as Florence James and trying to deal with a talented and now experienced company of actors and singers. Evamarii Johnson would later observe that, "Porter, although sympathetic to the group and its individuals, spoke and wrote of her work with the unit in a manner suggestive of a child who had been given a set of walking, talking black dolls to play with."[5] While Johnson's criticism of her may be unduly harsh, it's clear that Porter – in spite of her liberal credentials – was hampered by her own racial insensitivity. *Brer Rabbit* is a case in point.

Based upon a dramatization of the *Uncle Remus* stories by Ruth Mitchell and Alfred Allen, *Brer Rabbit and the Tar Baby* was adapted by Porter for a children's production for the Negro Company in spring 1938. Replete with conventional cliches about the "old South" and "the nursery up at the big house," *Brer Rabbit* was a problematic choice, but Porter and O'Connor thought that it would provide an excellent vehicle for the singing and dancing talents of the company. She compressed a number of the scenes by creating a Negro "mammy" character who sat in a rocking chair by the stage and gathered up children "characters" from the audience to take on a journey to Brer Rabbit's world. The scenery and clothes were colorful, and each episode in the production was built around improvised game playing by the acting company and original music from their young composer, Howard Biggs. Early in the rehearsals, however, Porter seems to have sensed the reluctance of some members of the company to play in this world. Whether she believed that "children's theatre" made the rules different or whether she was truly insensitive to the fact that this was the company that had *inhabited* their *Stevedore* production or been closed down after one night

7 The Federal Theatre Children's unit performing *Brer Rabbit and the Tar Baby*,
featuring Sara Oliver without her red bandanna.

of their remarkable *Lysistrata*, she forged ahead. In the end it was left to
Sara Oliver, the granddaughter of a slave, to resist when she discovered
that "Mammy" was to wear a red kerchief. "I'll do anything but I won't
put a red kerchief on my head."[6] Others chose high jinks and clowning
to mollify their resentment toward this idyllic world. Since a great deal of
the production was based upon game playing and improvisation, there was
ample time for the "cutups" to engage in byplay and sight gags which were
inappropriate. Finally Porter had to put her foot down and try to curb the
obstreperous cast. "You don't goose each other. Anything you want, but in
front of the children you don't goose each other."[7]

　　Ironically, *Brer Rabbit* was quite successful when it finally opened (May 7,
1938) and, while the records are sparse, it seems to have attracted audiences to
the out-of-the-way theatre and was reviewed favorably by two local papers.
More interesting, however, is the fact that Porter's patience and willingness
to allow the company to improvise and explore the text resulted in some
very fine theatre. "The scene of the rabbit children sneaking out of the let-
tuce head house with their mother asleep, so help me God, I timed them.

They could hold an audience spellbound watching their tricks for seven cold minutes."[8] It was this ability to invent, to create improvisationally, that led to excess and indulgence but also to some genuinely excellent work. O'Connor had curbed them in their November production of *Androcles and the Lion*, insisting that they learn the words exactly and play the text as written, but in *Black Empire* Porter had encouraged them to read widely, do individual research and prepare themselves for entering the world of the play. This was a way of working that they understood from the Jameses and which they carried forward into the development and creation of *Brer Rabbit*. It is significant that when Porter left them that spring, and they were once more adrift, they turned to their own strengths and skills to create one of their most moving pieces – *An Evening With Dunbar*. Flanagan had sent Esther Porter to Seattle to shore up what she perceived as a valuable but struggling unit and to inject some young and imaginative ideas into an organization that she saw becoming stodgy and conservative. She believed that Porter and O'Connor might be able to neutralize the old-fashioned George Hood and the unsympathetic WPA establishment. In spite of her misgivings about the location of the theatre,[9] Porter worked very hard and tried to fulfill Flanagan's goals. She directed the ex-vaudevillians in a children's production of *Mother Goose* (December 1937) and a combined group production of a rambling Living Newspaper called *Flight (*March 1938*)*. She did three productions with the Negro Company and made herself available to direct skits and entertainments for the National Organization of Social Workers and the Junior League. But she also chafed at what she saw as the conservatism on the project: the reluctance to engage new ideas and production styles. And she was not reluctant to express her point of view or voice her complaints. It was only a matter of time before she was perceived as anti-WPA and thus a threat to those people such as George Hood who wanted the project to mind its manners and stay in its place.[10]

In spite of his "Call To Arms," Hood had not prospered as the Head of the Federal Theatre in Washington State. He had been scolded by the Washington, DC office for irregularities in his budget requests and by the regional director of the FTP, Ole Ness, for inserting himself into the correspondence with Bernard Shaw over rights to *Androcles*. He had angered Fran Power by insisting that he (Hood) be present when receipts were counted, and both O'Connor and Porter believed that there were serious problems with the timekeeping on the project, perhaps even usury. And, as happened on many of the projects, he sided with the local WPA politicians against the Federal Theatre in most matters of substance. But it was his attitude toward the Negro Company which eventually forced an open confrontation with Porter and led to both their resignations.

While the record is not entirely clear, it seems certain that at some point in the winter of 1938 Porter asked Hood why he was not in sympathy with the Negro unit, and he responded that this reflected state WPA policy. She replied that if this was true "and could be proved she would see that Mr. Abel was removed as State Administrator."[11] Hood immediately reported this to Abel who had a long history of controversy with the theatre dating back to the *Lysistrata* closing and who was not about to be threatened by "their Miss Porter." Abel called for the resignations of O'Connor, Power and Porter for repeatedly trying to undermine George Hood. Flanagan, of course, balked because she had never had confidence in Hood and believed that if he were allowed to appoint his own people, the project would cease to function in any meaningful way. Ole Ness went to Seattle and met with the WPA officials, including Abel, to see if they could find a compromise position.

Ness told them that if O'Connor was forced out that they might not like the replacement; indeed it might be Florence James or someone from her "camp." Thereupon, Ness, admitting that Miss Porter had exercised "very poor judgement," suggested that *both* Hood and Porter go (along with Fran Power) and that the project be turned over entirely to Edwin O'Connor. What he did not reveal was that Porter was already scheduled to leave in June so that she could return to Vassar and run Flanagan's Experimental Theatre. After much bickering the deal was struck and Porter's tenure as caretaker for the Negro unit was terminated. It was a shrewd move by Ness and a victory for Federal Theatre, but once more the Negro Company – the most successful of any of the Seattle units – was abandoned. This time, however, being left on their own proved to be exhilarating.

That summer of 1938 the twenty-three surviving members of Seattle's Negro Company began planning a new production. Although they had cursory supervision from Edwin O'Connor, they were now creating their own work and making their own artistic decisions. They chose for this pioneering venture the life and poetry of Paul Laurence Dunbar, widely acclaimed as America's first African-American poet and a figure whose work was familiar to much of the company. It was an apt choice. Dunbar had grown up in the north (Dayton, Ohio) and had experienced much of the poverty and racism that characterized the lives of many members of the company. He was educated through high school in white classrooms and had earned his way through manual labor and operating elevators. But his passion for writing had eventually pulled him out of poverty and launched a career which made him famous. Championed at first by progressive whites and eventually respected critics such as William Dean Howells, Dunbar became a literary sensation in the last decade of the twentieth century and enjoyed the company of "polite society" up to and including President Teddy Roosevelt. In addition to thousands of lines of poetry, he wrote short stories and four novels as well as the book for the Bert Williams and George Walker musical *In Dahomey* (1902). He was also an accomplished platform speaker and performer, and before his premature death from tuberculosis in 1906, he appeared in various venues reciting his own work.

Like many black artists who had succeeded in America, Dunbar had a large white following. And in spite of the vast panorama of his work, he was most widely sought out and praised for his "plantation" poetry, verses which rendered the Negro voice into the "darkey" dialect associated with minstrel shows and caricatures of fawning ignorance. Even though such work had been initially praised for its true rendering of dialect and cadence, the early years of the twentieth century had not been kind to Dunbar's reputation. In a climate fueled by the emerging NAACP, the writings of W.E.B. Du Bois and the "New Negro" of the Harlem Renaissance, lyrical treatments of life on the plantation were no longer welcomed. Dunbar's reputation had skidded, his marital difficulties and alcoholic addiction discussed openly and his "whiteness" derided.

Still the very bulk of his work and its familiarity in working-class black communities kept his language alive, especially in the poverty and despair of depression America. People sang his songs at church ("I Come to the Garden Alone") and as they toiled, building roads and bridges. His wonderful narrative tales about romance and heartbreak, loss and the death of children struck a chord in much of black America even after the "deconstruction" of his reputation and accomplishments in the 1920s. He became a lonely and tragic figure, wasting away from illness and cognizant of the burden of those crinkly poems which he called "broken jingle" verses.

To make a play about Dunbar, the Negro Company first considered telling his story as a narrative tale, but as they read the material and experimented with staging ideas, it became clear that the limited space of their theatre precluded multiple settings or complex narratives. Led by Joseph Staton and Robert St. Clair, a former chorus member who had developed a fondness for writing and acting, they became intrigued by the idea of creating original music for a number of the poems and then fashioning a framework to hold them together. As they worked through the late summer and early fall, a shape began to emerge. Poems would be loosely grouped under three main categories: Church, Work and Play. Dunbar would be a character in the play observing and commenting but not participating in the action.

The job of writing and then orchestrating the music fell largely to Howard Biggs, the enormously gifted youngster who had joined the company shortly after its inception and who had directed their choirs, written original songs and generally contributed to their reputation as one of the Federal Theatre's stronger units. Like so many members of this company, little is known about Biggs after the demise of Federal Theatre. Evamarii Johnson, quoting Staton and others, says that he went to New York where he played with Nobel Sissle.[12] But that is probably a modest assessment. It's quite probable that he eventually formed his own orchestra and choir, featuring vocals by Johnny Hartman, for which there are several references in New York in 1952. In addition, "Howard Biggs" arranged music for the Silhouettes and the Penguins and in 1957 – with Richard Lewis – created one of the most successful "doo-wop" songs of the era – "Get a Job".[13] Staton and St. Clair are also credited with composing words and music for some of the songs in *Dunbar*, and Staton and other members of the company contributed to the dialogue which fleshed out some of the Dunbar poems and provided segues between the scenes.

By mid-September they had completed a draft and submitted it to the National Play Bureau for approval. Scene one featured a young Dunbar – played by Staton – reading his famous *Life* and then watching from his chair (stage left) while the company performed *The Rivals* and *Deacon Jones' Grievance*, both of which were set in or around a church. The company also sang *a capella* several of Dunbar's religious songs including "For My Lord" and "Two Wings." Scene two finds a considerably weakened Dunbar, now suffering from tuberculosis, reciting his poem, "Dawn" and watching the dramatization of two work songs, "Heavy Ol' Hammer" and "Bucket Boy." Although suggested by some of Dunbar's observations about Negro life, both these numbers were written and composed by Staton and St. Clair, and both proved very effective in performance. Staton remembered particularly the staging of "Bucket Boy":

I took one of his poems called *The Letter*. It was a letter that a little fellow wrote to his mother. We were on the chain gang, you see, and we had fluorescent paint on the hammers. And all the lights were off and you could see us hammering in unison, you know, and singing in unison. And the lights came on and we had a song that I put together called *Bucket*

Boy, something like *Water Boy*, you know, a little different. Then we read this letter that this fellow had written his parents and we tease the heck out of him about it and have a lot of fun. And somebody says, "The boss is comin'," so then we had to go back to work you know. And by that time the lights are getting dimmer and dimmer and dimmer and we go back to hammering and singing. And it turned out very nicely, very nicely. We did wonderful here.[14]

The final scene opens with a weak and very feeble Dunbar reading 'The Sum,' a brief four-stanza work which reflects on life and concludes: "Just dreaming, loving, dying so, The actors in the drama go – A fitting picture on the wall, Love, Death, the themes; but is that all?" There then follows an extended dramatization of his famous poem, *The Party*, which is a 200-line invocation of an exuberant and delightful get-together featuring colorful characters, a variety of fiddling and dancing and general high shenanigans. William Dean Howells had praised *The Party* in euphoric terms in *Harper's* and thought it one of the poet's finest works. The party atmosphere also allowed the participants to feature a number of Dunbar's other poems such as "Angeline" before time was returned to the "present" and his impending death. A single soprano voice began his "Good-Night" and was then joined by choral humming as the lights darkened and the curtain closed.

The Play Bureau approved *Dunbar* for production, and Staton and his company began the difficult task of converting their script into a musical/theatre piece. Part of the problem was the venue. Since their move to the Rainier Valley, attendance had been disappointing. Edwin O'Connor, who was now acting state director after Hood had been eased out, was concerned about their small houses, but he was also concerned about the rental costs if he should try to reserve the Metropolitan or one of the big downtown theatres. *Dunbar* was scheduled for their Federal Theatre and being rehearsed for their stage, but as O'Connor watched it come together he began to think that it might be powerful enough to attract audiences at a larger venue.

The advance sales were promising, and in early October O'Connor scheduled *Dunbar* for the Metropolitan to open on October 31 and run for a week. He knew that it was a gamble and he wrote to Howard Miller that, "Of course the rent is high. Not high for private enterprise but high for Federal Theatre in Seattle, but I simply had to do something. We tried all the tricks we knew to get them to come to our present location but to no avail...Naturally I expect big things from *Dunbar* or I would have remained in the Federal Theatre."[15]

For Staton and the Negro Company the change meant revising the ground plan and set pieces while they were still in the midst of rewriting and casting the show. The *esprit de corps* was high and enthusiasm about the production infectious. Casting was more difficult than on previous occasions because they were not constrained by the stereotypical roles of some of the "white" dramas. And in scenes such as "The Party" there was room for improvisation and richly textured characterizations. "Visualizing his (Dunbar's) characters and picking artists from our group to imitate them was a job," wrote Staton, "because, being of the same race as Dunbar, our people could do parts equally well."[16]

They were particularly concerned about making the transitions smooth and moving from one moment to the next as seamlessly as possible. With the cooperation of the NYA (National Youth Administration) members of the cast, they were able to work overtime and create a shift plan incorporating the dancers and singers.[17] Staton made the final casting decisions himself, and the company continued to revise and polish the script and score. They sought out "old-timers" in the community and questioned them about church behavior in the *ante bellum* South as well as dance steps and manners. Staton found a former chain gang member who talked to them about call and response singing. In late October they completed a third major revision based upon actors' suggestions and improvisations, and Howard Biggs wrote additional music to cover some of the more complicated transition moments. *"An Evening With Dunbar* is really beautiful," O'Connor wrote to Howard Miller.[18] What's more, it had the largest advance sale of any production since they had moved into their consolidated home.

They opened on October 31, 1938, to lavish critical praise. Reviewers commented on the rich ensemble playing as well as individual performers. Sirless Grove, Doris Booker, Sara Oliver and Staton all came in for special praise. But it was Biggs who received the most attention, not only for the orchestrations but for his superb direction of the choir. "Thunderous was the applause that greeted Howard Biggs who wrote the music and conducted the thirty-piece band during the play. His conducting of the chorus also was a thing of beauty to watch as he masterfully got just the tone and volume desired from them by a delicate gesture of his hand."[19] Biggs was finally recognized for the impressive work that he had been doing on the Project. "The work of the group is a tribute to the young maestro, for with just ordinary voices to work with, he has built, in our opinion, a smoother group of singers than some of the big name choruses that are famous all over the country."[20] Reviews also commented on the spirited staging, the wonderful

8 The finale from *An Evening With Dunbar*.

party scene complete with dazzling costumes and Staton's direction. The latter was also singled out in the *Seattle Star* for his "Heavy Ol' Hammer," "a masterpiece both musically and dramatically."[21]

Unfortunately, every reviewer undercut the production by linking its success to the Negro stereotypes which had haunted the company from the outset. And even at the height of what should have been their greatest triumph, they were marginalized and trivialized by the expectations of their racial heritage. There are numerous examples. "The show throughout is melodious, presented chiefly in the mixed chorus manner of singing for which the Negro is so famous."[22] Or: "the company offers cheering compositions and singing that are more than a credit to Seattle talent – done as only the Negro can do them."[23] Or: "And while they call it a folk opera, they don't just sing Negro spirituals, as well as their race always does that."[24] And:

> of humor there is aplenty in an entirely unprecedented party scene, in the unaffectedly joyous antics of several budding character artists and other bits that ring true to a typical funsome Negro – because the entire offering is arranged, acted, sung and played by negroes, giving vent to their natural flair for "play actin'" and to their natural love for idolization.[25]

Moreover, there was the issue of the credits. In the program Staton was acknowledged as the director of the production "under the supervision of Edwin G. O'Connor." But in the official production report filed with the national office Staton was credited as "assistant director." As Evamarii Johnson points out, this may have just been an administrative formality, but there is no question that O'Connor and others appropriated the successes of the Negro unit when it served their purposes. In a letter to Howard Miller prior to the opening of *Dunbar* O'Connor wrote, "I have worked hard to keep it natural, simple and completely devoid of staginess and feel that I have succeeded. The sets are my own and I will be anxious to learn what you think of them when you get the photographs."[26] In the program for *Dunbar* – and in the reviews – sets and costumes are credited to Blanche Morgan.

This is not to suggest that O'Connor was duplicitous. As director of the project he exercised considerable influence over all spheres of production. And since the venue had changed after rehearsals had begun, it is quite likely that he played some part in reconfiguring the production for the Metropolitan stage. He certainly seems to have supported the Negro Company and their personnel in all the records that have survived. Still it is dispiriting to see the ways in which their accomplishments were demeaned, undervalued or appropriated at the very moment that they had created an original work, a work rooted in three years of ensemble playing and the individual talents of this very unique group. As long as they were the Negro stereotypes happily playing out the natural abilities of their race, however, it seemed difficult to recognize them for what they had become: a truly talented company enacting Hallie Flanagan's original fantasy of what Federal Theatre might be.

8

Slums and syphilis

There is no doubt that the Seattle project, like many others, did some bad work. How could it be otherwise? Earnest amateurs and a smattering of professional artists, working against production deadlines on limited budgets, insured that the results were often mediocre. Warmed-over Broadway successes and tepid new plays dotted the national landscape of Federal Theatre. Howard Miller seems almost in despair reporting on a new play in Tacoma in 1936. "I think we should close it immediately."[1]

But there were also moments of compelling theatricality, of creative and imaginative leaps that justified the dollars spent and workforce created. And though these moments too were difficult to sustain over an entire evening, they occurred frequently in productions of the Living Newspapers. Like *Altars of Steel* in Atlanta or *Spirochete* in Chicago, the Living Newspapers attracted large audiences who applauded and quarreled over this unique theatrical form and like their cohorts elsewhere, the directors in Seattle wrestled with the task of adapting these sprawling New York-driven documents to the concerns of the local community.

Scheduling them, however, was not automatic because Flanagan and her staff of regional supervisors were concerned about the quality of the work, and from the outset they played a strong part in influencing season choices. Censorship, of course, had been an ongoing concern on the project ever since the cancellation of *Ethiopia* in 1935, and Flanagan had been accused by Joseph Losey and members of her own staff of a heavy hand in supervising several productions. However, Flanagan seemed most concerned, not about the occasional "red" messages but about the quality of the productions: the writing, acting, staging and design. She was committed to a professional theatre, not an amateur one, and even when the discrepancies became enormous – or when Glenn Hughes cautioned her about such a naive view – she exercised her influence to insure that local units not attempt what they seemed unable to achieve.

Before Guy Williams had resigned in July 1937, he had been negotiating the upcoming season with Howard Miller and a variety of other folks on his Seattle team. At the urging of the Jameses and others, he wanted to do *The Emperor Jones* utilizing the talents of Joe Staton, the antiwar sensation from the Group Theatre, *Johnny Johnson*, and *One-Third of a Nation*, the controversial new Living Newspaper on slums and poverty. Miller demurred, partly because he believed that the move to a new location in the "out of the way Rainier valley" might dictate more "popular" choices, and partly because Miller was not at all sure who would still be on board once the administrative changes were resolved. He suggested that the season might be stronger with a different O'Neill play, the comedy *Help Yourself* and Barrie Stavis's *The Sun and I*.[2]

Selecting plays was one of the most difficult and controversial tasks for all the regional units because they had so many masters to serve. And while Flanagan was very clear that part of their mission was to do plays about contemporary social issues, she and they were acutely aware of the need to have popular successes. Box office monies, after all, were one of the few ways that the theatres could improve their other than labor expenses. It was a battle that Flanagan and her aides confronted daily. In Seattle it was particularly difficult because even some of the theatre's most enthusiastic supporters were wary of its "political" agenda. After lunching with Anna Roosevelt Boettiger in November 1937, Flanagan confided to Helen Woodward:

> The general tenor of her remarks was that our theatre should never do anything controversial. She said this was because of the fact that 'Seattle was completely uninterested in such plays.' She said that *Stevedore* and *Power* were the wrong sort of things and urged light comedy.[3]

When Flanagan pointed out that these had been two of their biggest successes, Mrs Boettiger inquired about plans for a more active children's program.

O'Connor, however, was genuinely concerned about attracting audiences to the "distant" Federal Theatre, and in March 1938 he persuaded his supervisors to let him substitute *One-Third of a Nation* for the previously announced *Emperor Jones*. Although the stage requirements and cast needs would fully test their small auditorium, O'Connor was hoping that the celebrated and hugely successful Living Newspaper about urban slums would find an audience in Seattle just as *Power* had done a year before. *Power* had worked because its message was uniquely suited to the public utilities debate in the Northwest. And its provocative *mise en scène* captured the interests of local audiences. Similarly, the Seattle City Council was engaged in a campaign in 1938 to create a Housing Authority that would allow them to claim government funds under the National Housing Act to eradicate slums and build affordable public housing. It seemed an ideal moment and an ideal climate for a play that confronted the deplorable housing conditions in many American cities. But as they would shortly discover, Seattleites were not nearly as ready to own up to wealthy slum landlords as they were to engage in a debate over lower electricity rates.

One-Third of a Nation had been initially developed in a summer workshop at Vassar College and then fleshed out by Arthur Arent and his writing team for a New York production at the Adelphi Theatre. Featuring a towering slum tenement by the designer Howard Bay that ignited into an inferno in the first scene, the play had become a successful Broadway hit attracting large audiences and a mostly satisfied press. While there were those who carped about its simplistic notions and administration propaganda, it was widely hailed as a forceful critique of slum landlords, poverty, crime, disease and – in some quarters – private property.

Like many of the Living Newspapers, it had a wide chronological sweep moving back in time to illustrate how Manhattan real estate had been appropriated by churches and wealthy landowners. The play traced the northward movement of the working population as they were continually forced into substandard housing, rarely repaired, in spite of high rent and deteriorating conditions. Breeding disease and crime, the slums continued to prosper because there was a demand for living space even when that space was vile. Windowless rooms, acrid air shafts, rotting wooden structures all combined to create combustible buildings which could burn in a matter of minutes.

Reform, investigative committees, and crusading congressmen were only fitfully successful in fighting the slums because powerful interests were able to exempt existing structures from each successive attempt to regulate slum housing. Landlords profited by never selling and never repairing because somebody always needed a place to live. It was New Deal legislation that promised help, and low-interest federal funds which would aid urban America in fighting expanding slums and "Hoovervilles."

And Seattle had its share. Much of the residential housing had been built prior to the First World War, and the depression had led to hundreds of homemade shacks and overcrowded tenements. Seattle historian Richard Berner notes that "not a single permit had been issued for 1933 and 1934 for apartment house construction; only one in 1935, two more in 1936, and one in 1937."[4] Slums were not just confined to the inner city and poverty-level neighborhoods; they had crept out onto the muddy tide flats of the rivers that emptied into Elliott Bay. To address the problems the Seattle City Council had established an Advisory Housing Commission which would allow them to apply for long-term, low-interest loans to construct affordable housing. But the United States Housing Authority pointed out that the state of Washington lacked enabling legislation to set up such Commissions, and they would have to wait until legislation was passed before any loans could be granted. Since the legislature was not scheduled to meet until January 1939, and since there was much public debate about the advisability of such federal debt, the time seemed ripe to O'Connor and others to produce Arthur Arent's provocative living newspaper.

Esther Porter assisted O'Connor on *One-Third of a Nation* while she was rehearsing the Negro Company in *Brer Rabbit*. From the outset she envisioned a hard-hitting adaptation of the original script to focus on problems in Seattle. She and O'Connor discussed ways in which they could point the production toward the local scene. They wanted to find the equivalents of the New York slums in Seattle and localize the action. They planned to shoot photographs of the worst areas and then include them in the production. And they began adapting the script by creating a new character called "Seattle Cousin" who would comment on local conditions.

There were problems, however, in exposing the underskirts of Seattle's slum housing and landlords. Access to documents was difficult and the paper trail frequently frustrating. Working against production deadlines was difficult enough but here – unlike in *Power* – there was no convenient City Light ready to step in and smooth the way or distribute useful propaganda. Landlords and landowners were sometimes not the same people, and some of the most disreputable sites were tracked back to prominent Seattle citizens or churches. Porter, who was also functioning as technical director, soon realized that their ambitious plans could not accommodate the need to rehearse the sprawling text and open on time. It is difficult to tell when the focus began to shift, but once the slides from the New York production arrived, they were so clearly related to the script that O'Connor opted to put most of the Seattle photos into a lobby display. Six photos were blown up for the display and the remaining slides were projected in a converted coat room. "We transformed one of the cloakrooms in the lobby into a small projection booth. Here, before and after the show and during intermission, were more slides of housing conditions in Seattle passing across a small screen."[5]

(So much for Flanagan's "dangerous" theatre.) There were half a dozen places where the Loudspeaker interpellated statistics about Seattle housing, but as the production unfolded it focused principally on New York, retaining even the Harlem setting for the "hot bed" scene. Esther Porter later hinted darkly that there were forces at work which opposed too graphic an exposé of Seattle slum lords, but neither she nor O'Connor ever specified such charges. There was probably some concern on Hood's part about offending anyone while trying to build an audience in their new location. It is likely that given the production pressures and deadlines, there simply was not time to do the kind of investigative reporting that they had initially envisioned.

O'Connor was playing a major part (Little Man) as well as directing. Porter was doing the lighting and helping to oversee a massive publicity campaign that had almost no budget. In fact, outside salaries which were paid by the WPA, *One-Third of a Nation* had very little money for production. The converted movie house was highly unsuited to the flow of the text, and O'Connor was forced to play scenes on "side stages" built along the auditorium walls and eliminate numerous characters from the cast list. Still, he had more than forty performers to shepherd through the cramped setting.

The production opened on May 23, 1938, for a gala invitational audience which included the mayor, the Boettigers and the entire state housing commission. Ole Ness, who had replaced Howard Miller as Flanagan's West Coast regional director, was in attendance and reported that the production was very "interesting" and got off to an excellent start. "I noted a marked improvement in the staging and in the acting personnel."[6] The next night, however, the audience was considerably diminished, and in spite of some excellent press notices, O'Connor worried that their location would hurt them. He appealed to Hood for help, especially for paid newspaper advertisements, but there were no funds available. O'Connor had hoped to run the show for at least a month, however, so he and Porter undertook a campaign to spread the news and good reviews about the production. Twenty-seven organizations ranging from the United Federal Workers to the Sociology Department at the University of Washington were contacted to sell blocks of tickets. Signs were placed in the back windows of taxi cabs, and actors donated their time to read scenes over the radio. Teachers, social workers, doctors and lawyers were contacted by direct mail and O'Connor, Porter, Ormsby and others gave over a hundred talks at various meetings and organizations. In *Arena* Flanagan recalled that, "the press was guarded but the public turned out."[7] This is not entirely accurate. Some of the press was quite laudatory and as the production found its legs, much of the work was highly praised. But getting an audience was a constant struggle, and eventually the battle over attendance would force George Hood to resign as state administrator.

O'Connor was not happy with Hood's supervision. He believed that Hood just wanted to keep peace with the local WPA and would not do anything to promote Federal Theatre. Both he and Porter felt that their location was detrimental to their mission and Flanagan agreed. O'Connor complained to Ole Ness that there had been discussion about a possible new venue, but Hood turned it down because of its proximity and competition for local movie theatre owners.[8] When Hood seemed unable to help with the advertising for *One-Third of a Nation*, O'Connor appealed to Washington.

Ness had been lobbying Washington for some time to replace Hood, but he realized that as long as Hood had the support of Don Abel and the state WPA it would be a difficult task. Early in June 1938 Ness had written to Flanagan outlining the situation:

> Mr. Abel frankly feels that Mr. Hood is a competent man; that he has not been given a square deal by us; and holds firmly to the belief that Mr. Hood could do a good job if not hampered by outside interference. He refers, of course, to Mr. O'Connor and Miss Porter. While admitting Mr. Hood is an old "fogey," his work as liason (*sic*) officer between Federal Theatre and WPA (it is my impression that this 'work' was confined to the carrying of tales) is, in the opinion of Mr. Abel, of such value as to justify retention as State Director... Our main problem is to convince Mr. Abel that Mr. Hood is inefficient and that he has never come forward with one original idea for the promotion of the project.[9]

Apparently *One-Third of a Nation* gave them the opportunity. By the end of June 1938 they had played twenty-nine performances and taken in $672.90 or a little over $20 per show.[10] While Ole Ness admits that these figures are "decidedly low," he does point out that the production is now in its fifth week and attracting larger audiences. And he acknowledges that while the Seattle project has had difficulties with promotion and funding, he expects that things will improve. "You are probably aware of the fact that we have held Mr. George Hood, Acting State Director, *resigned as of June 30*, responsible for failure to properly acquaint Seattle with the value of the project."[11]

Given the politics of the Federal Theatre and the WPA – especially in Seattle where the Negro *Lysistrata* had been abandoned to Don Abel's

censorship – it seems odd that Hood was forced out over attendance problems. It is much more likely that there were other issues at play and that
One-Third of a Nation was the final straw. The record is incomplete, but
there are some tantalizing traces that suggest a narrative and help to explain
Hood's apparently sudden departure.

As part of his weekly report on the western region, Ole Ness wrote
to Flanagan in April 1938, "I am in receipt of a letter from Mr. Edwin
O'Connor, written with the knowledge of Miss Esther Porter, in which
he explains in detail the manner in which usury has been practiced on the
project. If his statements can be substantiated, the conditions are alarming
and must be investigated."[12] While that letter seems not to have survived,
and the details of an investigation are scant in the written record, it does
appear that an inquiry was undertaken. There are a number of vague and/or
veiled references to the charges in letters and reports and even one account
that "Mr. O'Connor is greatly concerned over an anonymous telephone
conversation concerning the direct operation of the Federal Projects by the
local WPA administration."[13] In May 1938, Ness met with WPA officials in
Seattle (Abel was out of town) and informed Flanagan that, "Both Mr. Kelso
and Mr. Erenburg were familiar with the charges alleging the practice of
usury, the sale of lottery tickets and irregularities in timekeeping procedure.
Nevertheless, save for a contemplated change of timekeepers, no steps have
been taken towards an investigation."[14] It is impossible to substantiate any
of these charges, but it is very likely that Hood was growing vulnerable
with the WPA because of his lack of oversight on the Project. As early as
December 1937, he had been scolded for not operating within the accepted
"man–month" cost formula and for not following the percentage guidelines
for his "other than labor" requests.[15] And when it was sorted out why there
were no advertising funds available for *One-Third of a Nation*, Hood was
expendable. Here is how Ness reported it to Howard Miller:

> The shortage of agent-cashier funds was due to a lack of coordination be-
> tween the State Finance office and our State Director and Agent-Cashier.
> As I understand the situation, several encumbrances for advertising were
> paid out of appropriated funds over a year ago. The error has been re-
> cently discovered and some $200 lifted from the A-C funds by the State
> Finance office in order to reimburse our appropriated account.[16]

It's difficult to believe that the agent-cashier, Fran Power, would not have
been aware of such "irregularities," since he was closely involved with the
operation of the theatre; a strong ally of O'Connor and about to wed Esther

9 This production shot from *Flight* (1938) shows the interior of the Federal Theatre, Seattle where Edwin O'Connor struggled to produce large productions such as *One-Third of a Nation* and *See How They Run*.

Porter. However, the WPA did respect the bottom line on their balance sheets, and Hood's supervision was suspect in this regard. Ultimately it was the wedge that allowed the Federal Theatre to replace him with Edwin O'Connor, who would guide the project till its demise a year later.

One-Third of a Nation played until July and became the longest-running production in the history of the theatre. And in spite of its frequently blatant propaganda on behalf of government subsidy, it was a remarkable achievement. Squeezed into a small venue, built on a budget of $242.75 and promoted by ingenuity and word of mouth, it, nevertheless, found an audience and struck a chord among those lobbying for housing reform in Seattle. Enabling legislation was easily passed by the state legislature in 1939, and the Seattle Housing Authority became one of the most active in the country creating, according to Richard Berner, an aggressive slum clearance program which resulted in the nation's first racially integrated public housing project.[17] Even Ole Ness, who was concerned about the physical demands of the script and O'Connor's ability to tell the story, was struck by much of the playing. "Mr. O'Connor has succeeded in taking the old vaudevillians, some burlesque and honky-tonk performers recently added to the project, the timekeeper and the janitors and whipping them into a production which would have done credit to any small project in the country."[18] A year later, O'Connor returned to the Living Newspaper format and armed with what he had learned from One-Third of a Nation, produced a spectacular version of Spirochete.

Spirochete

Spirochete originally was staged by the Chicago unit of the WPA theatre in April 1938 during a nationwide 'war' on syphilis that had been announced in December 1936 by Thomas Parron, the surgeon general of the United States.[19] The campaign included a national conference on venereal disease, newspaper and magazine articles, state laws requiring premarital blood tests, and a huge increase in the number of health clinics and treated cases of syphilis. In Chicago, the blood-test campaign, which had been initiated in 1937, was conducted in the lobby of the Blackstone Theatre where Spirochete was being performed. The campaign also included parades, radio programs, and an official "unlucky day for syphilis" on August 13 (a Friday). Later, officials estimated that, between 1937 and 1940, 31 percent of the population in Chicago was tested, resulting in the discovery and treatment of 56,000 cases of syphilis, all at public expense.[20]

The reason for this war was the epic proportions that syphilis had reached by the 1930s, thanks in part to public ignorance. Like AIDS, syphilis was a major killer aided in its lethal contagion by sexual taboos, notions of what constituted decorum, and a widespread view that the disease was ghettoized among perverts and Negroes. So fearful was the general population about syphilis that the word itself did not appear in print in commercial magazines until 1937 (*Colliers*). Newspapers, politicians, physicians, and others who undertook to educate the public ran the risk of an enormous backlash of popular opinion. In the Philadelphia production of *Spirochete*, for example, Christopher Columbus, a character in the play, was not identified by name because of heavy pressure from the Knights of Columbus, who did not wish him to be besmirched.[21]

In Seattle, the situation was typical of other regions of the United States. Incidents of reported syphilis cases had risen during the decade (from 847 in 1931 to 1,232 in 1939), and deaths averaged more than fifty a year.[22] There were inadequate clinical facilities to identify and treat infected persons – only two in the entire city in 1930 – and syphilis was routinely perceived by a large portion of the population to be a problem among the lower classes, Negroes and prostitutes. Washington, like many other states, had no laws requiring premarital or prenatal blood tests, and monthly reports about communicable diseases from the King County Medical Society did not have a category for venereal diseases.

By 1938, however, things had begun to change. The medical profession, in spite of fears of socialized medicine and "public" health, was beginning to support a more enlightened view about venereal disease, and state legislators were preparing bills to require mandatory blood tests for both expectant mothers and marriage applicants. Senate Bills 373 and 374 were officially entered into the debate of the Washington Senate in the fall of 1938 and made their way through the legislative process concurrently with the Federal Theatre run of *Spirochete*.

It was not a journey without controversy because Seattle, like other communities in the United States, also was embroiled in the debate about private vs. public medicine, and syphilis was the ideal field on which many of the issues were played out. The Seattle Provisional Health Committee, for example, recently had been organized to raise support for the Wagner National Health Act, which was bitterly opposed by the American Medical Association.[23] And the records of the King County Medical Society reflect the tension between organized private practice and the need to have an active public health presence to fight venereal disease.

Because syphilis was perceived as an immoral disease (or frequently as "punishment" for sin), doctor–patient confidentiality was paramount for many patients, and they and their doctors were totally opposed to government or public health interference. However, as Thomas Parran had argued so eloquently in his book, *Shadow on the Land*, the only way to wipe out the epidemic was to track down all the infected parties.[24] In addition, the economic aspects of the private–public debate were also consequential. Syphilis was expensive to treat and private practitioners could charge up to $25 per treatment, whereas an ordinary office visit might be three dollars. Treatment was cheaper at clinics where the medication salvarsan was available, but the patient lost anonymity. Moreover, the laboratory fees for such procedures as the Wasserman test could be set by the private doctors as opposed to the determined rates at public laboratories. It would be unfair to characterize all doctors profiting from this situation but, for many, syphilis was clearly a "cash cow."

An examination of the records kept at the King County Medical Society in Seattle as the premiere of the Federal Theatre's *Spirochete* approached provides some interesting facts. In February 1939, the Society *Bulletin* reported on the recent meeting of the Ladies Auxiliary of the Society, at which time there was a discussion of Senate Bills 373 and 374 (for prenatal and premarital syphilis testing). Dr Raymond Zeck is quoted as telling the members that, "the bill requiring blood tests before marriage will be backed by the medical profession but not pushed too hard as we might lose all in an attempt to accomplish too much."[25] This conservative position is very telling because it illustrates the dilemma of the medical profession when confronted with both the need to eradicate syphilis and the threat of government control and socialized medicine. The Wagner National Health Act, which had been introduced the year before and which provided, among other things, for nationwide subsidized health care, was still very much under discussion and attack by the American Medical Association (AMA).

The King County Medical Society, however, supported the syphilis bills and pushed for both education and understanding among its members. A February editorial in the *Bulletin* argued that for some time perceptions about syphilis had been changing and that, "the medical profession should do everything in its power to assist this spreading of information and education of the public"(8). Furthermore, under its Legislation column, the *Bulletin* assured readers that neither the prenatal bill nor the premarital bill is "intended to regulate the practice of medicine" and that the bills "should be of considerable interest to the medical profession and merit its consideration, thought and constructive criticism" (15). The *Bulletin* also discusses *Spirochete* and alerts its readers to the fact that the production has the full support of the various departments of health and that tickets have been reserved by the Ladies Auxiliary for a special 87-cent price on Monday, February 13. There was considerable anticipation about this play from the Federal Theatre that would address in honest terms the plague of syphilis.

For the Seattle unit, it was an apt moment. In spite of the loss of Esther Porter, O'Connor believed that he could revive the project, and that *Spirochete* was the kind of production that would be very successful in Seattle. He requested the loan of a talented young director from Los Angeles, Richard Glyer, to direct *Spirochete* and began to seek local support and sponsorship for the production. He enlisted the state and local medical associations, boards of health and the Ladies Auxiliary of the King County Medical Society. And he mapped out an aggressive campaign to sell the controversial play about venereal disease to the community.

O'Connor's principal concern was that the promotion of the play not concentrate on the "sex angle." At the same time, he wanted to attract large audiences and instructed the publicity department "to prevent the impression being formed that this was merely a kind of educational lecture." Approximately 35,000 handbills were distributed throughout the city – many from doctors' offices and hospitals – which stressed that this was not a show for "the prurient nor the prude." The handbill also stressed that the syphilis plague had been allowed to spread because of a "confused moral code." Audiences were assured, however, that they would experience "stage effects that have taken months in the building, with the best that can be brought to the stage of music, lighting, acting and stagecraft."[26]

Drawing on his experience from *One-Third of a Nation*, O'Connor had 3,500 posters placed on utility poles and in store windows throughout the city, and both the Board of Health and the medical associations bought air time for local radio programs. Ten programs – each fifteen minutes long – were produced using scenes from the play, while other stations made spot announcements. Streetcar advertising was also used, and special discount tickets were included in the pay checks for all King County WPA employees. O'Connor pointed out that this was the first time that the whole WPA workforce was targeted in this manner.

The dramatic "strategy" of *Spirochete* is to lead the viewer through a history of syphilis from the voyage of Columbus to the action of the Illinois legislature in 1937 via an everyday character called the 'Patient.' While the historical scenes are interesting in illustrating the pernicious nature of the disease, the play is most effective when it addresses contemporary notions of syphilis and tries to lay the groundwork for the passage of legislation affecting marriage laws. Consider, for example, the following scene between Dr. Metchnikoff and an indignant "reformer," which is set in 1906 but which resonates very clearly in the 1930s:

REFORMER: Syphilis is the penalty for sin! You are about to remove that penalty and plunge the world into an orgy of sinful living. Man will be free to pursue his lustful impulses with no thought of any physical wrath being inflicted on him.

METCHNIKOFF: And it's a horrible, ghastly penalty, you'll admit. A more horrible one could never be devised, could it?

REFORMER: I could think of none worse.

METCHNIKOFF: Then why in God's name hasn't it put an end to sin?... When all your moral prophylactics have failed to prevent the spread of this disease you wish to suppress a chemical one.

REFORMER: That's not the way to look at it.

METCHNIKOFF: Telling people it's sinful hasn't stopped it from striking one out of every ten persons you meet on the street!

REFORMER: Yes, but if they wouldn't sin...

METCHNIKOFF: If they wouldn't sin! The real sin would be to keep this discovery from the world. The real sin would be withholding a cure when one was available!

REFORMER: You must think of people's morals.

METCHNIKOFF: Morals be damned! You think of morals and I'll think of their illnesses.[27]

As the play attempts to demolish popular prejudices about the disease, it confronts the many taboos that had prevented the word "syphilis" from even being spoken in public. The following sequence is from the first legislature scene, which is based on actual deliberations from the Illinois legislature in 1933:

FIRST LEGISLATOR: The proposition is to add an amendment to the law in relation to marriage. This modern amendment to an old law would require persons of both sexes to present a medical certificate stating that they are free from venereal diseases. In submitting this amendment I wish to call attention to the great damage done by syphilis and gonorrhea each year. Statistics show that syphilis and gonorrhea...

SECOND LEGISLATOR: Mr. Speaker, I object to the terms being employed on this discussion.

FIRST LEGISLATOR: To what terms do you refer?

SECOND LEGISLATOR: It should be quite obvious to what terms I refer.
FIRST LEGISLATOR: Unless you can be more specific I shall continue the speech begun. I see nothing objectionable in it.
SECOND LEGISLATOR: Well, I do. I may be old-fashioned and come from a small town, but I still believe that the dignity of the legislature should not be besmirched by anything so patently revolting. The diseases to which references have been made are incompatible with anything above the level of bar-room talk. Furthermore, most of us are fathers of children who would sooner or later be subject to this infamous law. How many of us would wish them to be humiliated by an examination before the most sacred, the most holy moment of their lives?... In the name of decency I demand that this discussion be dropped at once!
FIRST LEGISLATOR: Mr. Speaker, with all due respect to my sensitive colleague, I insist that the greatest menace confronting public health today is syphilis. Each year its deadly effect on the social structure becomes more apparent.
SPEAKER: Pardon me, but are you really serious in what you're saying or is this some sort of joke?
FIRST LEGISLATOR: I've never been more serious in my life! (pp. 74–5)

At this point, a long scene illustrating how undiagnosed syphilis results in job loss, broken marriages, and even blindness in children interrupts the debate in the Illinois legislature, which in 1937 reached a climactic decision – a decision that was being anticipated in the state of Washington even as the events were unfolding on the stage of the Seattle Federal Theatre in 1939. The 'Second Legislator,' who figured so prominently in opposing the idea of premarital bills, now – four years later – has seen the light:

> I admit it. I admit my own former blindness to facts that ought to have been obvious to all of us...During the past four years I have learned many things. My eyes have been opened to the flagrant weakness of any system that allows its people to suffer year after year. Let's be truthful with ourselves...Nice people do get syphilis. And I say that the difference between those who do and those who don't is misfortune and nothing else. (pp. 89–90)

The legislation is passed unanimously and the Speaker of the House urges the people and the audience to take up the battle, to "stop whispering and begin talking about it... and talking out loud" (p. 90).

In spite of the fervor of *Spirochete*, there is a curious absence in the text that is important to note in placing this production in a larger cultural context. There is virtually no critique of the medical profession in the play. In fact, doctors are portrayed as heroic figures struggling against public ignorance. Nowhere is there reference to the battle lines that were being drawn between the AMA and New Deal social-welfare policies, or the difficulties of fighting syphilis because of the anonymity of doctor–patient confidentiality. The closest thing to a villain in the piece – other than ignorance – is a capitalist system that does not prize the worker, only the amount of labor that a worker can produce.

In Seattle, *Spirochete* was performed in the Metropolitan Theatre by thirty-seven cast members, with a great deal of doubling to fill out the seventy-nine speaking parts. In an effort to create a stronger sense of flow, a Hammond organ was placed in the orchestra pit with speakers flanking the stage, and Howard Biggs composed an original score to link the scenes and underscore action. Several sections in the text were rewritten or restructured to intensify the drama although, once again, Christopher Columbus was not identified by name. According to the Production Report, however, "we indicated the time, place and Columbus' rank as well as the type of his ship – caravel" (p. 4).

The biggest change from previous productions was the treatment of the legislative scenes. Unlike many of the Living Newspapers, *Spirochete* brought the events up to the present day and concluded with the legislators voting on the premarital bill. Glyer and O'Connor felt that the first legislative scene had to be rewritten so that the audience would not sympathize with the legislator who is arguing against passage of the bill. "We decided to satirize such a character, and in fact all the legislature . . . The entire scene was rewritten into a sort of doggerel blank verse of a rather low-comic variety . . . The pillars, the rostrum and even the legislators themselves were set off the vertical."[28] The final scene was also rewritten, but the satire was softened in order to stress the final important speech. The satire may have been lost on some viewers, or perhaps it was not as broad as O'Connor suggests. Z.A. Vane, the House Representative from the Twenty-Ninth District, wrote to O'Connor that "the Legislative scene naturally made quite an appeal to me and I must say quite authentic and effective . . . This scene was quite typical and very unique."[29] Vane also sent along several "prop" bills so that the actors could have added authenticity.

Spirochete was the biggest hit in the history of the Seattle project. Its total attendance – 2,956 – exceeded by nearly a thousand any previous production that the project had done in the Metropolitan Theatre.[30] The project grossed slightly more than $1,000, which was $400 more than it had made on any other show. People who were employed by the WPA were admitted for 10 cents, and they represented a large part of the turnout. Their total of 941 was more than the combined attendance of the three previous productions in the Metropolitan. Edwin O'Connor wrote Miller that it was the most successful thing in every respect that the Seattle Federal Theatre had ever done.

The newspaper reviews were less enthusiastic. Most commented on the structure of the piece or the technical production and praised many of the performers. J. Willis Sayre in the *Seattle Post-Intelligencer* reported that it was very entertaining but that "rather than a play it is an historical lecture."[31] And Gilbert Brown remarked that it was an important play but "infernally dull and rather sloppily acted."[32] Particularly interesting are the reactions of the medical profession to *Spirochete*. In April 1939, the *Bulletin* of the King County Medical Society reported on the event in its Ladies Auxiliary column.

> On Monday, February 13, the auxiliary took over a block of seats at the Metropolitan Theatre to see the Federal Theatre production of *Spirochete*. We sold 150 tickets which netted our treasury $37.50. In asking a number of those who attended that evening how they liked the play, I received a great difference of opinion. I did not enjoy it at all. It seemed to be an uninteresting play, very amateurishly done and accompanied by organ music that drowned out the voices and nearly split my ear drums with the constant vibration of the loud speaker hook-up. And I agreed with several who said, "If that man says 'In the Year of our Lord' once more, I'll simply scream!" I must confess that, although there were a number of people who seemed to be of the same opinion as I, there were also quite a few who said that they thought it was good for us to see it and even some said they really enjoyed it. So, maybe it was my dinner and not the play that was no good.[33]

Apparently, Hallie Flanagan would have agreed with this last remark. She saw a rehearsal of *Spirochete* and was so impressed that she could not believe that this was the same company that she had seen a year before.[34]

Legislation to mandate syphilis testing was passed by the Washington State House and Senate and signed by the governor in March, 1939. In order to give physicians time to familiarize themselves with the new laws, their effective date was set for January 2, 1940. The *Bulletin* of the King County Medical Society urged its members to comply with all aspects of the law and cautioned, "If the medical profession cannot prove itself willing and able to reduce the incidence of these diseases by a sincere effort in the public health phase of control, then some government agency will take over. It is up to us"(7).

Invigorated by the success of *Spirochete*, the Seattle unit began writing a new Living Newspaper based upon the lumber industry and America's vanishing forests. And they began rehearsing a brand new script by a local writer about politics and labor strife in a large Northwest city. *Timber* never opened. But *See How They Run* was destined to win a national playwriting prize and earn for the Seattle project considerable respect and additional controversy as they struggled to find an audience for a socially relevant theatre.

9

See How They Run

One of Hallie Flanagan's hopes was that Federal Theatre would produce new work, that they would discover new American playwrights. Accordingly, she co-sponsored with the Dramatists Guild a nationwide play competition that was officially announced on August 16, 1937. The contest was designed to "encourage young authors" and was "limited to those who have not achieved a commercial production on Broadway running more than three weeks, or 28 road performances."[1] While the subject matter was not proscribed, "scripts based on observations of the contemporary American scene are especially desired." The prize was generous: two hundred and fifty dollars and "a professional production with at least a two week run in New York." Federal Theatre would reserve the rights to produce the winning play in any of their theatres for up to six months, after which they would revert to the author. The judges were distinguished. Richard Lockridge, drama critic for the *New York Sun*, Lloyd Lewis of the *Chicago Daily News* and W.E. (Bill) Oliver of the Los Angeles *Herald Express*.

The deadline was set for September 21, 1937, little more than a month away. But even with this restriction, the scripts poured in. The deadline was extended for a month. More than 700 plays flooded the offices of the National Play Policy Board in New York. Readers were assigned to sort out those which showed some promise and move them up the ladder. After the initial cut the survivors would be read by Converse Tyler, head of the play department, Ben Russak, coordinator of new plays, and Francis Bosworth from the Play Bureau research office. Following that review, the scripts would be passed on to the newspaper critics for a final decision. It was an enormous task, especially on top of everyone's regular job. Some scripts got skimmed; others misplaced. Tempers erupted. After a particularly difficult weekend, Tyler fired off an interoffice memorandum expressing his frustration and displeasure:

I am astounded to find that practically the entire department, once again, shows its inability to note accurately the number of characters and scenes in a play. I suggest that we call a staff meeting for Thursday and thrash this thing out once and for all. You will find attached a complete listing of the cases where the readers made inaccurate production estimates.[2]

The total eventually ran to 733, although Tyler confided to John McGee that those above 600 only got a preliminary reading, and "there seems to be nothing of great importance among them."[3] On December 29, 1937, Tyler notified McGee that seven scripts had been identified as finalists for the judges. Each of them had been read "blind" and identified only by a number. In his letter to McGee he included a synopsis of each script and a summary of the Play Bureau critiques.[4]

Anyone who has judged a contest, selected a prize essay or given an award will appreciate the confusion and chaos that followed. In January all seven scripts were mailed to the judges with instructions to rank them "one through seven" and return them by the first week in February. Lockridge, who was probably the most prominent judge because of the success of his *Mr. and Mrs. North* characters, had no difficulty in declaring a winner. Number 523, a modern version of Noah's Ark transported to an ocean liner peopled with Boston Brahmins, was easily the class of the group. In fact, Lockridge informed Converse Tyler, "I can't honestly give you an alternative to the first choice, which seems to me, considering everything, clearly the best of the seven."[5] Unfortunately, Lloyd Lewis placed this "class of the group" in fifth place, and when Bill Oliver reported in on February 17, he had it ranked dead last.

Oliver preferred number 194, a melodrama about a future leftist revolution in America which had impressed some of the Federal Theatre staff, although Ben Russak found it "artificial" with only a "few dramatic moments." Lewis had ranked it third and Lockridge not at all, since he had only found three worthy of consideration. Tyler wrote to Lockridge and explained their dilemma. Finding little to recommend 194, he placed it fifth and added, "I am a little disturbed to find it necessary to go so far down the list to reach a decision; certainly if any of these last four is to be considered as a possible winner I'd like to be advised before any announcement is made."[6]

Tyler then tallied everyone's lists and found support for 397, a melodrama about the Texas oilfields that had authentic characters but "structural flaws" and which had been Lewis's first choice and Lockridge's second. However, Oliver had ranked it next to last. The only other possible choice appeared to be number 60, a serious study of labor strife in a large American city which mixed living newspaper techniques with traditional dramaturgy. It had a second, a third and a fourth. So Tyler asked everyone to vote again confining themselves only to numbers 194, 397 and 60. Even though Lockridge's first choice was eliminated by the decision, he did have his second (397) and his third (60), and he seemed hopeful that they now could reach an acceptable decision.

> I think, as a matter of fact, we've got the difficulty licked now. If each judge arranges the three surviving plays in his order of merit, we are, unless my figuring is cockeyed, going to come out with a two to one choice, which is fair enough. The play chosen will, obviously, be No. 397...
> Mr. Oliver, who rated 397 so low, may want to disassociate himself from the final decision, as I certainly would if the choice of the other two fell on No. 194 – a very sad jumble of good intentions, silly violence and improbable dialogue. But, with such wide disagreement, we'll not, I think, do much better than two to one. And Mr. Lewis, at any rate, ought to be fully pleased... I'm agreeably surprised, indeed, that anybody's first choice won, instead of everybody's third.[7]

Unfortunately, it was not to be. Lloyd Lewis acknowledged that he had debated a long time about whether to award first place to 397 or 60 and now decided to change his vote and go with 60. "If this will break the tie and solve the problem, consider my vote so cast."[8] Inexplicably he dropped 397 to third. Tyler now declared 60 the winner. Lockridge was beside himself. "Oh, all right. I'm not, you understand, very enthusiastic about the choice and I am pretty disappointed by Mr. Lewis's rather strange antics."[9] Lewis and Oliver telegraphed their confirmation. Number 60 (*See How They Run*) out of 733 had won.

In Seattle, George Milton Savage Jr. wondered if his political play about labor strife would ever get produced. He had submitted *See How They Run* to the Western Regional Office of the Federal Theatre Project nearly a year earlier and, at first, had received some very positive feedback. Georgia Fink, writing on behalf of the Regional Service Bureau, informed him in August 1937 that the play was tentatively scheduled for Denver, Des Moines and San Francisco, but the dates were not firm. Later she told him that it was "definite" for Denver in October and "tentative" for San Francisco in January 1938. By November, however, Denver was "delayed," although now San Diego looked like a possibility. Savage kept inquiring about a New York production, but Fink – and Howard Miller – seemed to think that

San Diego was their best bet, and they even discussed the contractual terms based upon a week's run beginning January 26, 1938.[10] In the meantime they had submitted the script for the Dramatists Guild competition.

See How They Run was not the work of a novice writer. Savage had written dozens of plays for amateur production and was published in a variety of anthologies. He also wrote under pseudonyms and collaborated with colleagues at the University of Washington where he was a professor of English. His forte, according to his son, George Savage III (with whom he also collaborated), was a kind of middle-class domestic drama with a mother, father and maid.[11] Like so many others who were propelled out of relative obscurity by Federal Theatre, Savage went on to have a distinguished career in the American theatre. After leaving the University of Washington in 1951, he taught playwriting for twenty years at UCLA where he counted among his students a host of successful actors and writers. In 1958 he was awarded a Fulbright grant to lecture at Bristol and later established the Samuel Goldwyn Award at UCLA. His numerous successes were recognized in 1962 when he was honored with a Margo Jones Award and entertained by President Johnson at the White House. He died in 1977.

As a youngster Savage had a privileged existence. His father was a de-manding and hard-working laborer who built a profitable construction com-pany. Determined to give his sons the education that he had missed, he sent young George to Exeter Academy where he struggled with a demanding curriculum but excelled. He read widely and wrote poetry and dialogue from an early age. Unfortunately, the depressed economy of the late 1920s and early 1930s prevented him from attending an Ivy League college. He had to settle for the local Washington State College, where he eventually earned a Ph.D in 1935 and stayed on to teach English composition and liter-ature. By this time he was also seriously interested in pursuing a career as a playwright.

He wrote constantly, and when Federal Theatre arrived in Seattle, Savage had already authored some thirty "amateur" plays. According to his New York agent, Frieda Fishbein, he contributed scripts regularly to *The High School Thespian* and the "new writers" sections of *Frontier* and *Midland*.[12] He taught at the University of Washington to pay the bills, but his real passion was the theatre and, as his ample surviving correspondence illus-trates, he yearned to be produced on Broadway, to be legitimatized as a real "professional." He was close to Glenn Hughes, but eventually realized that as long as Hughes was at the University, his own opportunities to be more active in the academic theatre life would be limited. With the arrival of the

Federal Theatre, however, Savage – like the Jameses and others – saw an opportunity to pursue his career in a different and funded venue. He saw the Seattle production of *Power* and was energized by the potential of the Living Newspaper format. He was intrigued by the short scenes and quick cuts, by the direct address and theatricality of the lights, sounds and loudspeakers. He was also fascinated by the way a narrative could be sustained in spite of the chronological jumps and brief snapshots of action. For some time Savage had been thinking about writing a contemporary play, a play that would confront the political realities of America in the depression years. Like other young writers on the left, he wanted to use the theatre to address social issues. He had imagined and dismissed several ideas and eventually worked his way back to what he knew best – a university setting. But this university would be in a community that was in the grip of labor unrest and confronted with the newest weapon of the working class: the sit-down strike.

The sit-down strike raised the ante in the struggle between management and labor in 1930s America. Picket lines – the traditional tool of labor – could be crossed and attacked. Scabs could be imported to keep the industrial machine running. But as radical rubber workers demonstrated in Akron in the winter of 1936, if you simply sat down at the machines and occupied the plants, the nature of the game was changed. Now the occupiers had to be forced out, attacked, or placed under siege. Management could cut off the heat, deny food and water, and hassle the CIO sympathizers who came to bear witness. But at a cost. The machines were the hostages in this battle, and a literal wrench in the assembly line could wound the entire plant.

The auto workers watched the successes at Firestone and Goodrich, and after some preliminary skirmishes in Atlanta and Kansas City, they moved against the great General Motors body plants in Flint, Michigan. Fisher Body Number One was occupied in December 1936, and a few days later Number Two was also seized. General Motors was defiant because they believed that the sit-down strike was a clear threat to the *idea* of private property, and that it would never be tolerated in a capitalist economy. For the emerging CIO, however, the stakes were equally high because they saw the opportunity to organize the entire industry and not allow separate plants to reach individual agreements. John L. Lewis joined the fight along with Walter Reuther. Striker's wives formed massive picket lines to prevent the eviction of – and to resupply – the embattled workers. On January 11, 1937, in a violent skirmish that's been immortalized as the "battle of running bulls,"[13] the Flint Police tried to storm the plant but were repelled by a hailstorm of tools and door hinges. Frank Murphy, the New Deal governor of Michigan, responded by summoning the National Guard. This time, however, their charge was not to evict the strikers but to end the violence on both sides and force everyone to the bargaining table. It was a critical moment in American labor history, igniting hundreds of battles in the following months. And even though the Supreme Court would eventually rule against the sit-down in 1939, the CIO rode the tactic to triumph throughout 1937. United States Steel surrendered without a fight.

In Seattle George Savage had seen the labor wars close up. The bitter confrontations that had plagued the waterfront since the 1934 strike continued to smolder. Dave Beck and his more conservative teamsters were trying to stave off Harry Bridges and the emerging ILA, while management and politicians scrambled to support the winning side. By 1936 violence and bombings were threatening to become commonplace. Savage watched as the sit-down strike and the rights of workers to organize under the Wagner Act collided with private property and free enterprise democracy. He pondered the dilemma and believed that he had found an answer. He may not have anticipated that his solution would be seen by some to be as controversial as *The Cradle Will Rock* had been a year before.

See How They Run is set in an "industrial American city" where all the factories have been closed by a sit-down strike. There is also a university of 12,000 students which is on the eve of "playing Pitt for a mythical national Championship" in football. The time is December 1936. The liberal university president, who is wise and widely respected, is drawn into the fray because he is about to announce a new Model Cities program funded from the will of a deceased industrialist. The committee authorizing the grant, however, finds a loophole and plans to deny the Model Cities program unless the President purges his liberal faculty and lends his authority to breaking the strike. Meanwhile, labor is divided into factions debating settlement, arbitration or a general strike. Its representatives also bring pressure on the university president, threatening campus violence if he interferes in their actions. In a wonderfully contrived final act, the President invites the plotters to his office on the eve of a radio broadcast celebrating the big game. There, they await his arrival, and unaware that the radio transmission is "on," betray their own venal interests over the airwaves. The strikers, learning that they have been betrayed by their leaders, threaten to riot. The President forces everyone to the table, and management settles. Enlightened educators, Savage asserts, are the best hope to end the turmoil and secure the future.

Savage's naive but passionate attempt to solve the labor problems grew out of his own experiences and are reflected vividly in the play:

> I wanted a contemporary theme because I am interested in the forces at work in America and think we need to understand them before we can make a better America. I knew the personality and temperament of some capitalists and politicians through my work with my father, a prominent contractor in the State of Washington. I knew the personality and temperament of the workers by actually working on the jobs my father had. I'd been water boy. I'd routed trucks. I'd lost money trying to do sub-contracting myself. And I knew something of the problems of a University for I have been teaching at the University of Washington for the past eight years... The academic world seemed a good one in which the forces of capital and labor might meet.[14]

What fascinated people about *See How They Run*, however, was not its "solution" to the labor wars – wise academics mediating among radical positions – but its structure and theatricality. Drawing upon techniques from film and the living newspapers, Savage created a *mise-en-scène* which included three specific settings and then dozens of "spots" or short takes which extended or commented on the action. These spots were sometimes brief scenes, such as workers dancing to ease the boredom of their strike, or sightseeing tourists passing the plants, or they could be brief vignettes such as when one of the labor leaders is shot. Frequently they were simply aural bridges to keep the action flowing: the sound of motors, sirens or machine-gun fire. Certainly part of the attraction of the piece was its careful scoring, the way that it broke out of the proscenium arch (several of the spots were played in the aisles of the auditorium) and its large and colorful cast. Savage later wrote that *See How They Run* was created, "to satisfy an inner need in myself: to write with no restrictions the best play I knew how to. I had written and marketed some thirty plays for the nonprofessional theatre. They were written with restrictions of setting, restriction of number of characters, restriction of ideas that the characters might have."[15] Now he wrote with a freedom that was exhilarating. In addition to the scenes and spots, *See How They Run* had roles for forty-one characters, thirty-seven of them men, representing every facet of the struggle between labor and management.

Savage learned that he had won the Federal Theatre–Dramatists Guild national competition on March 16, 1938. Five days later he received a check for $250 and was so delighted that he sat down and wrote several thank you notes, one of the most effusive to Richard Lockridge who, unbeknownst to Savage, was the most exasperated of the selection team.[16] Savage now believed that his long-awaited Broadway debut was imminent, and that the announcement would also facilitate other Federal Theatre productions.[17] Flanagan, who was under increasing pressure to account for communist activity on the project and preparing to face the Dies Committee, wrote to congratulate Savage and suggested that the premiere production take place in Seattle cosponsored by Federal Theatre and the University of Washington. If the notion of a federally funded play depicting the successful conclusion of a sit-down strike only months after the furor over *The Cradle Will Rock* troubled her, it was not immediately apparent.

Savage initially balked at a Seattle premiere, although it's not entirely clear why. Perhaps he thought that some of the characters might hit too close to home.[18] Perhaps he thought that it might detract from the glamor of his New York opening. Or perhaps, as he wrote to Flanagan, the facilities in Seattle were too limited and we just "do not have the right stages here." The prize announcement did stir San Francisco into action, however, and they began to plan for a September opening to be followed by a similar run in Oakland. Savage fully expected that the play would receive a New York production in the fall, but as the summer passed there was only interest from the Bay Area and locally. Edwin O'Connor, ever alert to draw crowds to their remodeled movie house, scheduled the play for September. Savage was convinced that they could learn a great deal from San Francisco and then adapt the script for Seattle and New York. He knew that his work could be strengthened in the rehearsal hall and wrote to Flanagan that by the time the Seattle run was completed it would be a significantly improved play and ready for Broadway.

In San Francisco Savage found an ally and a collaborator. Unlike most Federal Theatres, the unit in San Francisco was performing on a traditional stock two-week run, and Alan Williams chafed under the burden. He was interested in new plays and in having the time to develop and perfect them. *See How They Run* appealed to him because it was contemporary and original and because he was sympathetic with its leftist politics. Although he had lots of reservations about the script – the ending was too "pat" and many of the characters too cardboard – he was intrigued by the "spots" or "impressions" as he characterized them, and felt that they would serve as footnotes and emphasis points to the main story line. Charles Teevin, his supervisor, scheduled the play into their traditional two-week run and then arranged for it to transfer to the Oakland Federal Theatre if there seemed to be audience demand.

Williams was also keenly aware of the political situation in Washington, DC and the continual cries of communism which were now almost a daily occurrence. From August 19 to 21 the Dies Committee had heard a stream of invective against the Project, characterized most eloquently by Hazel Huffman, a former employee who had read other people's mail and was now an expert on un-American activities. Communism, she charged, was widespread on all the projects and reflected the prevailing philosophy of Flanagan and many of her associates. It was apparent in the plays and in the workplace. Flanagan was eager to rebut such charges, but as the summer waned the Dies Committee seemed content to amass only one side of the story. By early September, when *See How They Run* was preparing for its San Francisco premiere, Flanagan was desperately trying to convince the WPA officials that they couldn't allow the charges to go unchallenged. But she was repeatedly counseled – even by her friend and ally Eleanor Roosevelt – not to dignify the scurrilous accusations. When she was finally summoned by the Dies Committee in December 1938, much of the damage had been done.[19]

The cries of "communism" that inspired most of the daily headlines were usually prompted by the New York City units, but in fact all of the projects were vulnerable to the charges. Productions of *One-Third of a Nation* were routinely attacked as were any pieces which appeared to be critical of capitalism or the "American way of life." Theatres with Negro units were constantly fighting the criticism fueled by anger over Scottsboro (where the Communist Party had come to the defense of the "boys") and widespread rumors of mixing the races. In Cleveland, as early as January 1936, an actor, James F. Brooks, wrote to Washington that "being an old trouper, I was very glad that this project went through, to reestablish the legitimate stage and keep the old timers off relief rolls, but it seems that it is just a school for communists."[20]

While San Francisco had not provoked the same kind of censorship battles that racked Los Angeles, there had been letters of complaint about *Run, Little Chillun* and *One-Third of a Nation*, as well as criticism from the Left that the project was content with musical plays and the stock system. Thus, it was not surprising that Williams would lobby Teeven to produce the world premiere of *See How They Run*. And while Dies railed against the Federal Theatre in Washington, DC, Williams drilled his actors in sit-down tactics and the politics of a general strike. When they moved into the Alcazar Theatre for the techs and dresses, Savage trained down from

Seattle and joined the company for the final rehearsals. He expected to be an observer, but Williams and the company immediately involved him in the hectic process of mounting the play.

At this point Savage still believed that *See How They Run*, in spite of its pro-labor stance, would be produced for at least a two-week run on Broadway as stipulated by the terms of the contest. He had convinced Edward O'Connor to open a Seattle production two weeks after San Francisco. As a result, he was totally committed to making the script as strong as possible, and, taking his cue from Williams and company questions, he rewrote several speeches prior to opening. The next morning he met with Williams, Teevin and Ole Ness for a critique. He recorded the experience in a letter to Georgia Fink:

> They went over the script with me for the performance had revealed certain flaws – particularly in the last act and in the exposition of the first act. With their suggestions and help I rewrote the third act. This is what amazed me – the cast learned the new third act on Tuesday and put it on perfectly Tuesday night. No one objected to the added work. All seemed interested in making the play as good as it could be. I shouldn't have believed such a spirit possible.[21]

Williams' principal concern was to make the play less didactic and to work against the kind of *deus ex machina* nature of the third act in which the President tricks the racketeers and corrupt businessmen into revealing their plots over a live radio microphone. It was a difficult task because Savage had created each character as a kind of mouthpiece for a particular point of view and thus "humanizing" them became problematic. The ending "worked," but Williams wanted to see if they could arrive there behaviorally rather than from Savage's plotting skills. It was a problem that would haunt all the productions of *See How They Run*.

The press was mixed, but the word of mouth was good, and the audience built steadily during the first week. By Saturday night they had a sell-out. Interest was certainly triggered by the contemporary nature of the story, as well as the Dies hearings. Writing in the *San Francisco News* Robert Lee remarked, "Mr. Martin Dies would probably scream with joy should he happen to step into the Alcazar Theatre this week, for the Federal Theatre Project's new play *See How They Run* fairly bristles with social significance."[22] Lee, like some others, however, found the solution unconvincing: "Frankly, the play, as an effort to picture labor relations today, is so much flailing in the

10 Exterior of the Seattle Theatre; sign says "See How They Run Now Playing".

wind. Nothing new is said for capital or labor and there's no solution offered to today's industrial problems." But he did admire many of the performances and the general "entertainment" value of the script. The second Monday dropped off some but rebuilt during the week and closed to an enthusiastic audience. Teevin reported that the production played to more than 10,000 people or 70 percent of capacity.[23]

While Williams prepared a second production for the Oakland unit, Savage was busy in Seattle with O'Connor cutting and shaping so they could shoehorn the play into their tiny Federal Theatre. As with Williams, Savage found working with a director illuminating about the potential and the shortcomings of his play. But there were distinct differences of opinion and disagreement about how the play should be shaped. Neither Ole Ness nor O'Connor understood the "spots" in quite the same way that Williams had, or as Savage had originally intended. *See How They Run* has three distinct sets: the Mayor's office, the Union hall and the President's office. It also has some twenty-five spots or "flashes" which precede or follow the action in the main locales and which Savage imagined being played in the aisles or in corners of the house. Some are very brief or just sound effects; others are mini scenes of up to a dozen lines in specific places such as the inside of the plant. But they do not interrupt the main action of the play. Ness found them at odds with the traditional dramaturgy and wanted to cut or edit them. O'Connor wanted to extend some of them and play them on side stages in the auditorium so that they could help to clarify the action. But that involved more "locales" with accompanying props, etc. and tended to slow the action. O'Connor was convinced, however, that he could knit the piece together with sound and live choral effects – a strategy that the Seattle unit had explored since the original Negro productions. Savage trusted O'Connor, and by opening night in Seattle, the play was a grand hometown success.[24] The reviewers were positive and supportive noting that even though the author was a local professor, this was a prizewinning play which is a "robust and stimulating contemplation of chaotic modern America, rich in imagination and varied in entertainment appeal."[25]

Savage was delighted with the production and the reception. He wrote a long and enthusiastic letter to Hallie Flanagan detailing how much he had learned from working with two fine Federal Theatre directors and how the script had continued to evolve in the process:

> I wish you could see the production here about Saturday night... Mr. O'Connor has been willing to try anything. The last changes are going into rehearsals tonight and tomorrow I'll see what will probably be a final version. He's caught the spirit and meaning of the play so well that I only hope the New York production will be exactly like Seattle... I'm particularly pleased with the pacing of the play and with the sound effects. Mr. O'Connor did much with actual choral work. The sounds built amazingly effectively and held the play together... The choral effect

should, I think, surely be used in the New York production. It is much more effective than radio and phonograph effects... If the New York performance can duplicate Mr. O'Connor's production, I believe that you'll have a play that satisfies the public and the critics. I know it's one that completely satisfies the author.[26]

But the box office did not reflect either the positive reviews or Savage's enthusiasm for the production. Business lagged and confounded O'Connor. *See How They Run* was, in his estimation, some of the best work they had done, and it still could not attract patrons to their remote and cramped movie theatre. Before it closed, however, Savage received a letter from Hallie Flanagan about his New York production. He was stunned by her reply.

"I am very much surprised," she wrote on September 30, "at the inference of a New York production."

According to Flanagan, *See How They Run* would be considered for production by one of the New York units, but there was no guaranteed commitment. This position seemed, of course, to be at odds with the stated conditions of the prize competition, and Savage was both hurt and perplexed. He believed deeply in the worth of Federal Theatre. It had accorded him a unique and enlightening experience. He did not want to alienate Flanagan, or others who had helped him, but he also could not understand why the promises were being broken. He inquired again, and Flanagan informed him on October 19 that "no New York production" was being planned but reiterated that the play was being considered by the New York units. In the event that someone showed interest, she would let him know immediately. Savage took this to mean that she could not find an individual director who wanted to take on the show, so he suggested both through his agent, Frieda Fishbein, and directly to Flanagan, that Edward O'Connor be brought to New York for the purpose. Savage was also corresponding with Alan Williams who had been fired – "purged" was his word – after the Oakland production. Apparently Williams was so upset with the inept nature of the technical crews and performances that he gave Teevin an ultimatum, and Teevin accommodated him. Williams, however, was still very much interested in the play and the way that it seemed to endorse arbitration as a solution to the labor strife. He wanted to keep his hand in if there was to be a New York production.

Flanagan, meanwhile, was trying to save the Project. After her initial rebuke from the Dies Committee in August, she had given a rousing presentation to the Policy Board where she had talked about decentralizing and reinvigorating the individual units. She had suggested plays about local subjects, pageants honoring various state traditions and re-visioning classical works. She did not foreground political plays endorsing industrial unionization. In addition, she was preparing a rebuttal to the highly prejudiced Dies testimony which she believed misrepresented the Project, especially with regard to the number of political plays that they had presented.

Savage was cautious and diplomatic. He was hard at work on another manuscript that he hoped could also be done by Federal Theatre, and he was campaigning for the continuation of the Project and extension for another year of the play contest. His agent, however, was much more direct. She wrote to Flanagan pointing out that one of the conditions laid down in the terms of the prize competition was a production "with a run of at least two weeks in New York City."[27] Fishbein hoped that it would be honored. Flanagan caved. A month later, as Savage tried to work behind the scenes with Ole Ness, Fishbein informed him that, "Mr. Rubenstein had called on behalf of his client, Hallie Flanagan, to report that you are entitled to a New York production which will be following pretty soon."[28] Before it could be scheduled, however, Congress eliminated the Project. *See How They Run* went from first place to footnote. Savage, however, continued to be an avid supporter of Federal Theatre, and in the closing, hectic months he wrote numerous letters in the campaign to restore the full WPA budget. When Flanagan visited Seattle on her last official trip in March 1939, he entertained her at his home where they had a lively discussion about new plays. His telegram denouncing the end of the Project is one of the final documents in the Federal Theatre archives.

He continued to shop *See How They Run* but with little success. And eventually he imagined a history that allowed him to deal with the disappointment. In 1972 he told a columnist for the *Seattle Times* that the play, "was refused entry on Broadway because it was too controversial. It advocated the establishment of the Labor Relations Board."[29] After his death, his wife wrote to Lorraine Brown at the FTP Collection at George Mason University that the play, "was disliked by the Far Left and they were able to delay production. Others felt that any play sympathetic to the workers would offend the right."[30]

Given the political pressures of the time, it is a fascinating landscape to explore. Perhaps Flanagan was feeling the pressure of the attack on the project and thus "forgot" the promise of the play contest. Perhaps she just hoped to delay what promised to be another controversial production until the waters were calm. Or perhaps the poor box office in Seattle and Oakland, combined with the awkward dramaturgy, just did not justify continued support of the script. By the fall of 1938 there was no enthusiasm for a second national play competition. For whatever reasons, *See How They Run* simply did not have "legs," as Lockridge had predicted. Perhaps its politics would have been less of an issue if it had been more of a play. For Savage and others on the West Coast, it seemed filled with fire and a contemporary spirit. But Lawrence Langner may have summarized a more realistic point of view when he returned the play on behalf of the Theatre Guild in 1939, "I am sorry that the subject matter of the play does not interest me," he wrote, "I am quite sure it is an interesting play but I am heartily tired of capital and labor struggles on the stage."[31]

10

Flotilla of Faith

On the first day of the last year of Federal Theatre (1939) the Seattle project was funded at $53, 495 for labor costs.[1] This represented only a small decrease from the numbers in 1936 ($54,900) when the unit had been founded with high hopes and naive expectations. But they had survived, even flourished at times when other projects had floundered. Much had changed. Edwin O'Connor had brought stability to the theatre, and his reputation as a director was growing. Morale was improving. O'Connor put in long hours, and company members began to seek him out for advice and consolation. Some wanted his opinion about dating or divorce or mother-in-law problems. Others wanted him to hold money for them because they were afraid that if they put it in the bank and got a little ahead, they might jeopardize their relief status. And others wanted help with their drinking problems. Drinking on the job was a long-standing problem O'Connor confided to Howard Miller. "When I came here from Los Angeles the amount of drinking on project time was terrific but I never reported it for I felt that if I were given a free rein I could rectify it and I would like to report now that there is no drinking on the job."[2]

But some things had not changed. The company was still rigidly segregated, and issues of space, attendance and income continued to plague O'Connor. In March 1939 he had the opportunity to acquire the Jameses' Seattle Repertory Playhouse ("it has been offered to purchase outright at a price of twenty-five thousand and carry the seven thousand dollar mortgage, or at a flat rate of thirty thousand and the present owner will take care of the mortgage"[3]) but he felt that it was too small and too close to Glenn Hughes's university operations. Plus he was in the throes of his Showboat plans and really believed that the floating theatre would solve their problems. In March he directed a very successful production of *Ah, Wilderness!* with the white company in the Metropolitan Theatre and was able to bank over $500 ("This has never happened before," he told Miller). And he was readying the Negro Company for *Dragon's Wishbone*.

But what was occupying much of his time in the spring months of 1939 was figuring out ways that the Seattle unit could respond to Hallie Flanagan's charge to create work that was regional and expressive of the life of people in all parts of the United States. "Pageants" she had stressed in her speeches and letters to the state directors, and O'Connor wanted to support her vision. Unfortunately, Seattle had some baggage with regard to pageant making so O'Connor had to tread lightly.

Three years earlier Guy Williams had proposed a sort of Native American version of *Green Pastures*. As acting director of Region V, he had been seeking ways to activate the sparsely theatricalized Northwest (especially Montana, Idaho and Wyoming) and experiencing some frustration. He wrote to Hallie Flanagan that "it gets increasingly embarrassing to pretend that these states do not exist, but the unfortunate factor is that they have virtually no relief show-people."[4] However, he had had conversations with Professor Barnard Hewitt who was the head of the drama department at the University of Montana, and a local journalist named Frank Linderman who was an authority on "Indian life, customs and ceremonies."

Thus armed, Williams proposed to Flanagan that they create "a company of reasonably civilized Indians to put on under the aegis of the Federal Theatre Project a sort of Indian 'Green Pastures' – a theatrical expression of the race complete with music, ceremonials, dances and melodrama – frank and unashamed."[5] Unsure of how such a proposal might be greeted in official circles, Williams assured Flanagan that, "I sincerely feel that this is not altogether a goofy idea," and went on to exclaim that in time they might even present it during the tourist season at Yellowstone "building it up into a sort of Passion Play."

In spite of the universalizing and racist implications of this enterprise, Williams's proposal was taken quite seriously in Washington, DC. After a flurry of phone calls and correspondence, Nina Collier outlined the plan for the directors of the Federal Arts programs:

> Apparently the Blackfeet Indians could be employed to present a spectacle which, in a sense, would be an Indian "Green Pastures." This could be directed by members of the Federal Theatre Project with possibly a few additional persons. The university has agreed to provide stage equipment and other necessary expenses. It is possible that the Indian Bureau might pay the salaries of the 50 Indians to be employed from their rehabilitation funds – since this project would be definitely reimbursable in that gate receipts would pay for the salaries.[6]

But Clinton P. Anderson, a WPA field representative in Salt Lake City, thought that the idea was indeed "goofy" and wrote to Hallie Flanagan to tell her so:

It is his suggestion that the theatre of the University of Montana be used by a company of reasonably civilized Indians to put on a sort of Indian "Green Pastures," which Mr. Williams describes as a theatrical expression of the race, frank and unashamed. As I indicated to you in Washington, I have had some experience with the effort to make of the tribal Indian a vaudeville actor. Mr. Williams states that it might be possible to play the Indian show at Yellowstone during the tourist season, and that many of these Indians are already experienced showmen, due to their use in rodeos and county fairs.

Indian dances are a part of the religion of the Indian and no more deserving to be used as professional attractions than the religious cere-monies of other people who might happen to be on relief in this country at the present time.

I do not know what Mr. Williams means by "reasonably civilized Indians," but I do know that the more the Indians try to imitate the habits of their white neighbors, the more unfortunate it becomes for them . . .

I am sure that John Collier could give you a very strong statement, opposing the proposition which Mr. Williams has made. Mr. Collier has been objecting for many years to the commercialization of Indian festivals in the Southwest, to my definite knowledge, and I assume he has done the same thing in other parts of the country.

Therefore, I would say that Mr. Williams' idea ought to be judged by two tests: (1) Have we any Indian actors on relief who would fit into such a project, and (2) Is the project, itself, socially desirable?[7]

Apparently the Indian *Green Pastures* was dropped. William P. Farnsworth wrote to Clinton Anderson ten days later that it was no longer possible to proceed with the project because of "the March 5 ruling of Mr. Hopkins prohibiting further increase of employment on the Theatre Project. Thus, the question becomes purely academic."[8] Farnsworth went on to add, how-ever, that "Mr. Williams was here on Friday and Saturday and I had a long and interesting argument with him upholding your point of view."

Three years after the aborted Indian *Green Pastures*, Edwin O'Connor was presented with the opportunity of putting Region V back in the pageant business. And this time it was not only Northwest Indians who would peo-ple the stage, but also the controversial and powerful "Blackrobe" priests of the Catholic Church. O'Connor, in partnership with the Chamber of Commerce of Vancouver, Washington, and the Catholic Church in

Washington and Oregon, agreed to supervise the production of a gigantic pageant celebrating the 100th anniversary of the arrival of the Church in the Northwest. Focusing on the heralded journey of Fathers Demers and Blanchet and staged on the site of the Vancouver stockade of the Hudson Bay Company on the Columbia River, *The Flotilla of Faith* called for a cast of 45 core actors and approximately 200 extras. It would be viewed by an audience of approximately 8,000, broadcast over the NBC Red network and filmed for newsreel by Universal. An apostolic delegate would be sent by Pope Pius XII. It promised to be the largest outdoor theatrical production in the history of the former Northwest territories.

What is fascinating about the production, however, is not just the artistic contributions of the Federal Theatre, but the issues that it raises about the politics of the occasion. What led to this intriguing alliance between the Catholic Church and the Works Progress Administration in the spring of 1939? After all, many powerful Catholics believed that Roosevelt had simply ignored the persecution of the Church in Mexico, and his comradery with Winston Churchill and England spelled further heartbreak for the "cause" in Ireland. Roosevelt's efforts to recognize "red" Russia also discouraged church people who viewed Stalin and Hitler as equally barbaric. Finally, many Catholics – caught up in the fever of the Legion of Decency – viewed the "federalization" of the theatre as another New Deal tool with which to preach against their foes. What did the issues of 1939 have to do with the events of 1838? And had the representations of "Americans" changed since the ill-fated days of *Green Pastures*?

In the Northwest, Catholics were outnumbered by Protestants at a ratio of ten to one, and both Oregon and Washington State had significant Klan activity in the previous decade. It is important to recall that Oregon citizens had passed an outrageous antiparochial school bill in 1922 whereby parents could be charged with a misdemeanor if children between the ages of 8 and 16 did not attend public school. And while Washington defeated a similar bill in 1924 – and federal district and Supreme courts threw it out in Oregon – another battle erupted over busing children in both states in the 1930s. Certainly the prejudices were fired by statements such as the following from the Washington *Klamath Falls Herald*. "The birth of every male child in a Catholic family is celebrated by burying a gun and ammunition underneath the church, in preparation for the day when the government is to be overthrown on behalf of the pope."[9]

Thus, as the Church approached its Centenary celebration in the Northwest, it was still a decidedly minority voice in a section of the country where church attendance was historically low. In Seattle, however, Bishop Gerald Shaughnessy was working dramatically to change that. Originally consecrated in 1934, Shaughnessy had undertaken a series of programs and reforms which had a huge impact in the city. In 1936 he supervised the organization of Catholic Charities which was so successful that the national meeting of the organization was held in Seattle that August. Ten thousand people including twelve bishops gathered in the Civic Auditorium to hear speeches by the governor of Washington and the mayor of Seattle. That same summer he arranged for an aggressive program of "street preaching," sending priests with cars and amplifiers into the parks. A year later he shocked many of his colleagues when he acquired a trailer chapel which he hooked to the bumper of his car and drove to rural areas to celebrate mass. Shaugnessy also reestablished connections with the Native-American population sending priests to the long-neglected Quinault and Makah reservations.

The centerpiece of the centennial celebration was the dedication of Portland's Central Catholic High School, but when Shaughnessy heard that the Archdiocese wanted to stage an elaborate pageant to commemorate the arrival of Fathers Blanchet and Demers, he suggested that the Seattle unit of the Federal Theatre was the only professional organization with enough savvy to pull it off. Father Gallagher was appointed to liaise with the director, Edwin O'Connor, and was later supplemented by J. O'Connell, editor of the *Catholic Progress*.

No records survive of the early negotiations, but it seems clear that it was a fortuitous moment for Edwin O'Connor. Or least he presented it that way in a March letter to his boss J. Howard Miller:

> When my cooperation was solicited in the staging of this, I accepted, as I felt it would conform nicely with the plan of Mrs. Hallie Flanagan, stated in her National Directors letter of February 1st., in which she requests during the month of May, "that we make an effort to do something along the festival line, which would reflect the dramatic backgrounds of individual regions."[10]

As plans matured, however, O'Connor realized the public relations potential of the pageant, and he worked hard to exploit it. Ever mindful of the need to strengthen his ties to the state and regional officials, O'Connor believed that a successful production could have a great halo effect for the whole WPA. In a letter to Hallie Flanagan he later described their transit from Seattle to Vancouver:

Forty-five members of the Seattle Federal Theatre started the morning before the pageant was to be held. It was a glorious day and I had ten automobiles decorated with streamers and banners advertising the pageant, and of course Federal Theatre. All the actors were in costume. I thought wearing the costumes down there would attract a lot of attention to the caravan and it did. We had a State Patrol escort all the way through from Seattle to Vancouver. It was very nice advertising for 190 miles across the State.[11]

But perhaps an even greater "lure" was the fact that, from the beginning, cost was not an issue. Accustomed to the financial restraints of the Federal Theatre and the constant vigilance about non-labor spending, O'Connor seems slightly giddy about the surfeit of riches. "It certainly was a pleasure working with the Catholic Centenary Committee, no task was too difficult for them and the expenditure of money was never questioned. Whatever we needed was immediately given us without question as to cost."[12] After months of accounting for each phone call, telegram and advertising expense, O'Connor was able to request whatever he wanted. *The Flotilla of Faith* featured four bands, over two hundred costumed actors, five horses, a wagon team and dozens of hand and set props including pistols, rifles and cannon.

The plot is exquisitely simple. Outside the walls of the Vancouver fort Indians dance prior to the arrival of fur traders from the north and south. A renegade white man steals whiskey and incites the Indians against some new "Bostons" (American settlers). This rebellion is quelled by the head of the fort, John McLoughlin, who is a hero to all and the "father" of the Indians. There is a celebration as the traders arrive – Hawaiian dances; Scottish dances; and much singing. But the Indians want to know when the Blackrobes will come because they have been taught that the salvation of their people depends upon their instruction from the Catholic missionaries. Finally the "express" packet of the Hudson Bay Company is sighted, and Fathers Demers and Blanchet arrive in a canoe just as they did a hundred years earlier. They make speeches, raise a cross and the pageant ends with everyone singing patriotic songs.

There is no need to dwell on the historical accuracies of the story. With a modicum of research they are evident. The Blackrobes actually arrived at Fort Vancouver over six months later than the reenactment (November 24, 1838), and the legendary Chief Factor, John McLoughlin, was still in Europe on an extended tour and thus not even there to greet them. Moreover, the celebrated fathers are depicted so benignly that one gets no sense of the harshness with which they imposed some of their initial edicts. They separated all couples, for example, who had only the benefit of "fur trade" marriages until they could be properly instructed and reunited with priestly blessing.

In addition, the text paints the political situation so broadly that one gets little indication of the volatility of the whole area. The geographical struggle among England, Canada and the United States was a central trope in the activities of the Hudson Bay Company as was the ongoing rivalry between the Catholic and Methodist missionaries in their quests for converts among the native peoples. The Catholic historian Wilfred Schoenberg has remarked that, "the presence of Catholic missionaries, the [Hudson Bay] Company had learned, tended to pacify most Indians. Priests brought peace and order in their wake, and the company could do well to have them as allies in the event of trouble."[13]

And how does *The Flotilla of Faith* depict these events and native peoples? Has the attitude among the Federal Theatre personnel in Region V changed from the "reasonably civilized" days three years earlier? For the most part, the pageant draws upon traditional stereotypes. It opens with a rousing Indian dance which features three "smoke bombs" and builds to a "frenzied climax." Shortly after the white renegade sells them whiskey, the Indians perform a vigorous "War Dance." They are cowed, however, by the saintly McLoughlin who is "father" to all the tribes. He commands them not to attack the Americans and punishes the renegade who helped to excite them. There is also some comic business involving a fat squaw who keeps falling down when celebrating and enthusiastically kisses the wagon master of returning expeditions. Amongst this welter of cliches, however, there is a bit of dialogue – most of the pageant is visual and narrated – which is instructive.

After McLoughlin has secured the promise that the Indians will not attack the new white settlers, the "Chief" says:

White man come. King George man and French man and Boston man. More and more white man come. White man come. Red man die.
McLOUGHLIN
No. No.
CHIEF
My people die. They all die. Soon I will be a chief without a people.
McLOUGHLIN:
I'll do everything I can to help your people.

CHIEF
You help – no good. Your medicine no good. Red man's medicine no good.
Before the white man come, our medicine man make good medicine.
Our people well; our people happy. White man come. Teach my people
many things that are bad. Ignace La Mousse the Iroquois say my people
die because they live bad. He say we need the Blackrobe priests of the
Frenchman to teach us the good way to live.

McLOUGHLIN
I have sent for the Blackrobes.

CHIEF
Then why don't they come? Soon be too late.

McLOUGHLIN
They will come soon. And in the meantime, bring your people to my
house every Sunday and I will teach you what I can of the white man's
religion.

CHIEF
Blackrobe come, then my people live.

McLOUGHLIN
I am not sure that the Blackrobes can keep your people from dying.

CHIEF
Then my people die with the Blackrobe's blessing. Better that way.[14]

Among the estimated 8,000 audience members who viewed *The Flotilla*
were hundreds of priests and nuns; the bishops of Seattle, Spokane, Boise
and Great Falls; Archbishop Edward D. Howard of Portland and the Most
Reverend Amleto Giovanni Cicognani, the apostolic delegate from Pope
Pius XII to the United States. It must have pleased many of them to see the
Church depicted in such utopian garb. Not only did the ravaged Indians cry
out for the presence of the white Blackrobes, but they were so devoted to the
Christianity of the Catholic Church that they actually preferred to die with
the priest's blessing rather than continue life in their heathen ways. But this
was not just artful propaganda. And while it must have flattered the Church
to see itself represented as "saviors" in this imperialist endeavor, the Indians'
desire to bring the Blackrobes west was no dramaturgical device of the
Federal Theatre Project writers but a depiction of events which were played
out many times in nineteenth-century America. The Flatheads rejected
Methodist missionaries because they did not wear the black robes, carry
crucifixes or practice celibacy. The Nez Perce were deeply suspicious of the
Presbyterians for the same reasons, and "Old Ignace" was an actual figure
who made three arduous trips to Saint Louis in search of Blackrobes for

his people before meeting his death at the hands of the Sioux in Nebraska. Time and again Native American people petitioned the Church to send the priests because they had been taught that the smallpox had been sent by God to punish them for their wicked lives. Some of the story here was "right." And in spite of the wooden dialogue, there is a plaintive moment which is quite at odds with the rest of the pageant.

The Flotilla of Faith was written by "Mr. Wight of our staff," but he is silent in the record. Douglas Wight is credited on the title page of the manuscript that survives in the Library of Congress but little else is known about him. He had obviously done his homework, as numerous details in the script attest and he was also able – probably in collaboration with others – to negotiate some of the awkward landscape of the occasion. In attempting to recreate the impact of this huge event and to decipher the issues of representation and religious politics, two things stand out.

First, after all of the emphasis on the Blackrobes and the healing power of the Catholic Church the pageant had a powerfully secular ending, extraordinarily patriotic and nationalistic. After Father Blanchet blessed the assembled multitudes the stage directions require:

TRUMPET
All sing two verses of "America."
TRUMPET
All sing "Star-Spangled Banner."
TRUMPET
The band plays "God Bless America" and all march out singing.

In closing with a rousing version of the future of the Oregon territory and the victory of the United States over the British and Canadians, the pageant enacts a powerful irony on the events to come. For John McLoughlin, Chief Factor of Fort Vancouver and "leading man" in *The Flotilla* who wanted more than anything to see Canada triumph in the Northwest struggle, was "in real life" systematically stripped of his wealth, land, and finally his home by the "Americans" who came to power. In the end the "white eagle," as he was known by the many "Bostons" whom he protected, died a broken and penniless man.

More significantly, however, this symbolic linking of Church and State forecasts the doom of the Native Americans, legitimatizing the exploitation and loss of their lands. The Church was a powerful pacification tool in this process, and while the Jesuits have a strong missionary record, the Catholic establishment played a significant part in the evolution of the Reservation

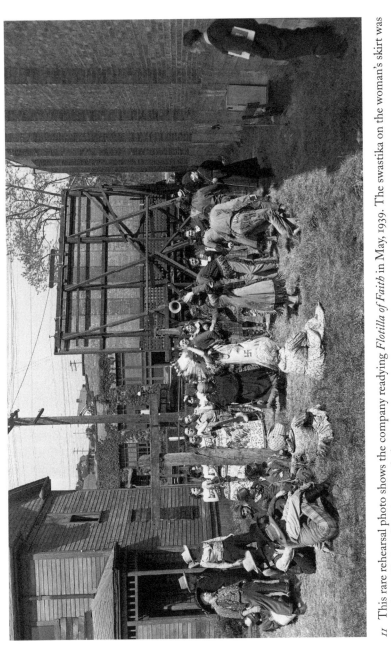

11 This rare rehearsal photo shows the company readying *Flotilla of Faith* in May, 1939. The swastika on the woman's skirt was a prominent Native-American symbol.

system. A hundred years later there is virtually no trace of the "Indian" in *The Flotilla of Faith*. The "natives" were played by the white actors of the Seattle Federal Theatre; their own distinguished Negro Company was at home rehearsing *Dragon's Wishbone*. But the two principal priests, Fathers Demers and Blanchet, were enacted by "real" priests (the Reverends William Robbins and Thomas Gill of Seattle). The stage had been emptied of the "real" Indians just as the land had a century before.

From all accounts, it was a grand success; the newspaper coverage was excellent, and the attendance surpassed their expectations. Even the weather cooperated, with sun and clear skies. Although not mentioned in any of the press reports or summaries, there was one potentially disastrous moment which O'Connor later confided to Hallie Flanagan:

> Of course the highlight of the pageant was the arrival down the Columbia River in a Bateau of the two Priests portraying the rolls of Father Blanchet and Father Demers. As the boat turned into shore it came near capsizing and one of the Priests came very near falling into the river. However, the audiences reaction was not comedy but taken very seriously and a great gasp arose.[15]

The Flotilla of Faith brought the Seattle theatre a remarkable wave of praise and goodwill. The Catholic Church was delighted. William O'Connell, editor of *Northwest Progress*, wrote to Don Abel, the WPA state administrator, praising the artistry of the Federal Theatre and singling out the directing, costuming and pre-show publicity. Ole Ness reported to Flanagan that, "The entire WPA staff was tremendously impressed with the good will and publicity which came as a result of our work with the pageant in Vancouver";[16] a point which Flanagan underscored later in *Arena*. And Ness also commented that the morale in Seattle was excellent "considering the season of the year."

O'Connor was elated. He had had a grand success in response to Flanagan's pageant directive, and he had established some wonderful connections in the Catholic community. In late May he invited the Reverend Father McFadden, superintendent of Catholic schools, to a performance of *Dragon's Wishbone* in the hope of arranging performances in seventeen Catholic grammar schools. "He went rather wild about the performance," wrote O'Connor, "and insists that he is returning next week to see it again."[17] He was also pursuing the State Progress Association to sponsor a statewide tour of *Ah, Wilderness!* and getting ready to direct a production of *Red Harvest* which he wanted to open in July during Seattle's big Naval Week celebration. And, finally, he was trying to clean up and play-doctor the final two productions of the theatre, both by the Negro Company and both directed by Richard Glyer who was neither sympathetic with, nor tolerant of, the shortcomings of the Negro performers.

While the white company was rehearsing and performing for a nationwide radio audience in *The Flotilla of Faith*, the Negro Company was presenting a fantasy under their "Children's Theatre" banner called *The Dragon's Wishbone* and rehearsing an updated "swing" version of *The Taming of the Shrew*. *Wishbone* by Joan and Michael Slane had been secured from the Play Bureau with the promise of an accompanying musical score, and *Shrew* had begun as an adaptation by the Negro Company but had been rewritten by Glyer. Neither went well in rehearsals, and Ole Ness reported in his regional review that they were uninteresting. The music never arrived for *Wishbone* so the talented Howard Biggs simply wrote a new score, but it was not enough to save the production. The actors tried, but their efforts were lost in a welter of scenic fantasy and inept directing. *Shrew* was equally disappointing, and even O'Connor's efforts could not bring it to life. Updated so that Petruchio was now "Pete" (a prizefighter who had sparred with Joe Lewis) and Kate, a feisty New Orleans ingenue, the production was difficult to follow and difficult to understand. In spite of Joe Staton's bravura performance as the "tamer," the critics found it embarrassingly amateur. It was a sad and painful endnote for a company that had been capable of theatrical magic.

Endgame for the Federal Theatre Project had begun in Washington, DC, although there is little recognition of it in Seattle. As the battles raged in Congress over the sins of the Theatre Project and the future of the WPA budget, O'Connor was occupied with the business of running a theatre. He was still chasing his dream of a traveling Showboat as well as planning a new season. Responding once again to Flanagan's desire for Living Newspapers of local subjects, he had encouraged two public relations writers to begin a dramatization of the timber barons and the decimation of America's forests. *Timber* would go into rehearsal for the new season. In DC the friends and foes of Federal Theatre lined up in the House and Senate rehearsing old charges, but in Seattle endgame was remote, and the record remarkably optimistic. There are occasional symptoms that a fever was raging. George Savage, ever optimistic about the promise of a Federal Theatre for writers, fired off a telegram in May to Harry Hopkins – now secretary of commerce – pleading for a reprieve. "Federal Theatre is a monument to your administration of WPA. Please exert every influence to preserve an institution that serves all the people."[18] But such blips were rare. O'Connor seemed confident that the triumph of *Flotilla of Faith* and the promise of his new season would solidify his position and his theatre. He had lost the Showboat battle, but he was impressed with the support that he now saw in the state and in the local WPA. The end was hard. He had just finished crafting a new budget.

Conclusion

Among the Eleanor Roosevelt papers at Hyde Park is a ten-page, single-spaced proposal titled, *Plan for a Government Supported Theatre*. It was written by Hallie Flanagan and dated April 26, 1939. Flanagan sent it to Eleanor Roosevelt on May 24, 1939, along with a two-page letter describing the people whom she had consulted in making the proposal, and asked for Eleanor's reaction. Eleanor gave it to the President sometime during the congressional debate that led to the end of the Federal Theatre. His memo in response is brief and to the point: "No use doing anything about this until the Relief Bill finally passes."[1]

The existence of such a plan is not new information. Flanagan talks about it briefly in *Arena*.[2] What is fascinating is the detail of the plan and the fact that it was prepared at the very time that the Federal Theatre was under heaviest attack. Flanagan knew that the project was in peril, and she was determined to save it, not by continuing it in its present structure, but by transforming it into something which would address the concerns raised in Congress and the country.

The centerpiece of the new proposal is a tax on admissions to plays and films. This tax, for which Flanagan provides ample precedent in several European countries, would then be used to employ theatre professionals, up to 75 percent of whom could qualify for welfare relief. (In *Arena* she says that 50 percent could be from welfare rolls.) Major theatre centers would be established in New York, Chicago and San Francisco to serve as artistic hubs and to coordinate activities in smaller cities. In addition, the Service Bureau of the present FTP would be retained to clear copyrights, circulate scripts and provide technical assistance. All the material resources of the Federal Theatre – lights, paint, props, costumes, etc. – would be transferred to this new organization along with its financial structure and agent-cashier offices. The proposed repertory would also be substantially retained, reflecting Flanagan's concern for children's and ethnic theatres, classical and contemporary works, Living Newspapers, religious plays and pageants. Her vision was that permanent theatres in twenty to thirty American cities would each perform a thirty-six-week season at affordable prices. And the three hubs, or central cities, would provide not only material help, but *ideas* and training for gifted young people. The ultimate goal would be for each theatre to raise enough local support so that it could become a permanent member of the community with active local sponsorship.

The plan is ambitious, carefully researched and presented. Flanagan is very articulate about the value of such a national theatre, arguing that it will have an impact on the theatre industry by building a larger audience base for the product. "It seems logical to believe that any person paying a tax on admission to a theatre, would do so willingly if he realized that this tax would go to stimulate the theatre industry."[3] Moreover, it will be a boon for the movie industry because it will "stimulate" activity by discovering new talent and promoting a vast and progressive audience. Not addressed, however, is why producers in the private sector would *want* to raise their ticket prices in order to support this enterprise, one which sounds very like the Federal Theatre that is about to be abolished. (Flanagan does propose that 10 percent of the tax be set aside each year for a fund which will be beneficial for the "theatre as a whole.")[4] And she was careful to have the whole plan vetted by a distinguished group of theatre professionals including producer Lee Shubert and Frank Gillmore, the president of Actors' Equity.

This new theatre would be run by a director and a board who would be appointed by the President and who would report to whatever government agency was finally authorized to oversee them. Flanagan hoped that there would be a cabinet-level position to supervise this and other national arts organizations. But she is clear in the proposal that she is not just looking for a way to extend current personnel. "The present personnel of the Federal Theatre Project, both relief and non-relief, should be reviewed by an impartial outside board of theatre people with the idea of retaining only such personnel as best can serve the new organization."[5]

The *Plan* is a fascinating document because it represents a critique of the Federal Theatre Project in its closing months by its own director. And, as such, provides an intriguing view of the project's accomplishments and shortcomings. For example, Flanagan seems quite comfortable with the basic structure. From the centrality of the Service Bureau to the three major "Hubs," the new theatre looks pretty much like the old. The mission is familiar: good, low-priced entertainment involving a variety of styles and subjects along with a commitment to touring through areas where theatre is not generally available, developing new plays, training young artists and exploring local subjects and legends. There is a commitment to review all current personnel, but it rings a bit hollow when you consider that every theatre, rehearsal space and laboratory, as well as all Federal Theatre tools, machines and telephones would simply become the property of the new organization. Even issues of local sponsorship, which had been central to the survival of smaller FTP units, are reinforced as desirable goals in the new arrangement, although they would now be augmented by patron subscription lists.

The biggest change would be to move the organization out of the WPA welfare apparatus all together and expand the role of the hub cities. By setting it up on a tax-supported basis, Flanagan believed that the principal difficulties would be ameliorated. Without welfare quotas, theatres would be able to employ up to 75 percent of their people from nonrelief status, thus making a better quality product. And without the WPA umbrella, political meddling in artistic decisions might be banished. (She does not mention censorship anywhere in the proposal.) It's not clear how she can be so optimistic given that the theatre would report to the administration in power, but she is confident that, "Such a plan would create a theatre which would not be dependent upon or swayed by any political party or faction" (3).

It is tempting to posit that some fundamental administrative changes could have converted Federal Theatre into a truly national program. Flanagan's critique, as culled from her 1939 proposal to the President, paints a very cheery picture and suggests that an administrative realignment and strengthening the hubs would enable a professional, national theatre to materialize. But this hypothesis – however promising – is not always useful in evaluating ways in which Federal Theatre participated in the life of various and varied communities. And it may be more fruitful to examine how the project functioned in local communities – in this case Seattle – to discover which goals it was able to maintain, modify or accomplish. In what ways does the experiment in Seattle support Flanagan's critique and optimism? Or, more importantly, what conclusions can we draw about the accomplishments of Federal Theatre based upon the record of its Seattle unit and, by extension, other units across the country?

First, in spite of its often extraordinary efforts, Federal Theatre in Seattle never discovered (or perhaps agreed on) who its audience was. Unlike the entrepreneurial Glenn Hughes who could target both a university and a community constituency – with different theatres and repertoires – Federal Theatre lurched from production to production without a clear sense for whom they were performing. And the state WPA compounded this problem by refusing to help them acquire venues which would stabilize or character- ize their mission. Like many units across the country, they were constrained in terms of nonlabor costs for advertising and promotion, but there were also powerful forces pulling them in different directions. Many of the well- established "New Dealers" such as Anna Roosevelt Boettiger were opposed to socio-political issues and were delighted with a theatre of comic pas- time. Others such as Florence James, however, wanted a theatre more in keeping with Flanagan's often-stated notion of a relevant and committed institution. And many others were content with box office and good show business regardless of the politics involved. Given these tensions, it is not surprising that Federal Theatre could not put down the kind of long-lasting roots in Seattle that Flanagan desired. The repertory reflects the tensions. With a powerful Negro Company, what could have been a more exciting choice than *Big White Fog*, for example? But each time it was considered it was ultimately discarded in favor of something with more song and dance.[6]

Of course, it is easy to reach this conclusion in hindsight. But what is fascinating is that the contradictions were vividly apparent to many people at the time. Of all the hundreds of documents involved in the preparation of this study, none is more insightful than the following review of a little- known play in 1938:

There is a certain element of national irrelevance about many of the productions of the Federal Theatre in Seattle and elsewhere thruout [*sic*] the country that worries me.

Like a good many other Americans, in the past I've looked forward hopefully to the day when we'd have a national theater in this country. But now that we seem to be getting just such an institution handed to us, I wonder.

Every time I think of the government of the United States hiring a man to put on grease paint and impersonate a down-at-heel Austrian baron, for instance, I get a confused feeling.

It seems perfectly natural when a theatre operated on federal money puts on plays and presentations dealing with great national economic and social questions, tho here the question of propaganda is bound to rear its ugly head. But when the government invites me to come and see a melodrama dealing with the financial troubles of a Viennese produce man who's been helping himself to the firm's money, I don't understand what it's all about.[7]

In spite of all the rhetoric about creating a new audience and the very visible transfusion of energy and talent from the network of workers' theatres in

New York City, Federal Theatre in Seattle was not initially aligned with the progressive elements of theatre, but rather with the university – carriage trade alliance that Glenn Hughes had forged. And even though some of their first efforts were produced in conjunction with Florence and Burton James, there was a tension between many of the populist goals of the Project and the demands for a kind of legitimatizing visibility that came with the name and accomplishments of Glenn Hughes. Later, when Edwin O'Connor and others tried to break with that tradition, they were unable to construct a new identity more in keeping with the original mission. O'Connor's complaints were frequently geographical ("our little out-of-the-way theatre"), but by 1938 they had become a theatre in search of an identity that was more than geographical.

Second, with regard to the repeated cries of communism and un-American activities that hectored the Federal Theatre to its demise, there is scant evidence of serious involvement in Seattle. The life of Federal Theatre coincides with the "popular front" in the United States when the Communist Party decided that fascism was a bigger enemy than capitalism, and through its mouthpiece, the Comintern, approved of an alliance with Roosevelt and the New Deal. Moreover, the Federal Theatre – especially in New York – coopted many of the radical/workers' theatres who were unable to subsist on their own. So it is not surprising that there were communists in the program, just as there were in many other organizations and activities. In Seattle, they were much less prominent and not terribly influential. Certainly there were interested parties and moments of opportunity, especially during the period when Florence and Burton James were active. The Jameses, who embraced a widely progressive agenda on many fronts, were suspected of subversive views by numerous people and were ultimately destroyed by the fraudulent Washington State Canwell hearings in 1948. Although much of the official language from the memos of the 1930s is coded, it seems clear that several members of the Federal Theatre in Seattle did not want the Project to fall into the hands of Florence James following the skirmishes after *Power*.[8] When Howard Costigan, the president of the ultra-left Washington Federation, lobbied Edwin O'Connor to get Florence James back on the Project, O'Connor wrote to Flanagan that, "I in turn gave him my reasons for thinking that such an assignment would prove detrimental. After hearing my side of it he assured me that I would hear no more on that score and he felt that I was right."[9] None of the reasons are ever spelled out, but it's clear that the innuendo which eventually led to the convictions of both Florence and Burton for contempt of the Canwell Committee was gathering momentum a decade earlier. The specter of communism was weighty enough to influence policy and personnel selection. But there was no communist presence strong enough to subvert the goals of the enterprise or to justify the suspicions of insecure and/or vengeful people.

Third, reaching any conclusions about the *quality* of the work in Seattle is daunting – especially given Flanagan's initial concession to allow companies to be created – but the notion of "professional" in association with Federal Theatre is problematic. Much of the work was painfully amateurish. Admittedly, there are both semantic and aesthetic judgements at play here, and it would be folly not to recognize the implications of class and hierarchies in reaching any final assessments. Loren Kruger and others have pointed out the varying degrees of "professionalism" on the project.[10] For Flanagan, it was sometimes a negative term, when associated with the traditional Broadway reluctance to experiment or refusal to accept techniques of popular entertainment. But it was also a touchstone for much of her rhetoric about a degree of performance that would help to transform a new American audience. In Seattle, in spite of some inspired performances and some truly provocative productions, the quality of the work was not consistently professional. By this I mean that the histrionic capabilities of many of the performers did not compel one to engage, but rather to groan. Even the Negro Company, which was capable of splendid moments, never seemed to overcome some fundamental speech and articulation shortcomings. The orchestras were especially awful and are repeatedly singled out for derision and lampoon in reviews and commentary. And while there are delightfully heroic stories, such as Florence James turning an unemployed cleaning man into the spitting image of Wendell Wilkie in *Power*, the fact is that, beyond a handful of competent actors, the performance quality was often thin.

Fourth, in spite of these shortcomings (and with inconsistent support from the local WPA), the Seattle unit had some genuine success in developing a theatre that was reflective of, or at least responsive to, local, state and regional issues. All three of the Living Newspapers attempted to underline the hometown situation, whether it was the power from Grand Coulee or enabling legislation for subsidized housing. *See How They Run* was an effective look at both local and national labor problems. *Stevedore* captured the fabric of local waterfront confrontations. And both the *Flotilla of Faith* and *Timber* were direct responses to Flanagan's increasing concern that these theatres become part of the fabric of their individual communities. Owing to frequent rehearsal pressures and other time/money restraints,

these "localizations" were never as complete or incisive as they had been envisioned. But Flanagan's notion of a network of national theatres responding
to regional issues was both credible and prescient. It still complicates the
repertories of modern League of Resident Theatres as they struggle with
season choices that reflect their regional interests as well as their status as
significant professional theatres.[11]

Fifth, the appearance and success of a Negro repertory company in a
remote northern corner of the continental United States was truly an extraordinary event. And the fact that they flourished and graduated alumni
such as Theodore Brown and Howard Biggs into mainstream professional
careers is further testimony to their startling presence. In spite of its liberal
traditions, Seattle could be a deeply racist community, and the history of
the company attests to the paternalism and prejudices which dogged and
thwarted its work. However, the Negro Company survived throughout the
complete tenure of the project, battling for recognition and performing a series of sometimes startling productions. It was a monumental achievement.
In the final analysis, the Negro Repertory Theatre was the centerpiece of
the Seattle unit and symptomatic of what was fundamentally forward looking and decent about the whole New Deal enterprise. That the President
of the United States was unable to sign anti-lynching legislation for fear
of offending his constituency in the south is loathsome. However, that he
was able – with Eleanor's prodding – to campaign for a different kind of
racial project, which would ultimately help to manufacture an ideology of
inclusion, is noteworthy.

Sixth, the research programs were enormously successful. Monies were
allocated and spent appropriately. The theatre history record is detailed and
thorough and was completed on schedule. It remains a valuable resource for
students and scholars of theatre in the Northwest. The models project was
also a splendid accomplishment, and even in their current distressed setting,
they stand as visual tribute to the vision and the craftsmanship of the whole
enterprise. Perhaps the University of Washington will ultimately recognize
their significance and display them in an appropriate museum setting.

Seventh, the legacy of a theatre for children, which is characterized today
by an internationally renowned company in Seattle, owes much to Federal
Theatre productions and accomplishments. While the record is not complete with regard to all the FTP Children's Theatre – especially in the parks
and playgrounds – it is clear that it was an important part of their mission,
particularly in the latter years under Edwin O'Connor and Esther Porter.
Moreover, in a wonderfully ironic way, Glenn Hughes's ability to capture

WPA funds for his own fledgling department would ultimately generate the very community roots that Flanagan was desirous of obtaining with her Federal Theatre. Seattle today owes much of its theatrical vigor to artists who were trained in the university drama school.

And finally, to return to the above-cited Gilbert Brown review of *Tomorrow's a Holiday* for a moment:

> These reflections, of course, have nothing to do with the laudable primary purpose of the Federal Theatre as a WPA project, to provide a modicum of self-respecting work for actors and actresses stranded by the depression and the simultaneous death – or near-death – of the American stage.
>
> *Tomorrow's a Holiday* is a rattling good show, produced and presented remarkably well considering the handicaps under which the Federal Theatre project operates. Along with some merely adequate acting and a few instances of distinctly inferior acting, it offers several rousingly good performances in key roles.
>
> Young Barbara Bettinger, in the leading feminine role, and David Carroll, as the gambling baron who saves Toni, the hero of the play, from discovery and disgrace, turn out corking performances... May be if the Federal Theatres can keep on bringing to light such promising young talent as Barbara Bettinger and David Carroll evidently possess, the whole program won't seem quite so irrelevant as it now does.[12]

Brown touches here on the heart of the program. How can you measure giving a man or a woman "self-respect" as a "professional" in their field? How could black actors imagine themselves as professionals in a field which a year earlier did not exist? The Federal Theatre, like every theatre, fulfilled its goal with each performance, providing a space for unemployed actors to live and create through their imaginations. Each night the stage was emptied, not only of the Barbara Bettingers and David Carrolls, but of *all the artists* who made the work. Like "carving our initials in a block of ice on a summer day," in Arthur Miller's wonderful words, Federal Theatre was here and then gone. Perhaps it shares today in the legacy of the National Endowment for the Arts (NEA) or the Regional League of Resident Theatres (LORT) theatres, or other as yet unconnected phenomena, but it does not need that justification to shore up its achievements. In Seattle, at least, the record is clear. Federal Theatre made a space for actors to perform for audiences in a time and place where they weren't before. This book has tried to reclaim some of what happened, but their achievement was that they were there, and they were paid for their labor with a modest salary, audience approval and their own self-respect.

Appendix A: production calendar

Even though the activities of the Federal Theatre units were reported religiously to Washington, DC, there are still numerous problems involved in regularizing the production calendar. Delayed or postponed openings were sometimes not noted. Specific songs in the children's programs or the vaudeville presentations were mistakenly reported as different *productions*. "Mother Goose on the Loose," for example, is sometimes recorded as a separate play rather than a number in *The Curtain Goes Up* and then confused with the full production of *Mother Goose Goes to Town*. Often programs that played only "on the road" were not included in the record. The following is a list of productions which were presented under the auspices of the Federal Theatre *in* the theatre between 1936 and 1939, for which I have been able to verify an opening night and director. The single exception is *Flotilla of Faith* which played only on the banks of the Columbia River.

Name	Opened	Director
Noah	4-28-36	Burton James
Stevedore	5-13-36	Florence James
Noah (Revival)	6-15-36	Florence James
Stevedore (Revival)	6-16-36	Florence James
Swing, Gate, Swing	6-23-36	Burton James
Lysistrata	9-17-36	Florence James
Hit the Road	9-20-36	Harry Pfeil
It Can't Happen Here	10-27-36	Florence James
The Curtain Goes Up	11-9-36	Guy Williams
Natural Man	1-28-37	Florence James
Blind Alley	3-10-37	Clarence Talbot
In Abraham's Bosom	4-21-37	Florence James

158

Cont.

Name	Opened	Director
The Warrior's Husband	5-26-37	Clarence Talbot
Power	7-6-37	Florence James
O Say Can You Sing	8-5-37	Harry Pfeil
The Clown Prince	8-10-37	Harry Pfeil
The Beggar Prince	8-26-37	Harry Pfeil
Help Yourself	10-5-37	Florence James
Androcles and the Lion	11-1-37	Edwin O'Connor
Pursuit of Happiness	11-22-37	Edwin O'Connor
Mother Goose Goes To Town	12-23-37	Esther Porter
Is Zat So?	12-27-37	Esther Porter
Counsellor-At-Law	1-31-38	Edwin O'Connor
Black Empire	2-14-38	Esther Porter
Flight	3-5-38	Esther Porter
Tomorrow's a Holiday	3-29-38	Edwin O'Connor
Brer Rabbit and the Tar Baby	5-7-38	Esther Porter
One-Third of a Nation	5-23-38	Edwin O'Connor
See How They Run	9-19-38	Edwin O'Connor
An Evening With Dunbar	10-31-38	Joe Staton
Mississippi Rainbow	1-24-39	Herman Moore
Spirochete	2-13-39	Richard Glyer
Ah, Wilderness!	3-29-39	Jan Norman
Flotilla of Faith	5-10-39	Edwin O'Connor
The Dragon's Wishbone	5-13-39	Richard Glyer
Taming of the Shrew	6-19-39	Richard Glyer

Appendix B: glossary of names

Abel, Donald – State director of the WPA during the heyday of the Federal Theatre, he was most famous for the abrupt cancellation of *Lysistrata* and for his opposition to Edwin O'Connor's attempts to secure a showboat.

Biggs, Howard – A musical prodigy, he wrote and composed for the Negro theatre and later had a successful career in New York as a band leader and composer.

Brown, Theodore – Original member of the Negro Company, he acted in *Noah*, wrote *Natural Man* and later was a founding member of the Negro Playwright's Company in Harlem.

Glyer, Richard – Borrowed from the Los Angeles unit after the departure of Esther Porter, he directed the very successful *Spirochete* and then *The Dragon's Wishbone* and *Taming of the Shrew* with the Negro Company.

Hood, George T. – Former theatre manager and producer, he was appointed state supervisor in 1938 to try and bridge some of the personnel gulfs on the project. Considered "old school" by Flanagan and others, he was ousted after the controversy surrounding publicity and ticketing for *One-Third of a Nation*.

Hughes, Glenn – Head of the University of Washington drama department, he was the original director of the Federal Theatre Project in Region V and later one of the most successful producer/teachers in the history of the Northwest.

James, Burton – Co-founder of the Seattle Repertory Playhouse, he was instrumental in creating the Negro Theatre and directed – along with his wife, Florence – their early productions. Burton was later hounded by the Canwell Committee for un-American activities and subsequently lost his health and their theatre in the aftermath of the hearings.

James, Florence – Social activist and theatre director who was responsible for the early successes of the Project. She directed *Power* and later was promoted by many as artistic director of the Seattle project. She, too, was indicted for contempt by the Canwell Committee and after Burton's death moved to Calgary where she continued to direct.

Miller, Howard – One of Hallie Flanagan's trusted confidants, he was a regional director in the West and later deputy national director for the entire Theatre Project.

Ness, Ole – Howard Miller's replacement as regional director, he started on the project in Los Angeles and later reported to Flanagan on all the West Coast units.

O'Connor, Edwin – The last artistic director, O'Connor was widely respected and responsible for stabilizing the project. He directed, among others, *One-Third of a Nation*, *See How They Run* and *Flotilla of Faith*.

Porter, Esther – A former student of Hallie Flanagan at Vassar, she came to Seattle to work with the Negro Company and the Children's Theatre. She directed *Black Empire*, *Mother Goose* and *Flight* and then resigned in the fallout following *One-Third of a Nation*.

Power, Francis – Agent-cashier for the company, Power was a supporter of the Florence James faction and also resigned when George Hood was appointed acting director. Power later married Esther Porter.

Pfeil, Harry – One of the original members of the project, Pfeil directed and produced the vaudeville units and musical entertainments. He also supervised the touring units in the CCC camps and was instrumental in writing and arranging the vaudeville shows.

Talbot, Clarence – Director of the Tacoma, WA production of *It Can't Happen Here* and the ill-fated Northwest New Playwrights series, he also directed *Blind Alley* and *The Warrior's Husband* for the Seattle unit.

Savage, George – Winner of the first – and only – Federal Theatre national playwriting contest, he taught English at the University of Washington and lobbied for a New York production of his prize-winning labor drama, *See How They Run*.

Staton, Joseph – Principal actor of the Negro Company, he played many leading roles and was instrumental in creating and directing one of their most successful plays, *An Evening With Dunbar*.

Williams, Guy – Student of Glenn Hughes, he was active in setting up the Project and eventually served as state director when Hughes, frustrated with red tape, withdrew from active participation in Federal Theatre. Flanagan later named Williams to supervise touring shows in the Northwest.

Notes

Introduction

1. While the *Ethiopia* incident was a blow, Flanagan sought to put the best face on it. In fact the first "official" historian of the project, Willson Whitman, described it this way barely two years later: "[that ruling] was a wise one...It is difficult enough to make Nazi or Fascist powers understand that a free country assumes no responsibility for the remarks of mayors or the press. It would be almost impossible to explain an insult attributable to a government-supported theatre." Willson Whitman, *Bread and Circuses* (New York: Oxford University Press, 1937), p. 94.

2. Federal Theatre Project Report, *Relation of Admission Receipts to Project Costs*, June 9, 1939, Record Group (RG) 69, National Archives (NA).

3. Audience Survey Report, *Help Yourself*, Seattle, Washington, Oct. 10, 1937, RG 69, NA. Unfortunately these surveys were discontinued in 1937 and many others were lost after the project was closed, but the ones that survive provide fascinating insights. The "occupational classifications" include Professional, The Arts, Trades and Manual Labor, Commercial, Office and Miscellaneous. This latter included housewives, students and social workers.

4. George Jean Nathan, "A Government in Greasepaint," *Newsweek* (April 18, 1938): 25.

5. A notable exception to much of the record is Paul Sporn's 1995 study of the Midwest units, *Against Itself* (Wayne State University Press) in which he also examines the Federal Writers Project from a "worm's eye view" and against the background of American capitalism and what he terms "industrial regionalism."

6. Loren Kruger, *The National Stage* (University of Chicago Press, 1992), p. 183.

1 A showboat for the people

1. O'Connor reported to his boss Ole M. Ness that "several labor groups" were anxious to sponsor Federal theatre but they ran into the same complaints about propaganda. Edwin O'Connor to Ole M. Ness, Nov. 18, 1938, RG 69, NA.

2. O'Connor to Ness, Nov. 18, 1938, RG 69, NA.

3. *Ibid.*

4. *Ibid.*

5. Hallie Flanagan to George Kondolf, June 17, 1937, RG 69, NA.
6. Jane Mathews, *The Federal Theatre, 1935–1939* (Princeton University Press, 1967), p. 192.
7. Edwin O'Connor to Howard Miller, Dec. 31, 1938, RG 69, NA.
8. Abel had closed the Negro unit's production of *Lysistrata* in 1936 after one performance because it was reported to be "offensive." See Chapter 5. After a huge controversy, his ruling stood and he agreed to refrain from further interference. Still, like WPA state administrators everywhere, Abel resented having his authority questioned. In a 1965 interview for the Smithsonian *Archives of American Art*, he told Dorothy Bestor that "There were always, or practically always, one or more assistants of Mr. Hopkins in the State of Washington, checking on various phases of the work and informing myself as well as the national offices as to the operation. But, generally speaking, the State Administrator had complete authority to hire and fire and carry out the functions of the WPA." (See Abel interview, p. 1.)
9. Edwin O'Connor to Hallie Flanagan, March 24, 1939.
10. *Ibid.*
11. Hallie Flanagan to Glenn Hughes, Oct. 4, 1937, RG 69, NA.
12. Quoted in O'Connor to Flanagan, March 24, 1939, RG 69, NA.
13. *Ibid.*
14. *Ibid.*
15. Quoted in William F. McDonald, *Federal Relief Administration and the Arts* (Columbus: Ohio State University Press, 1969), p. 131.
16. *Ibid.*, p. 519.
17. Hallie Flanagan to Harry Hopkins, May 1, 1936, FDR Library, Hyde Park, New York.
18. McDonald, *Federal Relief Administration*, p. 111.
19. For a discussion of some of the censorship battles see Barry Witham, "Censorship in the Federal Theatre," *Theatre History Studies*, 17 (1997): 3–14.
20. These "parallel" business programs were staffed by unemployed workers in closed plants where products could be sold in company stores for script.
21. Howard Costigan to Hallie Flanagan, April 26, 1939, RG 69, NA.
22. John Boettiger to FDR, May 19, 1937, Roosevelt Correspondence, FDR Library, Hyde Park, NY.
23. *Ibid.* Bridges was investigated on several occasions for possible deportation but managed to outfox his persecutors. In 1993 the University of Washington honored him by creating the Harry Bridges Chair in Labor Studies.
24. Mary Dewson to Anna Roosevelt Boettiger, Dec. 9, 1936, Roosevelt Correspondence, FDR Library, Hyde Park, NY.
25. Howard Costigan to Hallie Flanagan, May 15, 1939, RG 69, NA.
26. Anna Roosevelt Boettiger to Hallie Flanagan, May 19, 1939, RG 69, NA.
27. The actress's father was Speaker of the House and her uncle a prominent Senator from Alabama. Talullah's heartfelt pleas to save the program were widely reported in the press and chronicled in Jane Mathews, *The Federal Theatre*, p. 284.
28. Hallie Flanagan to Howard Costigan, June 13, 1939, RG 69, NA.

2 Glenn's plan

1. Gordon Craig to Hallie Flanagan, Aug. 9, 1935, RG 69, NA. Flanagan had met Craig in Copenhagen in 1926 where he was directing *The Pretenders*. She attended some rehearsals and later dined with him at the Copenhagen Oyster House where he charmed her with his wit and theatrical imagination. Her account of their meetings became a delightful chapter in her first book, *Shifting Scenes of the Modern European Theatre* (New York: Coward-McCann, 1928).
2. Rice was the author of a number of successful Broadway productions including *On Trial* (1914), *The Adding Machine* (1923) and *Street Scene* (1929). But he was also widely admired for his commitment to social causes such as the National Child Labor Committee and the American Civil Liberties Union.
3. Barrett Clark to Glenn Hughes, Aug. 8, 1935, RG 69, NA.
4. The National Theatre Conference still exists and meets annually at the Players Club in New York City to socialize and discuss issues of concern to American theatre. Among its important achievements were the publication of a series of influential texts including Richard Boleslavski's, *Acting: The First Six Lessons* (1933) and Stanley McCandless's *A Method of Lighting the Stage* (1932); a series of fellowships which enabled talented theatre people to travel or study; and, currently, achievement and playwriting awards. Membership is limited to 125 "leaders of the American Theatre." See Tino Balio and Lee Norvelle, *The History of the National Theatre Conference* (New York: National Theatre Conference, 1968). Hallie Flanagan was a member of the executive committee in 1943–44 and a trustee in 1948–49.
5. Flanagan, *Arena* (New York: Duell, Sloan and Pearce, 1940), p. 29. She estimated that there would be approximately 10,000 people at the outset.
6. Hallie Flanagan to Glenn Hughes, Aug. 9, 1935, RG 69, NA.
7. Flanagan, *Arena*, p. 30.
8. Enclosed as part of a letter from Glenn Hughes to Hallie Flanagan, Aug. 17, 1935, RG 69, NA.
9. In the state of Washington he identified ten cities (including Seattle) with the appropriate population bringing the total number of proposed theatres to thirteen.
10. Hallie Flanagan to Glenn Hughes, Aug. 24, 1935, RG 69, NA.
11. Jane Mathews, *The Federal Theatre* (Princeton University Press, 1962), p. 35.
12. Hallie Flanagan to Glenn Hughes, Sept. 13, 1935, RG 69, NA.
13. Glenn Hughes to Hallie Flanagan, Sept. 12, 1935, RG 69, NA.
14. Glenn Hughes to Hallie Flanagan, Sept. 16, 1935, RG 69, NA.
15. Glenn Hughes telegram to Hallie Flanagan, Sept. 18, 1935, RG 69, NA.
16. Flanagan to Hughes, Sept. 20, 1935, RG 69, NA. My italics.
17. Flanagan, *Arena*, p. 45.
18. *Ibid*.
19. *Ibid*.
20. Flanagan to Hughes, Oct. 14, 1935, RG 69, NA.
21. Toinette Swan to Hallie Flanagan, Oct. 18, 1935, RG 69, NA.
22. Burton James to Hallie Flanagan, Oct. 7, 1935, RG 69, NA.
23. Hughes to Flanagan, Oct. 16, 1935, RG 69, NA.

24. Paul Sporn provides a graphic description of the administrative web which frustrated and thwarted many of the original members of the project. "In order to get the Michigan Theatre Project started, authorization documents had to be sent from three different sources to administrators at three different points in the organizational structure of the WPA. In a letter dated October 14, 1935, Flanagan commissioned Thomas Wood Stevens, regional director of the FTP for the Midwest, to oversee theatre projects in Michigan. At the same time, she informed the Michigan director of the WPA, Harry Lynn Pierson, of Stevens's commission. Four days later, Bruce McClure, the national director of Professional and Service Projects, sent Pierson his seal of approval authorizing Stevens's work in Michigan. Almost a month later, on November 12, Flanagan addressed a memo to McClure and Jacob Baker, the assistant administrator for Federal One, informing them that Stevens was about to start a theatre project with fifty people in Detroit at the Bonstelle Playhouse and hence $20,000 should be allotted for six months. Presumably, either Baker or McClure or both authorized the state WPA to release money for the theatre project, but unfortunately documents to demonstrate this are now waylaid in the maze." Paul Sporn, *Against Itself* (Detroit: Wayne State University Press, 1995), p. 168.
25. Hughes to Flanagan, Oct. 23, 1935, RG 69, NA.
26. Flanagan to Hughes, Nov. 4, 1935, RG 69, NA.

3 Hoofers, mystics and a singing bird

1. Williams to Flanagan, April 13, 1936, RG 69, NA.
2. Vaudeville routines from "two liners" and more which built quickly to a punch line followed by an immediate light blackout. "Have you got worms?" "Yup, but I'm going fishin' anyway."
3. MPTONW to George Gannon, Feb. 3, 1936, RG 69, NA.
4. George Gannon to Glenn Hughes, Feb. 6, 1936, RG 69, NA.
5. Flanagan, *Arena*, p. 158. Flanagan was incensed about the false newspaper reporting and recorded, "Thus 165 professional people on relief rolls and qualified for theatre work were thrown out of their chance for re-employment by a newspaper falsehood about a woman who was never on the Federal Theatre in any capacity whatsoever."
6. *Ibid.*, p. 174.
7. The extent to which some people in the theatre mistrusted the CCC is apparent in the production of *Young Go First*, the initial offering of New York's Theatre of Action in May 1935. This expose of the abuse of young men at the Blue Hill Mountain Camp marked the directorial debut of Elia Kazan. It was written by Peter Martin, George Scudder and Charles Friedman with designs by Mordecai Gorelik and ran for thirty-nine performances.
8. Robert Ermentrout, who commanded a camp in Wisconsin, recalled that, "a thief caught in the act was whipped with belts up and down the center of the barracks. When the barracks leader judged the thief had had enough, the end door was opened allowing the thief to escape. He never came back. After thirty days he was awarded a dishonorable discharge for desertion." See *Forgotten Men* (Smithtown, NY: Exposition Press, 1982), p. 90.

9. *Manual of Recreational Activities for Young Men's Work Camps* prepared by the National Recreation Association, 315 Fourth Ave., New York. n.d., 65–6.
10. These statistics are from a monograph titled *The Civilian Conservation Corps in the State of Washington*, compiled by Margaret E. Thomas and published by the Department of Social Security, State of Washington, Olympia, WA, May, 1937.
11. The following narratives are from *Weekly Reports of CCC Revue Tour* kept by Company Manager, Harry Pelletier, RG 69, NA.
12. Guy Williams to Hallie Flanagan, April 13, 1936, RG 69, NA.
13. Howard Miller to Hallie Flanagan, May 21, 1936, RG 69, NA. Miller is referring to George Gannon who had been replaced by Don Abel.
14. Memorandum from Harry Pfeil to William Muehlman, July 20, 1936, RG. 69, NA.
15. Memorandum from Mr. McCulloch to Harry Pfeil, Aug. [n.d.], 1936, RG 69, NA.
16. The account was prepared to be published in the *Federal Theatre Magazine* and thus has a certain self-serving and self-conscious quality but it does provide an intriguing glimpse of the space and event.
17. I believe the reference here is to class, referring to the speech of educated Easterners with their Boston accents.
18. Guy Williams, RG 69, NA.
19. Report from Fran Power to Harry Pfeil on "Hill Billy Unit," May 2, 1936, RG 69, NA.
20. Memorandum from Harry A. Pfeil, Supervising Director to Mr. Fran Power, Treasurer, May 2, 1936, RG 69, NA.
21. Beyond routine press releases not much information has survived about the Baron Knights. However, Syvilla Fort, who appeared with them in *Transom Blues*, later had a distinguished career as a dancer with the Katherine Dunham Company and then ran her own studio in New York.
22. Report from Harry Pfeil to Guy Williams, June 7, 1937, RG 69, NA.
23. Report from Fran Power to Guy Williams, April 2, 1937, RG 69, NA.
24. William Farnsworth to Lawrence Morris, Feb. 20, 1937, RG 69 NA.

4 Typists and models

1. Interview with Barbara Sauntry, May 7, 1998, Seattle, WA.
2. Flanagan, *Arena* (New York: Duell, Sloan and Pearce, 1940), p. 98.
3. *Ibid.*, p. 267.
4. The research project was initially identified as 815-1 but as the classification system changed it became 1951-1 in May 1936 and then 7002-E in September 1936.
5. Glenn Hughes, "Foreword" to *The Story of Seattle's Early Theatres*, compiled by Howard F. Grant (Seattle: University Bookstore, 1934).
6. Memo from Howard Grant to Guy Williams, State Director, December 16, 1936, RG 69, NA.
7. *Ibid.*
8. Grant to Williams, "Report of Work Accomplished," Dec. 16, 1936, RG 69, NA.
9. The article, "The Pioneer Theater in Washington," was published in *The Pacific Northwest Quarterly*, April 1937, 115–36 and provides an excellent synopsis of the materials in the collection.

10. Glenn Hughes, "Foreword" to Eugene Clinton Elliott, *A History of Variety-Vaudeville in Seattle* (Seattle: University of Washington Press, 1944).

11. Mary Katherine Rohrer, *The History of Seattle Stock Companies* (Seattle: University of Washington Press, 1945), xi.

12. Hallie Flanagan to Ellen S. Woodward, Nov. 4, 1937, RG 69, NA. Although Hughes later concluded that the whole project was "essentially ephemeral," he was generous in his appraisal of Flanagan: "She was social-minded, idealistic, incorruptible and fearless." Glenn Hughes, *A History of the American Theatre, 1790–1950* (New York: Samuel French, 1951), p. 423.

13. Flanagan to Woodward, Nov. 4, 1937, RG 69, NA.

14. Hughes to Flanagan, Nov. 25, 1935, RG 69, NA. My italics.

15. Lester Lang to Glenn Hughes, Jan. 31, 1936, RG 69, NA.

16. Guy Williams to Lester E. Lang, Feb. 17, 1936, RG 69, NA.

17. J. Howard Miller to Guy Williams, July 23, 1936, RG 69, NA.

18. Over the next few month, however, three more "supervisors" on nonrelief status were added to this project. This probably reflected the need to accomplish the detail painting as well as the largesse of the FTP in its first year. Before the big cuts came in 1937 some units were exempting up to 25 percent of their workers from relief certification.

19. Report from Fran Power to Guy Williams, Dec. 2, 1936, RG 69, NA.

20. *Ibid.*

21. *Ibid.*

22. Report from Fran Power to Guy Williams, April 2, 1937, RG 69, NA.

23. Flanagan to Woodward, Nov. 4, 1937, RG 69, NA.

24. *Ibid.*

25. Glenn Hughes to George Hood, Dec. 7, 1937, RG 69, NA.

26. Glenn Hughes to J. Howard Miller, Feb. 28, 1939, RG 69, NA.

27. Glenn Hughes to Edwin G. O'Connor, Feb. 19, 1939, RG 69. NA.

28. Edwin G. O'Connor to Glenn Hughes, March 1, 1939, RG 69, NA.

29. J. Howard Miller to Ole Ness, Jan. 4, 1939, RG 69, NA.

5 A Negro theatre

1. Interview with lighting designer Marion McGinnis, Bellevue, WA, Nov. 13, 1987.

2. Hallie Flanagan, "Personal Notes, 1935–39," Nov. 2, 1937, New York Public Library.

3. "Drastic Plan for Reduction Based on Hopkins Letter," June 8, 1937, RG 69, NA.

4. Richard Glyer, "Director's Report," *The Dragon's Wishbone*, Seattle, WA, May, 1939, Federal Theatre Collection (FTC), Library of Congress (LOC).

5. See Barry Witham, "The Playhouse and the Theatre," in Sue-Ellen Case and Janelle Reinelt, eds., *The Performance of Power* (University of Iowa Press, 1991), pp. 146–62 and Mark Jenkins, *All Powers Necessary and Convenient* (University of Washington Press, 1999).

6. Glenn Hughes to R.P. Ballard, Jan. 29, 1928, Seattle Repertory Playhouse Files, University of Washington.

7. Glenn Hughes to Burton James, Aug. 31, 1928, Seattle Repertory Playhouse Files, University of Washington. He also reported on his playgoing and pronounced

The Royal Family amusing, *Diamond Lil* a washout, *Volpone* very good and *Porgy* excellent.

8. Glenn Hughes to Jeffrey Heiman, March 29, 1934, SRP Files, UW
9. Esther Hall Mumford, *Seven Stars and Orion* (Seattle: Ananse Press, 1980), p. 70.
10. Burton James to Hallie Flanagan, Oct. 7, 1935, RG 69, NA.
11. It is curious that there did not seem to be any interest in the thousands of Native Americans whose treaties had been broken, whose lands had been appropriated and who were a substantial minority population in Seattle rather than several hundred blacks who had been imported from the east and south.
12. Evamarii Johnson suggests that Jackson and Frederick Darby, an aspiring actor, had submitted their own proposal for a Negro unit but had been denied because they had no facilities nor could they identify experienced Negro performers. See Evamarii A. Johnson, "A Production History of the Seattle Federal Theatre Project Negro Company, 1935–39," Ph.D dissertation, University of Washington, 1981, p. 24.
13. Hood to Flanagan, Dec. 9, 1935, RG 69, NA.
14. Flanagan to Messrs. Baker and McClure, Jan. 13, 1936, RG 69, NA. She attached telegrams from George Gannon and Glenn Hughes to support her request and added that "I feel that the work of this project merits such an additional non-relief exemption."
15. Hood to Fran Power, Jan. 31, 1936, SRP Papers, UW.
16. Johnson, "Production History," p. 41.
17. Hood to Burton James, Feb. 12, 1936, SRP Papers, UW.
18. The producer, stage manager, technical director, musical director, and accompanist were all listed as nonrelief.
19. Flanagan to Woodward, Nov. 4, 1937, RG 69, NA.
20. Quoted in Mumford, *Seven Stars*, p. 72.
21. Production book, Technical reports, FTC, LOC.
22. Mumford, *Seven Stars*, p. 76.
23. Interview with Joe Staton conducted by John O'Connor, Seattle, WA, Jan. 7, 1976, p. 18.
24. Fran Power to Guy Williams, April 2, 1937, NA.
25. Robert St. Clair to Hallie Flanagan, Sept. 19, 1936, RG 69, NA.
26. Guy Williams to Hallie Flanagan, Sept. 19, 1936, RG 69, NA.
27. Transcript of telephone conversation between William Farnsworth and Guy Williams, Sept. 23, 1936, RG 69, NA.
28. Miller to Hallie Flanagan, Sept. 26, 1936, RG 69, NA.
29. *Ibid.*
30. *Ibid.*
31. For an analysis of the *Lysistrata* closing see Ron West, "Others, Adults, Censored: The Federal Theatre Project's Black *Lysistrata* Cancellation," *Theatre Survey*, 37:2 (Nov., 1996): 93–113.
32. Miller to Flanagan, Sept. 28, 1936, RG 69, NA.
33. Flanagan to Miller, Oct. 5, 1936, RG 69, NA.
34. Miller to Flanagan, May 12, 1936, RG 69, NA.
35. Production Report, FTP Collection, LOC.
36. *Seattle Argus*, Oct. 31, 1936.

37. *Seattle Commonwealth News*, Oct. 31, 1936.
38. *Natural Man* was subsequently produced by the American Negro Theatre in Harlem on May 7, 1941. Theodore Brown was active in the company which was founded in 1940 by Abram Hill and Frederick O'Neal.
39. Mumford, *Seven Stars*, pp. 72–3. My italics.
40. *Ibid.*
41. For an excellent discussion of the Negro units of the FTP, particularly with regard to their "natural" ability to sing and perform, see Rena Fraden, *Blueprints for a Black Federal Theatre, 1935–1939* (Cambridge, 1994), pp. 168–95.

6 *Power* and control

1. The origins and impact of this documentary form have been debated by a variety of scholars and historians. Certainly Flanagan was aware of the Russian "blue blouses," since she had seen them perform in Russia and recorded her impressions in *Shifting Scenes* (New York: Coward-McCann, 1978). But she was adamant that the FTP version was as "American as Walt Disney, the March of Time and the *Congressional Record*" (Flanagan, *Arena* [New York: Duell, Sloan and Pearce, 1940], p. 70). For an excellent overview of the Living Newspapers, particularly with regard to how they functioned within the ideological structure of the FTP, see Kruger, *The National Stage* (University of Chicago Press, 1992), pp. 158–84.
2. Flanagan, *Arena*, p. 70.
3. For an analysis of race relations in Seattle see Quintard Taylor, *The Forging of a Black Community* (Seattle: University of Washington Press, 1994).
4. Scrapbook collection of City Light, 1936, Manuscript Division, University of Washington Libraries.
5. *Radio Broadcasts*, July, 1937, Library of Seattle, City Light, Seattle, Washington.
6. Arthur Arent, *Power*. Promptbook for the Seattle production, Papers of the Seattle Repertory Playhouse, University of Washington Libraries.
7. Production report on *Power* in Seattle, FTC, LOC.
8. Letter from Bob Beck to J.D. Ross, May 4, 1937, Seattle City Light Papers, UW.
9. W.J. McKeen to J.D. Ross, May 25, 1937, Seattle City Light Papers, UW.
10. Beck letter, May 4, 1937.
11. Pete Spowart to J.D. Ross, June 16, 1937, Seattle City Light Papers, UW.
12. Memorandum from J.W. Ferguson to W.J. McKeen, June 16, 1937, Seattle City Light Papers, UW.
13. They failed along with dozens of others who pleaded for exceptions that week, including Orson Welles and John Houseman in New York.
14. Florence James, "Fists Upon a Star," unpublished manuscript, Florence James Papers, UW, ch. 6, p. 10.
15. *Ibid.*, p. 11.
16. Charges of "mixing" the races were prominent in testimony against her during the infamous Canwell hearings in 1948. See Vern Countryman, *Un-American Activities in Washington State*, Ithaca: Cornell University Press, 1951.
17. Flanagan, *Arena*, p. 306.
18. *Seattle Times*, July 7, 1937.

19. *Seattle Post-Intelligencer*, July 7, 1937.
20. *Seattle Argus*, July 31, 1937.
21. *Seattle Post-Intelligencer*, July 8, 1937.
22. Clarence Talbot to Howard Miller, Aug. 27, 1937, RG 69, NA.
23. Hallie Flanagan to Helen Woodward, Nov. 4, 1937, RG 69, NA.
24. "Greetings" memorandum from George Hood to Federal Theatre employees, Sept. 16, 1937, RG 69, NA.

7 *Dunbar* and the children

1. Hallie Flanagan to Ellen Woodward, Nov. 4, 1937, RG 69, NA.
2. The issue of control and leadership of the numerous Negro units has been a subject of ongoing investigation and controversy. With respect to the New York project and the decision to appoint John Houseman rather than the black actress Rose McClendon, Rena Fraden comments that, "It would seem that no one in the upper echelons of the FTP (all of whom were white) believed that a black person had the necessary clout and respect to run a Negro unit; and since the black community itself was unsure on this point, codirection seemed a viable compromise." Fraden, *Blueprints for a Federal Black Theatre, 1935–1939* (New York: Cambridge University Press, 1994), p. 96.
3. Letter from Esther Porter to Barry Witham, Oct. 6, 1992.
4. Reprinted in Production Report, FTC, LOC.
5. Evamarii Johnson, "A Production History of the Seattle Federal Theatre Project Negro Company, 1935–1939," Ph.D dissertation, University of Washington, 1981, p. 117.
6. Interview with Esther Porter, quoted in Johnson, "A Production History," p. 140. Porter later admitted that the choice to pursue an Aunt Jemima image was probably thoughtless, and she characterized Oliver's reaction as "fascinating."
7. *Ibid.*, p. 144.
8. *Ibid.*
9. "The Federal Theatre had rented this little old theatre place way out east of main Seattle on the road to Mount Rainier, a lovely walk in the morning, you know straight towards the mountain on clear days. But I can't explain how suburban the location was . . . It's like kind of a movie theatre alone by itself – I can't even remember any stores around. Just sort of a space, way out east." Porter quoted in Johnson, "A Production History," p. 115.
10. Porter also fell in love with – and later married – John Francis ("Fran") Power who was the agent-cashier on the Seattle project and one of those who had been closely allied with the "James faction" after the production of *Power*. Fran Power died in 1941. Porter to Witham, July 3, 1992.
11. Ole Ness to Hallie Flanagan, *Weekly Report*, n.d. From internal evidence April 21, 1938, RG 69, NA. Ness reviews for Flanagan the whole bitter dispute between the two factions in Seattle and advances a compromise to address the major issues.
12. Johnson, "A Production History," p. 51.
13. Howard Biggs later played piano for Ruthie Brown and Charles Mingus and wrote 'I'm Gonna Sit Right Down & Cry (Over You)' which was recorded by a number of artists including Elvis Presley and The Beatles.
14. Staton interview, p. 5.

15. O'Connor to Miller, Oct. 29, 1938, RG. 69, NA.

16. Staton, Production Report, FTC, LOC.

17. The National Youth Administration was funding three female members of the company and they had strict regulations about working hours. As in many of the projects, there was tension between the NYA who wanted to return youngsters to regular employment and the FTP who wanted to hold on to talented performers.

18. O'Connor to Miller, Oct. 29, 1938, RG 69, NA.

19. *"An Evening with Dunbar* Smash Hit," *The Northwest Enterprise*, Nov. 4, 1938.

20. *Ibid.*

21. Ken Lightburn, "Negro Folk Opera Has Opening," the *Seattle Star*, Nov. 1, 1938.

22. "Negro Players Open Folk Opera at Metropolitan," the *Seattle Times*, Nov. 1, 1938.

23. Lightburn, "Negro Folk Opera."

24. J. Willis Sayre, "WPA Negro Troupe Seen in New Play," *Seattle Post-Intelligencer*, Nov. 1, 1938.

25. Lightburn, "Negro Folk Opera."

26. O'Connor to Miller, Oct. 29, 1938, RG 69, NA.

8 Slums and syphilis

1. Miller to Flanagan, May 12, 1936, RG 69, NA.

2. Miller to Guy Williams, July 30, 1937, RG 69, NA.

3. Flanagan to Ellen Woodward, Nov. 4, 1937, RG 69, NA.

4. Richard C. Berner, *Seattle, 1921–1940, From Boom to Bust* (Seattle: Charles Press, 1992), p. 183.

5. Production Report, FTC, LOC.

6. Ole Ness to Hallie Flanagan, June 1, 1938, FTC, LOC.

7. Flanagan, *Arena* (New York: Duell, Sloan and Pearce, 1940), p. 309.

8. Ness to Flanagan, June 2, 1938, FTC, LOC.

9. Ness to Flanagan, June 1, 1938, RG 69, NA.

10. Figures are quoted from Ness to Howard Miller, June 29, 1938, RG 69, NA.

11. *Ibid.* My italics.

12. Ness to Flanagan, Weekly Report, April 30, 1938, RG 69, NA.

13. Ness to Flanagan, Weekly Report, Feb. 19, 1938, RG 69, NA.

14. Ness to Flanagan, Weekly Report, May 22, 1938, RG 69, NA.

15. Ness and Taylor Snow to George T. Hood, Dec. 14, 1937, RG 69, NA.

16. Ness to Miller, June 29, 1938, RG 69, NA. These re-paid funds were probably from the box office receipts of *One-Third of a Nation*.

17. Berner, *Seattle, 1921–1940*, p.186.

18. Ness to Flanagan, June 1, 1938, RG 69, NA.

19. For a review of the Chicago and Philadelphia productions, see John S. O'Connor, *"Spirochete* and the War on Syphilis," *The Drama Review* 21:1 (March, 1977): 91–8.

20. See Alan M. Brandt, *No Magic Bullet* (New York: Oxford University Press, 1985), p. 152.

21. John S. O'Connor, *"Spirochete,"* 96. In subsequent productions and the printed text of the play there is reference to "a sea captain in 1493."

22. Ragnar T. Westman, ed., *Annual Report and Survey* (Seattle: Health and Sanitation Department, 1939).

23. See letter from Harriet Silverman of the New York Conference to Cynthia Ulrich of the Seattle Committee outlining plans for New York support of the Wagner Act dated April 28, 1939 in Robert E. Burke Collection, University of Washington Libraries.

24. Thomas Parron, *Shadow on the Land* (New York: Kendal and Hitchcock, 1937).

25. *Bulletin* of the King County Medical Society (Feb. 6, 1939): 21.

26. Handbill from *Spirochete*, Seattle, 1939, RG 69, NA.

27. Arnold Sundgaard, ed., *Spirochete* in *Federal Theatre Plays* (New York: Random House, 1938), p. 62.

28. *Spirochete* Production Report, FTC, LOC.

29. Z.A. Vane to Edwin O'Connor, Feb. 21, 1939, FTC, LOC.

30. See Edwin O'Connor to Howard Miller, Feb. 28, 1939, RG 69, NA.

31. *Seattle Post-Intelligencer*, Feb. 14, 1939.

32. *Seattle Star*, Mar. 9, 1939.

33. *Bulletin* (April 1939): 19.

34. Flanagan, *Arena*, p. 309.

9 See How They Run

1. From the press release quoted in the *Des Moines Register*, Aug. 17, 1937, FTC, LOC.

2. Converse Tyler to Ben Russak, *Inter-Play Bureau Memorandum*, Oct. 4, 1937, FTC, LOC.

3. Converse Tyler to John McGee, Dec. 29, 1937, FTC, LOC.

4. It appears that the anonymity was honored throughout the contest. In the subsequent judging the plays are only referred to by number. There is a single master list in the FTP collection at the Library of Congress which identifies the authors: #20 – Charles Allen Smart; #60 – George M. Savage; #194 – Walter Abbott; #221 – Irving W. Baker; #397 – Atlee and Van Zandt; #523 – Whitfield Cook; and #552 – Isabel Barber.

5. Richard Lockridge to Converse Tyler, Feb. 8, 1938, FTC, LOC.

6. Lockridge to Tyler, Feb. 21, 1938, FTC, LOC.

7. Lockridge to Tyler, Feb. 25, 1938, FTC, LOC.

8. Lloyd Lewis to Converse Tyler, March 2, 1938, FTC, LOC.

9. Lockridge to Tyler, March 11, 1938, FTC, LOC.

10. Fifty dollars for a full week of six to eight performances. See Fink to Savage, Dec. 16, 1937, George Savage Papers, University of Washington Libraries.

11. Personal interview, Seattle, WA, May 24, 2000. Savage, who was only two when *See How They Run* was produced, speaks warmly about his father's ability to "listen and be an excellent play doctor." He believes that his best play is *The Garbage Hustler*.

12. Fishbein to Converse Taylor, March 15, 1938, Savage Papers, UW.

13. For a detailed account see Sidney Fine, *Sit-Down: The General Motors Strike of 1936–37* (Ann Arbor: University of Michigan Press, 1969).

14. Production Book for *See How They Run*, FTC, LOC.

15. *Ibid.*

16. Savage was a prolific letter writer and his correspondence regarding *See How They Run* is preserved in his papers at the University of Washington Libraries Special Collections.

17. Between Aug. and Dec., 1937 the play had been tentatively scheduled for Denver, Des Moines, San Diego, San Francisco and Oakland. In San Diego the contracts had been drawn and the opening date announced for Jan. 26, 1938. But at the time of the award no production had taken place.

18. During the waterfront strike in Seattle in 1934 management attempted to hire strike-breakers from among the students at the University. Then President Hugo Winken-werder opposed the action and vowed to fight such practices. See Berner, *Seattle, 1921–1940* (Seattle: Charles Press, 1992), p. 338.

19. There are numerous accounts of the congressional investigations of the Federal Theatre Project. Jane Mathews, *The Federal Theatre, 1935–39* (Princeton University Press, 1962) remains one of the best.

20. See James Brooks to Jim Farley, Jan. 29, 1936, WPA Records, FDR Library. Farley, the Postmaster General, investigated and reported to Hopkins that there was no basis for the accusations although the Project, having no permanent home, had leased the stage of the Peoples Theatre, a "left wing group" perhaps causing some confusion. The lease was subsequently voided. See Farley to Hopkins, Feb. 16, 1936. WPA Records, FDR Library.

21. George Savage to Georgia Fink, Sept. 18, 1938, Savage Papers, UW.

22. *San Francisco News*, Sept. 7, 1938.

23. Teevin to Savage, Sept. 19, 1938, Savage Papers, UW.

24. The Oakland production, directed by Alan Williams, opened the same night (Sept. 19, 1938) and was by his account a technical disaster. The press agreed and was harsh in its assessment of Savage's ideas and the dramatic structure.

25. *Seattle Times*, Sept. 20, 1938.

26. Savage to Flanagan, Sept. 26, 1938, Savage Papers, UW.

27. Frieda Fishbein to Hallie Flanagan, Oct. 5, 1938, Savage Papers, UW.

28. Fishbein to Savage, Nov. 18, 1938, Savage Papers, UW.

29. *Seattle Times*, July, 17, 1972.

30. Mrs. Savage to Lorraine Brown, Oct. 6, 1975, Savage Papers, UW.

31. Lawrence Langner to George Savage, Feb. 8, 1939, Savage Papers, UW.

10 *Flotilla of Faith*

1. WPA Form 330, Dec. 21, 1938, Theatre Collection, UW.

2. O'Connor to Miller, May 28, 1939, RG 69, NA. In this long and reflective letter O'Connor details how he had threatened, cajoled and conned various members of the company to curb or abandon their drinking. "To two others counsel meant nothing. I knew they were Catholics and I told them that if they didn't take a pledge immediately they were through. I know the Catholic mind and know that if they take a pledge they will keep it. They took the pledge six months ago and are still on the wagon and will be for six months more until the pledge expires. Will give them a couple of days then to absorb their fill and then I'll chase them up to church again for another year's pledge."

3. O'Connor to Miller, April 3, 1939, RG 69, NA.

4. Williams to Flanagan, Feb. 24, 1936, RG 69, NA.

5. *Ibid.*

6. Memorandum from Nina P. Collier to Mr. McClure and the Federal Arts Directors, March 24, 1936, RG 69, NA.

7. Clinton P. Anderson to Hallie Flanagan, March 9, 1936, RG 69, NA.

8. William P. Farnsworth to Anderson, March 19, 1936, RG 69, NA.

9. Quoted in Wilfred P. Schoenberg, *A History of the Catholic Church in the Pacific Northwest, 1743–1983* (Washington, DC: The Pastoral Press, 1987), p. 528.

10. O'Connor to Miller, March 21, 1939, RG 69, NA.

11. O'Connor to Flanagan, May 15, 1939, RG 69, NA.

12. *Ibid.*

13. Schoenberg, *History of the Catholic Church*, p. 26.

14. Douglas Wight, *The Flotilla of Faith*, FTC, LOC, p. 7.

15. O'Connor to Flanagan, May 15, 1939, RG 69, NA.

16. Ole Ness to Flanagan, May 30, 1939, RG 69, NA.

17. O'Connor to Miller, May 28, 1939, RG 69, NA.

18. Telegram from George Savage to Harry Hopkins, May 27, 1939, Roosevelt Papers, FDR Library, Hyde Park, NY.

Conclusion

1. Memo from F.D.R. to E.R., June 16, 1939, Eleanor Roosevelt Papers, FDR Library, Hyde Park, NY.

2. Flanagan, *Arena* (New York: Duell, Sloan and Pearce, 1940), pp. 328–9. Flanagan also quotes FDR to Senator Claude Pepper to the effect that "we are not ready for so advanced a plan."

3. Hallie Flanagan, *Plan for a Government Supported Theatre*, Eleanor Roosevelt Papers, FDR Library, Hyde Park, NY. Dated April 26, 1939, p. 3.

4. She gives two specific examples of this: bringing the Comedie-Francaise for a visit or touring a distinguished play such as *Abe Lincoln in Illinois*.

5. Flanagan, *Plan*, 4.

6. *Big White Fog* by Theodore Ward was one of the most controversial and remarkable productions of the Negro units. Originally produced in Chicago in 1938, the play dealt with an urban family pulled in various ideological directions by capitalism, communism and the teachings of Marcus Garvey.

7. Gilbert Brown, Review of *Tomorrow's a Holiday*, *Seattle Star*, March 30, 1938.

8. The word communism is rarely mentioned in any of the letters and memos. However, there are frequent references to things that "stink" or other metaphors. Clarence Talbot wrote to Miller in reference to the "James Faction," that, "something is wrong with the local picture . . . the boat seems to be sinking although you can't find the hole to plug up." Aug. 27, 1937, RG 69, NA.

9. O'Connor to Flanagan, May 1, 1939, RG 69, NA.

10. Kruger, *The National Stage* (University of Chicago Press, 1992), p. 154. Kruger rightly observes that, "The art and college theatre practitioners, from whose ranks Flanagan herself came, resisted both the commercial theatre's exclusive claim to professionalism in the narrow sense of marketable expertise and labor's and the Left's interest in the idea of an art ministry, on the grounds that both moves tainted the autonomy of art."

11. As dramaturg for the Seattle Repertory Theatre in 1983, I recall numerous discussions about opening a new theatre with Michael Weller's *Ballad of Soapy Smith* and how its gold rush stories would resonate in the Northwest. I also remember Artistic Director Dan Sullivan cautioning everyone in his gentle way that we weren't gonna do "just plays about salmon and timber."

12. Brown, Review of *Tomorrow's a Holiday*, *Seattle Star*, 1938.

Bibliography

Archives

The bulk of the research for this book was carried out in RG (Record Group) 69 at the National Archives in Washington, DC and at the Federal Theatre Collection at George Mason University and later at the Library of Congress. Additional valuable papers and letters were examined in the Franklin Delano Roosevelt Library in Hyde Park, New York and in the Manuscripts and Special Collections at the University of Washington in Seattle. Other important resources are the Seattle Public Library, the Federal Repository on Sand Point Way in Seattle, The Washington Historical Society, the Museum of History and Industry in Seattle and the Washington State Archives, Olympia, Washington.

Interviews

Abel, Don (June 10, 1965) Conducted by Dorothy Bestor for the Smithsonian *Archives of American Art*. Available on-line at http://artarchives.si.edu/oralhist/ abel65.htm.
Brown, Theodore (Oct. 22, 1975, Roxbury, MA.) Conducted by Lorraine Brown for the Federal Theatre Collection at George Mason University.
Buttitta, Anthony (Dec., 1990, New York City).
Harrington, Donal (Nov. 15, 1986, Seattle, Washington).
Oliver Jackson, Sara (1976, State of Washington Oral/Aural History Project) Conducted by Esther Hall Mumford and later reprinted in Mumford, *Seven Stars and Orion*, pp. 66–76.
Lane, Esther Porter (Feb. 16, 1993, telephone).
McGinnis, Marion (Nov. 13, 1987, Bellevue, WA).
Sauntry, Barbara (May 7, 1998, Seattle, WA).
Savage, George M. III (May 24, 2000, Seattle, WA).
Schram, Noel (May 4, 1989, Seattle, WA).
Staton, Joe (Jan. 7, 1976, Seattle, WA) Conducted by John O'Connor for the Federal Theatre Collection at George Mason University.
Valentinetti, Aurora (April 25, 1990, Seattle, WA).

Books

Abramson, Doris E. *Negro Playwrights and the American Theatre, 1925–1959*. New York: Columbia University Press, 1969.

Ames, William E. and Roger A. Simpson. *Unionism or Hearst: The Seattle Post-Intelligencer Strike of 1936*. Seattle: Pacific Northwest Labor History Association, 1978.

Arian, Edward. *The Unfulfilled Promise: Public Subsidy of the Arts in America*. Philadelphia: Temple University Press, 1989.

Baker, Houston. *Afro-American Poetics: Revisions of Harlem*. Madison: University of Wisconsin Press, 1988.

Balio, Tino and Lee Norvelle. *The History of the National Theatre Conference*, New York: National Theatre Conference, 1968.

Bentley, Joanne. *Hallie Flanagan: A Life in the American Theatre*. New York: Knopf, 1988.

Berner, Richard C. *Seattle 1921–1940: From Boom to Bust*. Seattle: Charles Press, 1992.

Blake, Ben. *The Awakening of the American Theatre*. New York: Tomorrow Publishers, 1935.

Blumell, Bruce D. *The Development of Public Assistance in the State of Washington During the Great Depression*. New York: Garland, 1983.

Brandt, Alan M. *No Magic Bullet*. New York: Oxford, 1985.

Broadus, Mitchell. *Depression Decade: From New Era Through New Deal, 1929–1941*. New York: Rinehart, 1947.

Brown, Lawrence Guy. *Immigration: Cultural Conflicts and Social Adjustments*. New York: Arno Press, 1969.

Brown, Lorraine and John O'Connor, eds. *Free, Adult, Uncensored: The Living History of the Federal Theatre Project*. Washington, DC: New Republic Books, 1978.

Burke, Padraic. *The History of the Port of Seattle*. Seattle: Port of Seattle, 1976.

Buttitta, Tony and Barry Witham. *Uncle Sam Presents*. University of Pennsylvania Press, 1982.

Cahill, Holger, Foreword. *Art for the Millions: Essays From the 1930s by Artists and Administrators of the WPA Federal Art Project*. Ed. and intro. Francis V. Connor. 1973. Boston, MA: New York Graphic Society, 1975.

Case, Sue-Ellen and Janelle Reinelt, eds. *The Performance of Power*. Iowa City: University of Iowa Press, 1991.

Caute, David. *Joseph Losey: A Revenge on Life*. New York: Oxford University Press, 1994.

Chandler, Lester Vernon. *America's Greatest Depression*. New York: Harper & Row, 1970.

Charles, Searle F. *Minister of Relief: Harry Hopkins and the Depression*. Syracuse, NY: Syracuse University Press, 1963.

Conroy, Jack and Curt Johnson. *Writers in Revolt: The Anvil Anthology, 1933–40*. New York: Laurence Hill, 1973.

Countryman, Vern. *Un-American Activities in Washington State*. Ithaca: Cornell University Press, 1951.

Cowley, Malcolm. *The Dream of the Golden Mountains: Remembering the 1930s*. New York: Viking, 1980.

Davidson, Donald. *The Attack on Leviathan: Regionalism and Nationalism in the United States.* Chapel Hill: University of North Carolina Press, 1938.

Davis, John H. *The Guggenheims: An American Epic.* New York: William Morrow, 1978.

Draper, Theodore. *The Roots of American Communism.* New York: Viking Press, 1957.

Duffy, Susan. *American Labor On Stage.* Westport, CT: Greenwood Press, 1996.

Dunbar, Paul Laurence. *The Complete Poems of Paul Laurence Dunbar, with the Introduction to "Lyrics of the Lowly Life," by W.D. Howells.* New York: Dodd, Mead and Co., 1913.

Dunbar, Paul Laurence. *The Paul Laurence Dunbar Reader.* Ed. Jay Martin and Gossie H. Hudson. New York: Dodd, Mead, 1975.

Eagleton, Terry. *Marxism and Literary Criticism.* Berkeley: University of California Press, 1976.

Ekirch, Arthur A. *Ideologies and Utopia: The Impact of the New Deal on American Thought.* Chicago: Quadrangle Books, 1969.

Elliott, Eugene Clinton. *A History of Variety-Vaudeville in Seattle.* Seattle: University of Washington Press, 1944.

Engle, Ron and Tice L. Miller, eds. *The American Stage.* Cambridge University Press, 1993.

Ermentrout, Robert Allen. *Forgotten Men: The Civilian Conservation Corps.* Smithtown, NY: Exposition Press, 1982.

Evans, Walker. *Walker Evans, America.* New York: Rizzoli, 1991.

Fast, Howard. *Being Red.* Boston, MA: Houghton Mifflin Company, 1990.

Fearnow, Mark. *The American Stage and the Great Depression.* Cambridge University Press, 1997.

Federal Theatre Project: A Catalog-Calendar of Productions. Westport CT: Greenwood Press, 1986.

Ficken, Robert E. and Charles P. LeWarne. *Washington: A Centennial History.* Seattle: University of Washington Press, 1988.

Fine, Sidney, *Sit-Down: The General Motors Strike of 1936–37.* Ann Arbor: University of Michigan Press, 1969.

Flanagan, Hallie. *Arena.* New York: Duell, Sloan and Pearce, 1940.

Flanagan, Hallie. *Dynamo.* New York: Duell, Sloane and Pearce, 1943.

Flanagan, Hallie. *Shifting Scenes of the Modern European Theatre.* New York: Coward-McCann, 1928.

Fraden, Rena. *Blueprints for a Black Federal Theatre, 1935–1939.* New York: Cambridge University Press, 1994.

France, Richard. *The Theatre of Orson Welles.* Lewisburg, PA: Bucknell University Press, 1977.

Fraser, Steve and Gary Gersfee, eds. *The Rise and Fall of the New Deal Order, 1930–1980.* Princeton University Press, 1989.

Freidel, Frank B. *Franklin Delano Roosevelt: A Rendezvous with Destiny.* Boston, MA: Little, Brown, 1990.

Friedheim, Robert L. *The Seattle General Strike.* Seattle: University of Washington Press, 1964.

Galbraith, John Kenneth. *The Great Crash, 1929.* 2nd edn. Cambridge, MA: Houghton Mifflin, 1961.

Galenson, Walter. *The CIO Challenge to the AFL: A History of the American Labor Movement, 1935–41.* Cambridge, MA: Harvard University Press, 1960.

Gard, Robert Edward. *Community Theatre: Idea and Achievement.* New York: Duell, Sloan and Pearce, 1959.

Gard, Robert Edward. *Grassroots Theater: A Search for Regional Arts in America.* Madison: University of Wisconsin Press, 1955.

Gill, Glenda. *White Grease Paint on Black Performers: A Study of the Federal Theatre, 1935–1939.* New York: Peter Lang, 1988.

Gillingham, J. B. *The Teamsters Union in the West.* Berkeley: Institute of Industrial Relations, University of California, 1956.

Goldstein, Malcolm. *The Political Stage: American Drama and Theater of the Great Depression.* New York: Oxford University Press, 1974.

Grant, Howard F., ed., *The Story of Seattle's Early Theatres.* Seattle: University Book Store, 1934.

Gunns, Albert F. *Civil Liberties in Crisis: The Pacific Northwest, 1917–40.* New York: Garland, 1983.

Hay, Samuel A. *African American Theatre: An Historical and Critical Analysis.* New York: Cambridge University Press, 1994.

Himelstein, Morgan Y. *Drama Was a Weapon: The Left-Wing Theatre in New York, 1929–1941.* New Brunswick: Rutgers University Press, 1963.

Hines, Neal O. *Denny's Knoll: A History of the Metropolitan Tract of the University of Washington.* Seattle: University of Washington Press, 1980.

Holcombe, A. N. *The New Party Politics.* New York: W. W. Norton, 1933.

Hopkins, Harry Lloyd. *Spending to Save: The Complete Story of Relief.* New York: W. W. Norton, 1936.

Houseman, John. *Run-Through: A Memoir.* New York: Simon and Schuster, 1972.

Houseman, John. *Entertainers and the Entertained.* New York: Simon and Schuster, 1986.

Howard, Donald S. *The WPA and Federal Relief Policy.* New York: Russell Sage Foundation, 1943.

Howe, Irving and Louis Closer. *The American Communist Party: A Critical History.* Boston, MA: Beacon Press, 1957.

Hughes, Catharine. *Plays, Politics, and Polemics.* New York: Drama Book Specialists, 1973.

Hughes, Glenn. *A History of the American Theatre, 1790–1950.* New York: Samuel French, 1951.

Hughes, Glenn. *The Story of the Theatre: A Short History of Theatrical Art From Its Beginning to the Present Day.* New York: Samuel French, 1928.

Hughes, Glenn. *The Penthouse Theatre: Its History and Technique.* Seattle: University of Washington Press, 1958.

Jenkins, Mark. *All Powers Necessary and Convenient.* Seattle: University of Washington Press, 1999.

Kazacoff, George. *Dangerous Theatre: The Federal Theatre Project as a Forum for New Plays.* New York: Peter Lang, 1989.

Klehr, Harvey. *The Heyday of American Communism: The Depression Decade.* New York: Basic Books, 1984.

Kruger, Loren. *The National Stage*. University of Chicago Press, 1992.

Larson, Gary O. *The Reluctant Patron: The United States Government and the Arts, 1943–1965*. Philadelphia: University of Pennsylvania Press, 1983.

Larrowe, Charles P. *Harry Bridges: The Rise and Fall of Radical Labor in the United States*. New York: Lawrence Hill, 1972.

Leuchtenburg, William E. *Franklin D. Roosevelt and the New Deal, 1932–1940*. New York: Harper Row Torchbooks, 1963.

Levine, Ira A. *Left-Wing Dramatic Theory*. Ann Arbor: UMI, 1985.

Levine, Lawrence. *Black Culture and Black Consciousness*. New York: Oxford University Press, 1977.

Locke, Alain Le Roy. *The Negro and His Music*. 1936. New York: Arno Press, 1969.

Loften, Mitchell. *Black Drama: The Story of the American Negro in the Theatre*. New York: Hawthorne Books, 1967.

MacDonald, Norbert. *Distant Neighbors: A Comparative History of Seattle and Vancouver*. Lincoln: University of Nebraska Press, 1987.

McConachie, Bruce, and Daniel Freidman, ed. *Theatre for Working-Class Audiences in the United States, 1830–1980*. Westport, CT: Greenwood Press, 1985.

McCreery, Kathleen and Richard Stourac. *Theatre as a Weapon: Workers' Theatre in the Soviet Union, Germany, and Britain, 1917–1934*. London: Routledge & Kegan Paul, 1986.

McDonald, William F. *Federal Relief Administration and the Arts: The Origins and Administrative History of the Arts Projects of the Works Progress Administration*. Columbus: Ohio State University Press, 1969.

McElvaine, Robert S. *The Great Depression*. New York: Times Books, 1984.

McKinzie, Richard D. *The New Deal for Artists*. Princeton University Press, 1973.

Manchester, William. *The Glory and the Dream*. New York: Bantam, 1974.

Manual of Recreational Activities for Young Men's Work Camps. New York City: National Recreation Association, n.d.

Mangione, Jerre. *The Dream and the Deal: The Federal Writers' Project, 1935–1943*. Boston, MA: Little Brown, 1972.

Marling, Karal Ann. *Wall-to-Wall America: A Cultural History of Post-Office Murals in the Great Depression*. Minneapolis: University of Minnesota Press, 1982.

Mathews, Jane De Hart. *The Federal Theatre, 1935–39: Plays, Relief, and Politics*. Princeton University Press, 1962.

Mersand, Joseph. *The American Drama, 1930–40*. 1941. Rpt. New York: Kennikat, 1968.

Metcalf, E. W. Jr. *Paul Laurence Dunbar: A bibliography*. Metuchen, NJ: Scarecrow Press, 1975.

Miller, Jordan Y. and Winifred L. Frazer. *American Drama Between the Wars: A Critical History*. Boston, MA: Twayne, 1991.

Miller, Lillian. *Patrons and Patriotism: The Encouragement of the Fine Arts in the United States, 1790–1860*. University of Chicago Press, 1966.

Minihan, Janet. *The Nationalization of Culture: The Development of State Subsidies to the Arts in Great Britain*. New York: New York University Press, 1971.

Montgomery, David. *The Fall of the House of Labor: The Workplace, the State, and American Labor Activism, 1865–1925*. Cambridge University Press, 1987.

Morgan, Murray. *Skid Road: An Informal Portrait of Seattle*. Seattle: University of Washington Press, 1982.

Mumford, Esther Hall. *Seven Stars and Orion*. Seattle: Ananse Press, 1980.

Murphy, Brenda. *American Realism and American Drama, 1880–1940*. Cambridge University Press, 1987.

Nannes, Caspar H. *Politics in the American Drama*. Washington, DC: Catholic University of America Press, 1960.

Netzer, Dick. *The Subsidized Muse: Public Support for the Arts in the United States*. New York: Cambridge University Press, 1978.

O'Connor, Francis, ed. *Art for the Millions: Essays from the 1930s by Artists and Administrators of the WPA Federal Art Project*. Boston, MA: New York Graphic Society, 1975.

O'Connor, Francis, ed. *Federal Support for the Visual Arts: The New Deal and Now*. Boston, MA: New York Graphic Society, 1969.

O'Connor, John and Brown, Lorraine. *Free, Adult and Uncensored*. Washington, DC: New Republic Books, 1978.

Odell, George C.D. *Annals of the New York Stage*. 15 Vols. New York: Columbia University Press, 1927–49.

Odum, Howard W. *American Regionalism*. New York: Henry Holt, 1938.

Overmeyer, Grace. *Government and the Arts*. New York: W. W. Norton, 1939.

Parron, Thomas. *Shadow on the Land*. New York: Kendal and Hitchcock, 1937.

Peeler, David P. *Hope Among Us: Social Criticism and Social Solace in Depression America*. Athens, GA: University of Georgia Press, 1987.

Pells, Richard. *Radical Visions and American Dreams. Culture and Social Thought in the Depression Years*. Middleton, CT: Wesleyan University Press, 1973.

Penkower, Noam. *The Federal Writers' Project. A Study in Government Patronage of the Arts*. Urbana: University of Illinois Press, 1977.

Perry, Joseph McGarity. *The Impact of Immigration on Three American Industries, 1865–1914*. New York: Arno Press, 1978.

Piscator, Erwin. *The Political Theatre: A History, 1914–1929*. New York: Avon Books, 1978.

Poggi, Jack. *Theater in America: The Impact of Economic Forces, 1870–1967*. Ithaca, NY: Cornell University Press, 1968.

Rabkin, Gerald, *Drama and Commitment: Politics in the American Theatre of the Thirties*. Bloomington: Indiana University Press, 1964.

Rice, Elmer. *Minority Report: An Autobiography*. New York: Simon and Schuster, 1963.

Reynolds, Clay. *Stage Left: The Development of the American Social Drama in the Thirties*. Troy, NY: Whitston Press, 1986.

Rohrer, Mary Katherine. *The History of Seattle Stock Companies From Their Beginnings to 1934*. Seattle: University of Washington Press, 1945.

Rothbard, Murray Newton. *America's Great Depression*. Los Angeles: Nash Publishers, 1972.

Sales, Roger. *Seattle: Past to Present*. Seattle: University of Washington Press, 1976.

Sanders, Jane. *Cold War on the Campus: Academic Freedom at the University of Washington, 1946–64*. Seattle: University of Washington Press, 1979.

Scharine, Richard G. *From Class to Caste in American Drama: Political and Social Themes Since the 1930s.* Westport, CT: Greenwood Press, 1991.

Schoenberg, William P. *A History of the Catholic Church in the Pacific Northwest, 1743–1983.* Washington, DC: The Pastoral Press, 1987.

Schwartz, Lawrence H. *Marxism and Culture: The CPUSA and Aesthetics in the 1930s.* Port Washington, NY: Kennikat Publishers, 1980.

Schwarz, Jordan A. *The New Dealers,* New York: Alfred A. Knopf, 1993.

Selden, Samuel. *Frederick Koch, Pioneer Playmaker: A Brief Biography.* Chapel Hill: University of North Carolina Library, 1954.

Sernett, Milton C. *Afro-American Religious History: A Documentary History.* Durham, NC: Duke University Press, 1985.

Sherwood, Robert E. *Roosevelt and Hopkins: an Intimate History.* New York: Grosset and Dunlap, 1950.

Slonim, Marc. *Russian Theater: From the Empire to the Soviets.* Cleveland, OH: World Publishing Company, 1961.

Smiley, Sam. *The Drama of Attack: Didactic Plays of the American Depression.* Columbia: University of Missouri Press, 1972.

Smith, Susan Harris. *American Drama: The Bastard Art.* New York: Cambridge University Press, 1997.

Sobel, Mechal. *Trabelin' On: The Slave Journey to an Afro-Baptist Faith.* Princeton University Press, 1988.

Sohn-Rethel, Alfred. *Intellectual and Manual Labour.* Trans. Martin Sohn-Rethel. Atlantic Highlands, NJ: Humanities Press, 1978.

Spearman, Walter. *The Carolina Playmakers: The First Fifty Years.* Samuel Selden, asst. Chapel Hill: University of North Carolina Press, 1970.

Sporn, Paul. *Against Itself.* Detroit: Wayne State University Press, 1995.

Stearns, Marshall W. *The Story of Jazz.* New York: Oxford University Press, 1956.

Stoneman, William E. *A History of the Economic Analysis of the Great Depression in America.* New York: Garland, 1979.

Stott, William. *Documentary Expression and Thirties America.* University of Chicago Press, 1986.

Stourac, Richard and Kathleen McCreery. *Theatre as a Weapon: Workers' Theatre in the Soviet Union, Germany and Britain, 1917–1934.* London: Routledge & Kegan Paul, 1986.

Sundgaard, Arnold. *Spirochete* in *Federal Theatre Plays.* New York: Random House, 1938.

Swados, Harvey, *The American Writer and the Great Depression.* Indianapolis: Bobbs-Merrill, 1966.

Taylor, Quintard. *The Forging of a Black Community.* Seattle: University of Washington Press, 1994.

Thomas, Margaret E., ed. *The Civilian Conservation Corps in the State of Washington.* Olympia, WA: Department of Social Security, State of Washington, May 1937.

Wainscott, Ronald H. *The Emergence of the Modern American Theater, 1914–1929.* New Haven, CT: Yale University Press, 1997.

Westman, Ragnar T., ed. *Annual Report and Survey.* Seattle: Health and Sanitation Department, 1939.

Whitman, Willson. *Bread and Circuses.* New York: Oxford University Press, 1937.

Williams, Jay. *Stage Left*. New York: Charles Scribner's Sons, 1974.
Williams, Raymond. *Problems in Materialism and Culture*. London: Verso Editions, 1980.
Wilmeth, Don B. and Christopher Bigsby. *The Cambridge History of American Theatre*, vol. 11 New York: Cambridge University Press, 1999.
Witham, Barry B., ed. *Documents of American Theatre History*, vol. 1. Cambridge University Press, 1996.

Articles, Essays, and manuscripts

Bennett, Marilyn D. "The Glenn Hughes Years, 1927–1961," unpublished Ph.D dissertation, University of Washington, 1982.
Botkin, B. A. "WPA and Folklore Research." *Southern Folklore Quarterly* 3 (1939): 7–14.
Brown, Lorraine. "A Story Yet to Be Told: The Federal Theatre Research Project." *Black Scholar* 10:10 (1979): 70–8.
Bulletin of the King County [WA] Medical Society, Feb. 6, 1939.
Cantwell, Robert. "America and the Writers' Project." *New Republic* (April 26, 1939): 323–5.
Cobb, Gerry. *"Injunction Granted* in Its Time: A Living Newspaper Reappraised." *New Theatre Quarterly* 6:23 (Aug., 1990): 279–96.
Cole, John Y. "Amassing American "Stuff": The Library of Congress and the Federal Arts Projects of the 1930s." *Quarterly Journal of the Library of Congress* 40:4 (fall, 1983): 356–89.
Duffy, Susan and Bernard K. "Theatrical Responses to Technology During the Depression: Three Federal Theatre Project Plays." *Theatre History Studies* 6 (1986): 143–64.
Dycke, Marjorie Louise. "The Living Newspaper: A Study of the Nature of the Form and Its Place in Modern Social Drama." Ph.D dissertation. New York University, 1948.
Elion, Harry. "A Playwriting Group." *Workers' Theatre* (Sept.-Oct. 1932): 7–8.
Federal Theatre Magazine, vols. 1 and 2 (1936–7).
Flanagan, Hallie. "A Theatre is Born." *Theatre Arts Monthly* (Nov., 1931): 908–15.
Fox, Daniel. "The Achievement of the Federal Writers' Project." *American Quarterly* 13 (1961): 3–19.
Fraden, Rena. "The Cloudy History of *Big White Fog:* The Federal Theatre Project, 1938." *American Studies* 29:1 (spring, 1988): 5–27.
Glicksberg, Charles. "The Federal Writers' Project." *South Atlantic Quarterly* 37 (1938): 157–69.
Grant, Howard. "The Pioneer Theater in Washington." *The Pacific Northwest Quarterly* (April 1937): 115–36.
James, Florence. "Fists Upon A Star" Unpublished manuscript, Special Collections, University of Washington Library.
Jeliffe, Rowena Woodham. "A Negro Community Theatre." *New Theatre* (July, 1935): 13, 32.
Johnson, Evamarii A. "A Production History of the Seattle Federal Theatre Project Negro Company, 1935–1939" Ph.D dissertation, University of Washington, 1981.
Knuuti, Rosa Alexander. "The Workers' Play." *Industrial Pioneer* 3: 7 (1925): 268.

Kreizenbeck, Alan. "The Radio Division of the Federal Theatre Project." *New England Theatre Journal* 2:1 (1991): 27–37.

Mathews, Jane De Hart. "Arts and the People: The New Deal Quest for a Cultural Democracy." *Journal of American History* 62 (1975): 316–39.

McDermott, Douglas. "The Theatre Nobody Knows: Workers' Theatres in America, 1926–1942." *Theatre Survey* 6:1 (May, 1965): 65–82.

McKinzie, Kathleen O'Connor. "Writers on Relief: 1935–1942." Unpublished Ph.D dissertation. University of Indiana, 1970.

Nadler, Paul. "Liberty Censored: Black Living Newspapers of the Federal Theatre Project." *African American Review* 29:4 (winter, 1995): 615–22.

Nathan, George Jean. "A Government in Greasepaint," *Newsweek* (April 18, 1938): 25.

O'Connor, John S. "*Spirochete* and the War on Syphillis." *The Drama Review* 21:1 (March, 1977): 91–98.

Redd, Tina. "Staging Race: The Seattle Negro Unit Production of *Stevedore*." *Journal of American Drama and Theatre* 7:2 (Spring, 1995): 66–85.

Sklar, George, "Negro Theatre in America." *New Theatre* (July, 1935): 3.

Vacha, J. E. "The Night *It Can't Happen Here* Happened." *Gamut* 20 (1987): 14–24.

Vallillo, Stephen M. "The Shakespeare Productions of the Federal Theatre Project." *Theatre History Studies* 3 (1983): 29–54.

Watson, Morris. "Sitdown Theater." *New Theater and Film* 4:2 (1937): 5–6.

West, Ron. "Others, Adults, Censored: The Federal Theatre Project's Black *Lysistrata* Cancellation." *Theatre Survey* 37:2 (Nov., 1996): 93–113.

Witham, Barry B. "The Living Newspaper's *Power* in Seattle." *Theatre History Studies* 9 (1989): 23–35.

Witham, Barry B. "Backstage at *The Cradle Will Rock*." *Theatre History Studies* 12 (1992): 213–19.

Witham, Barry B. "The Playhouse and the Theatre." In Sue-Ellen Case and Janelle Reinelt, eds., *The Performance of Power*. University of Iowa Press, 1991, pp. 146–62.

Witham, Barry B., "Censorship in the Federal Theatre." *Theatre History Studies* 17 (1997): 3–15.

Witham, Barry B., "Pandemic and Popular Opinion: *Spirochete* in Seattle." *Journal of American Drama and Theatre* 5:2 (spring, 1993): 86–95.

Witham, Barry B., "The Economic Structure of the Federal Theatre Project." in Engle and Miller, eds., *The American Stage*. Cambridge, 1993, pp. 200–14.

Index